DAY TRADING
AND SWING TRADING
THE CURRENCY MARKET

DAY TRADING AND SWING TRADING THE CURRENCY MARKET

Technical and Fundamental
Strategies to Profit from Market Moves

Third Edition

Kathy Lien

WILEY

Published by John Wiley & Sons, Inc., Hoboken, New Jersey.

The first edition was published as *Day Trading the Currency Market* by John Wiley & Sons, Inc. in 2005. The second edition was published as *Day Trading and Swing Trading the Currency Market* by John Wiley & Sons, Inc. in 2008.

Published simultaneously in Canada.

For general information on our other products and services or for technical support, please contact our Customer Care Department within the United States at (800) 762-2974, outside the United States at (317) 572-3993, or fax (317) 572-4002.

Wiley publishes in a variety of print and electronic formats and by print-on-demand. Some material included with standard print versions of this book may not be included in e-books or in print-on-demand. If this book refers to media such as a CD or DVD that is not included in the version you purchased, you may download this material at http://booksupport.wiley.com. For more information about Wiley products, visit www.wiley.com.

Library of Congress Cataloging-in-Publication Data:
Names: Lien, Kathy, 1980- | Lien, Kathy, 1980- . Day trading the currency market.
Title: Day trading and swing trading the currency market : technical and fundamental strategies to profit from market moves / Kathy Lien.
Description: Third edition. | Hoboken : Wiley, 2015. | Series: Wiley trading | Revised edition of the author's Day trading and swing trading the currency market, 2009. | Includes index.
Identifiers: LCCN 2015031925 | ISBN 9781119108412 (paperback) | ISBN 9781119220107 (ePDF) | ISBN 9781119220091 (ePub)
Subjects: LCSH: Foreign exchange futures. | Foreign exchange market. | Speculation. | BISAC: BUSINESS & ECONOMICS / Investments & Securities.
Classification: LCC HG3853 .L54 2015 | DDC 332.4/5—dc23 LC record available at http://lccn.loc.gov/2015031925

Cover Design: Wiley
Cover Image: © John Lund/Getty Images

Printed in the United States of America

10 9 8 7 6 5 4 3 2 1

Dedicated to My Son Jackson,
Who I Hope Will Share His Momma's Love for the Markets
And to My Husband and Wonderful Family, for Their Love and Support

CONTENTS

vii

PREFACE

Day Trading and Swing Trading the Currency Market is one of the most popular books for new and experienced forex traders. In the third edition, all of the content has been updated with new chapters and strategies. After having taught seminars across the country on how to trade currencies, I am repeatedly approached about recommendations for good books on currency trading. *Day Trading Strategies for the FX Market* addresses that need by not only providing technical and fundamental strategies for trading FX, but also giving traders more detailed insight into how the currency market works. This book is designed for both the beginner and advanced trader. There is something for every type of reader. Aside from the basic market overview, the book covers the best times to trade currencies, the most market moving economic data cross-market correlations, and unique currency characteristics just to name a few. For technical traders, there are strategies for both breakouts and range trading that work particularly well in the FX market.

Kathy Lien is managing director of FX strategy for BK Asset Management and co-founder of BKForex.com. As a financial market prodigy, she graduated from New York University's Stern School of Business at the age of 18. After graduation, she joined JPMorgan Chase's interbank foreign exchange trading desk. This early start has given Kathy more than 15 years of experience in the foreign exchange market. At JPMorgan, she helped to make markets in G20 currencies and later moved to the bank's cross markets proprietary trading group where she traded FX spot, options, interest rate derivatives, bonds, equities, and futures.

In 2003, Kathy joined FXCM and started DailyFX.com, a leading online foreign exchange research portal. As chief strategist, she managed a team of 10 analysts dedicated to providing research and commentary on the foreign exchange market. In 2008, Kathy joined Global Futures & Forex Ltd as director of Currency Research, where she provided research and analysis to clients and managed a global foreign exchange research team with analysts in the United States, London, and Japan. In 2012, she became an official CNBC contributor and served as a guest host for *Money in Motion*.

As an expert in G20 currencies, Kathy travels around the world teaching investors to trade forex. She is often quoted in the *Wall Street Journal, UK Telegraph,* and *Sydney Morning Herald*, and by Reuters, Bloomberg, Marketwatch, Associated Press, AAP, and other leading news sources. She also appears regularly on CNBC US, Asia, and Europe, and on Sky Business.

Kathy is an internationally published author of the best-selling book *Day Trading and Swing Trading the Currency Market; The Little Book of Currency Trading;* and *Millionaire*

Traders: How Everyday People Beat Wall Street at Its Own Game—all published through Wiley.

Kathy's extensive experience in cross-markets analysis, trading strategy development, and predicting economic data surprises has made her known in the forex community as the "queen of the macro forex trade."

CHAPTER 1

Foreign Exchange— The Fastest Growing Market of Our Time

The foreign exchange market is the largest and fastest growing market in the world. Traditionally, it is the platform through which governments, businesses, investors, travelers, and other interested parties convert or "exchange" currency. At its most fundamental level, the foreign exchange market is an over-the-counter (OTC) market with no central exchange and clearing house where orders are matched. FX dealers and market makers around the world are linked to each other around-the-clock via telephone, computer, and fax, creating one cohesive market. Through the years, this has changed with many institutions offering exchange traded FX instruments, but all of the prices are still derived from the underlying or spot forex market.

In the past two decades, foreign exchange, also known as *forex* or *FX,* became available to trade by individual retail investors, and this access caused the market to explode in popularity. In the early 2000s, the Bank of International Settlements reported a 57% increase in volume between April 2001 and 2004. At the time more than $1.9 trillion were changing hands on a daily basis. After the financial crisis in 2008, the pace of growth eased to a still-respectable 32% between 2010 and 2013, but the actual volume that changed hands was significantly larger at an average of $5.3 trillion per day. To put this into perspective, it is 50 times greater than the daily trading volume of the New York Stock Exchange and the NASDAQ combined.

While the growth of the retail foreign exchange market contributed to this surge in volume, an increase in volatility over the past few years also made investors more aware of how currency movements can impact the equity and bond markets. If stocks, bonds, and commodity traders want to make more educated trading decisions, it is important for them to also follow forex movements. What follows are some of the examples of how currency fluctuations impacted stock and bond market movements in past years.

EURUSD and Corporate Profitability

For stock market traders, particularly those who invest in European corporations that export a tremendous amount of goods to the United States, monitoring exchange rates are essential to predicting earnings and corporate profitability. Throughout 2003 and 2004, European manufacturers complained extensively about the rapid rise in the euro and the weakness in the U.S. dollar. The main culprit for the dollar's selloff at the time was the country's rapidly growing trade and budget deficits. This caused the EURUSD exchange rate to surge, which took a significant toll on the profitability of European corporations because a higher exchange rate makes the goods of European exporters more expensive to U.S. consumers. In 2003, inadequate hedging shaved approximately EUR$1 billion euros from Volkswagen's profits, while DSM, a Dutch chemicals group, warned that a 1% move in the EURUSD rate would reduce profits by EUR$7 million to EUR$11 million. Unfortunately, inadequate hedging is still a reality in Europe, which makes monitoring the EURUSD exchange rate even more important in forecasting the earnings and profitability of European exporters.

Nikkei and U.S. Dollar

Traders exposed to Japanese equities also need to be aware of the developments that are occurring in the U.S. dollar and how that affects the Nikkei rally. Japan recently came out of 10 years of stagnation. During this time, mutual funds and hedge funds were grossly underweight Japanese equities. When the economy began to turn around, global macro funds rushed to make changes to their portfolios in fear of missing out on a great opportunity to take advantage of Japan's recovery. Hedge funds borrowed significant amount of dollars to pay for increased exposure, but the problem was that their borrowings were very sensitive to U.S. interest rates and the Fed's monetary policy tightening cycle. Increased borrowing costs for the dollar could derail the Nikkei's rally because higher rates will raise the dollar's financing costs. Yet with the huge current account deficit, the Fed might need to continue raising rates to increase the attractiveness of dollar-denominated assets. Therefore, continual rate hikes, coupled with slowing growth in Japan, may make it less profitable for funds to be overleveraged and overly exposed to Japanese stocks. As a result, how the U.S. dollar moves also plays a role on the future direction of the Nikkei.

George Soros

Known as "the man who broke the Bank of England," George Soros is one of the most well-known traders in the FX market. We discuss his adventures in more detail in Chapter 2, but in a nutshell, in 1990, England decided to join the Exchange Rate Mechanism (ERM) system because it wanted to take part in the stable and low-inflation environment created by the Bundesbank, the central bank of Germany. This alliance tied the pound to the deutschmark, which meant that the United Kingdom was subject to the monetary policies enforced by the Bundesbank. In the early 1990s, Germany aggressively increased interest rates to avoid the inflationary effects related to German reunification. However, national pride and the commitment of fixing exchange rates within the ERM prevented England from devaluing the pound. On Wednesday, September 16, also known as *Black Wednesday,* George Soros leveraged the entire value of his fund ($1 billion) and sold $10 billion worth of pounds to bet against the ERM. This essentially "broke" the Bank of England and forced it to devalue the pound. In a matter of 24 hours, the British pound fell approximately 5%, or 5000 pips. The Bank of England promised to raise rates in order to tempt speculators to buy pounds. As a result, this caused tremendous volatility in the bond markets, with 1-month UK LIBOR rates rising 1% and then retracing those gains over the next 24 hours. If bond traders were completed oblivious to what was going on in the currency markets, they would have probably found themselves dumbstruck in face of such rapid gyration in yields.

Chinese Yuan Revaluation and Bonds

For Treasury traders, there's another currency-related issue that is important to follow and that is the gradual revaluation of the Chinese yuan. For most of its history, the yuan or renminbi (RMB) was pegged to the U.S. dollar. In the 1980s, the RMB was devalued to promote growth in China's economy, and between 1997 and 2005 the People's Bank of China artificially maintained a USDRMB rate of 8.27. At the time, it received significant criticism because keeping the peg meant that the Chinese government would artificially weaken its currency to make Chinese goods more competitive. To maintain the band, the Chinese government had to sell the yuan and buy U.S. dollars each time their currency appreciated above the band's upper limit. These dollars were then used to purchase U.S. Treasuries, and this practice turned

China into the world's largest holder of U.S. Treasuries. In 2005, however, China ended its dollar peg and linked the value of the yuan to a basket of currencies and allowed it to fluctuate within a narrow band that was reset every day. While the exact percentage of the basket is unknown, it is largely dominated by the U.S. dollar and includes other currencies such as the euro, Japanese yen, South Korean won, British pound, Thai baht, Russian ruble, and Australian, Canadian, and Singapore dollar.

Through the years China has gradually widened the band that the yuan can trade in, but if China were to end the float and allow the RMB to trade freely on the global foreign exchange market, the impact on the fixed income markets would be significant because it would reduce the government's need to purchase Treasuries and other fixed-income securities. An announcement of this sort would send yields soaring and prices tumbling. While it could be years before this happens, it will be important for bond investors to follow these developments if they want to effectively manage the risk.

■ Comparing the FX Market with Futures and Equities

The foreign exchange market has not always been a popular market to trade because for many decades, it was restricted to hedge funds, commodity trading advisers who manage large amounts of capital, major corporations, and institutional investors due to regulation, capital requirements, and technology. Yet it was the market of choice for many of these large players because the risk was fully customizable. Trader A could use a 50 times leverage, and Trader B could trade cash on cash. When the market opened up to retail traders, many brokerage firms swept in to provide leveraged trading along with free instantaneous execution platforms, charts, and real-time news. This access to low-cost information helped foreign exchange trading surge in popularity, increasing its attractiveness as an alternative asset class to trade.

Many equity and futures traders also turned to currencies, adding the asset class to their trading portfolios. Before you choose to do so, however, it is important to understand some of the key differences between the forex and equity markets.

Characteristics of FX Markets

1. It is the largest market in the world with growing liquidity.
2. The market is open 24 hours, 5.5 days a week for trading.
3. Profits can be made in both bull and bear markets.
4. There are no trading curbs, and short selling is permitted without an uptick.
5. Instant executable trading platform minimizes slippage and errors.
6. Leverage can be extremely high, which can magnify profits as well as losses.

Characteristics of Equities Market

1. There is decent market liquidity, but that can depend on a stock's daily volume.
2. The market is only available for trading 9:30am to 5pm NY Time, with limited after-hours trading.
3. The existence of exchange fees results in higher costs and commissions.
4. There is an uptick rule to short stocks, which many day traders find frustrating.
5. The number of steps involved in completing a trade can increase slippage and error.

As one of the most liquid markets in the world, the volume and liquidity present in the FX markets has allowed traders to access a 24-hour market with low transaction costs, high leverage, the ability to profit in both bull and bear markets, minimized error rates, limited slippage, and no trading curbs or uptick rules. Oftentimes, traders can use the same strategies for analyzing the equity markets in the FX market. Fundamental traders will find that countries can be analyzed like stocks. Technical traders will find that the FX market is perfect for their style of analysis because of the abundance of tick data and because it is already one of the most commonly used analysis tools by professional traders. Now let's take a closer look at the individual attributes of the FX market to really understand why this is such an attractive market to trade!

24-Hour Market

One of the primary reasons why the FX market is popular is because for active traders, it is the ideal market to trade. It's 24-hour nature offers traders instant access to the markets at all hours of the day for immediate response to global developments. This characteristic also gives traders the added flexibility of determining their own trading day. Active day traders no longer have to wait for the equities market to open at 9:30am NY Time to begin trading. If there is a significant announcement or development either domestically or overseas between 4pm NY Time and 9:30am NY Time, most day traders will have to wait for the exchanges to open at 9:30am to place trades. In all likelihood, by that time, unless you have access to electronic communication networks (ECNs) such as Instinet for premarket trading, the market would have gapped up or gapped down against your favor. This is particularly frustrating when important data are released at 8:30am NY Time, such as nonfarm payrolls. Professionals would have already priced in the outcome before the average trader can even access to market.

In addition, many people who want to trade also have a full-time job during the day. The ability to trade after hours makes the FX market a much more convenient market for all traders. Different times of the day will offer different trading opportunities, as the global financial centers around the world are all actively involved in foreign exchange. With the FX market, trading after hours with a large online FX broker provides the same liquidity and spread as any other time of day.

As a guideline, at 5pm Sunday NY Time, trading begins as the markets open in Sydney, Australia. Then, the Tokyo markets open at 7 pm NY Time. Next, Singapore and Hong Kong open at 9 pm NY Time followed by the European markets in Frankfurt (2am) and then London (3am). By 4am the European markets are in full swing, and Asia has concluded their trading day. The U.S. markets open first in New York around 8am Monday as Europe winds down. By 5pm, Sydney is set to reopen once again.

The majority of trading activity happens when the markets overlap; for example, Asia and Europe trading overlaps between 12am to approximately 2am, Europe and the United States overlaps between 8am to approximately 12pm NY Time, while the United States and Asia overlap between 5pm and 9pm. During New York and London hours, all currency pairs trade actively. During the Asian hours, however, the trading activity for pairs such as the GBPJPY and AUDJPY tend to peak.

Lower Transaction Costs

Lower transaction costs also makes forex an attractive asset class to trade. In the equity market, traders must pay a spread and/or a commission and with online equity brokers, commissions can run upwards of $20 per trade. This means that for positions of $100,000, average roundtrip commissions could be as high as $120. The over the counter (OTC) structure of the FX market eliminates exchange and clearing fees, which, in turn, lowers transaction costs. Costs are further reduced by the efficiencies created by a purely electronic market place that allows clients to deal directly with the market maker, eliminating both ticket costs and middlemen. Because the currency market offers round-the-clock liquidity, traders receive tight competitive spreads day and night. Equity traders are more vulnerable to liquidity risk and typically receive wider dealing spreads, especially during after-hours trading.

Low transaction costs make online FX trading the best market to trade for short-term traders. For an active equity trader who typically places 30 trades a day, at $20 commission per trade, you would have to up to pay $600 in daily transaction costs. This is a significant amount of money that could take a large cut out of profits or deepen losses. The reason why costs are so high is because there are a lot of people involved in an equity transaction. More specifically, for each trade, there is a broker, the exchange, and the specialist. All of these parties need to be paid, and their payment comes in the form of commission and clearing fees. In the FX market, because it is decentralized with no exchange or clearinghouse (everything is taken care of by the market maker), these fees are not applicable.

Customizable Leverage

Even though many people realize that higher leverage comes with risks, traders are humans, and few of them find it easy to turn away the opportunity to trade on someone else's money. The FX market caters perfectly to these traders by offering the highest leverage available for any market. Most online currency firms offer 50 times leverage on regular-sized accounts and up to 200 times leverage on miniature accounts (abroad leverage can be as high as 400 times). Compare that to the 2 times leverage offered to the average equity investor and the 10 times capital that is typically offered to the professional trader, and you can see why many traders have turned to the foreign exchange market. The margin deposit for leverage in the FX market is not seen as a down payment on a purchase of equity, as many perceive margins to be in the stock markets. Rather, the margin is a performance bond, or good-faith deposit, to ensure against trading losses. This is very useful to short-term day traders who need the enhancement in capital to generate quick returns. For the more risk-averse investor, leverage is completely customizable, which means that if they only feel comfortable with 10 or 20 times leverage or no leverage at all, they can elect to do so. It is extremely important to understand that leverage is a double-edged sword—it can magnify profits but also losses.

Profit in Both Bull and Bear Markets

In the FX market, profit potentials exist in both bull and bear markets. Since currency trading always involves buying one currency and selling another, there is no structural bias to the market. Therefore, if you are long one currency, you are at the same time short another. As a result, equal profit potential exists in both upward-trending and downward-trending markets. This is different from the equities market, where most traders go long instead of short stocks, so the general equity investment community tends to suffer in a bear market.

No Trading Curbs or Uptick Rule

The FX market is the largest market in the world, forcing market makers to offer very competitive prices. Unlike the equities market, there is never a time in the FX markets when trading curbs would take into effect and trading would be halted, only to gap when reopened. This eliminates missed profits due to archaic exchange regulations. In the FX market, traders would be able to place trades 24 hours a day with virtually no disruptions.

One of the biggest annoyances for day trades in the equity market is the fact that traders are prohibited from shorting a stock in a downtrend unless there is an uptick. This can be very frustrating as traders wait to join short sellers, but are only left with continually watching the stock trend down before an uptick occurs. In the FX market, there is no such rule. If you want to short a currency pair, you can do so immediately; this allows for instant and efficient execution.

Online Trading Reducing Error Rates

A shorter trade process minimizes errors. Online currency trading is typically a three-step process. A trader would place an order on the platform, the FX dealing desk would automatically execute it electronically, and the order confirmation would be posted or logged onto the trader's trading station. Typically, these three steps would be completed in a matter of seconds. For an equities trade on the other hand, there is generally a five-step process. The client would call his broker to place an order, the broker sends the order to the exchange floor, the specialist on the floor tries to match up orders (the broker competes with other brokers to get the best fill for the client), the specialist executes the trade, and the client receives a confirmation from the broker. The elimination of a middleman minimizes the error rates in currency trades and increases the efficiency of each transaction.

Limited Slippage

Unlike the equity markets, many online FX market makers provide instantaneous execution from real-time, two-way quotes. These quotes are the prices where the firms are willing to buy or sell the quoted currency, rather than vague indications of where the market is trading, which may or may not be honored. Orders are executed and confirmed within seconds. Robust systems would never request the size of a trader's potential order, or which side of the market he's trading, before giving him a bid/offer quote. Inefficient dealers determine whether the investor is a buyer or a seller, and shade the price to increase their own profit on the transaction.

The equity market typically operates under a "next best order" system, under which you may not get executed at the price you wish, but rather at the next best price available. For example, let's say Microsoft is trading at $52.50. If you enter a buy order at this rate, by the time it reaches the specialist on the exchange floor, the price may have risen to $53.25. In this case, you will not get executed at $52.50; you will get executed at $53.25, which is essentially a loss of ³/₄ of a point. The price transparency provided by the some of the better market makers assures that traders always receive a fair price.

Perfect Market for Technical Analysis

For technical analysts, currencies rarely spend much time in tight trading ranges and have the tendency to develop strong trends. Over 80% of volume is speculative in nature and as a result, the market frequently overshoots and then corrects itself. Hence, technical analysis works well for the FX market, and a technically trained trader can easily identify new trends and breakouts, which provide multiple opportunities to enter and exit positions. Charts and indicators are used by all professional FX market traders, and candle charts are available on most charting packages. In addition, the most commonly used indicators such as Fibonacci retracements, stochastics,

MACD, moving averages, RSI, and support/resistance levels have proven valid in many instances.

In the USDJPY chart shown in Figure 1.1, it is clear that Fibonacci retracements, moving averages, and stochastics have at one point or another given successful trading signals. For example, the 61.8% retracement level served as resistance for USDJPY in December 2014, January 2015, and February 2015. The moving-average crossovers of the 10- and 20-day simple moving averages also successfully forecasted the rally in USDJPY in late October, along with the decline in early January. Equity traders who focus on technical analysis have the easiest transition, since they can implement the same technical strategies that they use in the equities market into the FX market.

Analyze Stocks Like Countries

Trading currencies is not a big challenge for fundamental traders either, because countries can be analyzed like stocks. For example, if you analyze growth rates of stocks, you can use gross domestic product (GDP) to analyze the growth rate of countries. If you analyze inventory and production ratios, you can follow industrial production (IP) or durable goods data. If you follow sales figures, you can analyze retail sales data. As with a stock investment, it is better to invest in the currency of a country that is growing faster and fund it with a currency of a country that is growing slower. Currency prices reflect the balance of supply and demand for currencies. Two of the primary factors affecting supply and demand of currencies are interest rates and the overall strength of the economy. Economic indicators such as GDP, foreign investment, and the trade balance reflect the general health of an economy and are therefore responsible for the underlying shifts in supply and demand for that currency. There is a tremendous amount of data released at regular intervals, some of which are more important than others. Data related to interest rates and international trade is the most closely followed.

If there is uncertainty regarding the direction of interest rates, any bit of news on monetary policy can directly affect how the currency trades. Traditionally, if a country raises its interest rate, the currency of that country will strengthen in relation to other countries as investors shift assets to that country to gain a higher return. In contrast, an interest rates hike is generally bad news for stocks because it means that borrowing costs have risen. In response, some investors will transfer money out of a country's stock market when interest rates are increased, causing the country's currency to weaken. Determining which effect dominates can be tricky, but generally there is an advance consensus on how interest rates will move. Indicators that have the biggest impact on interest rates are producer prices, consumer prices, employment, spending, and GDP. Most of the time monetary policy announcements are known in advance with meeting dates by the Bank of

FOREIGN EXCHANGE—THE FASTEST GROWING MARKET

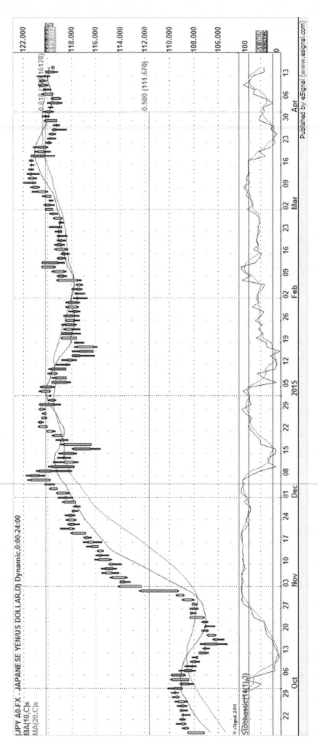

FIGURE 1.1 USDJPY Chart

Source: eSignal

England (BoE), the Federal Reserve (FED), European Central Bank (ECB), Bank of Japan (BoJ), and other central banks posted on their respective websites.

Another piece of data that can impact how currencies move is the trade balance, which shows the net difference over a period of time between a nation's exports and imports. When a country imports more than it exports, the trade balance will show a deficit, which is generally considered unfavorable. For example, if U.S. dollars are sold for other domestic national currencies (to pay for imports), the flow of dollars outside the country will depreciate the value of the dollar. Similarly, if trade figures show an increase in exports, dollars will flow into the United States and appreciate the value of the dollar. From the standpoint of a national economy, a deficit in and of itself is not necessarily a bad thing. If the deficit is greater than market expectations however, it can trigger a negative price movement.

FX versus Futures

Trading spot forex is also different from trading futures, and like equity traders, many futures traders have also added currency spot trading into their portfolios. We know that the spot forex market has the following attributes:

Characteristics of FX Markets
1. It is the largest market in the world with growing liquidity.
2. The market is open 24 hours, 5.5 days a week for trading.
3. Profits can be made in both bull and bear markets.
4. There are no trading curbs and short selling is permitted without an uptick.
5. Instant executable trading platform minimizes slippage and errors.
6. Leverage can be extremely high, which can magnify profits as well as losses.

Characteristics of Futures Markets
1. There is limited market liquidity depending on the month of contract trades.
2. The presence of exchange fees results in more costs and commissions.
3. Market hours for futures trading are much shorter than spot and are dependent on the product traded; each product may have different open and closing hours, and there is limited after-hours trading.
4. Futures leverage is higher than equities, but still only a fraction of the leverage offered in FX.
5. There tends to be prolonged bear markets.
6. Pit trading structure increases error and slippage.

Like in the equities market, traders can implement the same strategies they use in analyzing the futures markets in the FX market. Most future traders are technical traders, and the FX market is perfect for technical analysis. In fact, it is the most popular analysis technique used by professional FX traders. Taking a closer look at how the futures market stacks up, we see the following.

Comparing Market Hours and Liquidity

The volume traded in the FX market is estimated to be over five times that of the futures market. The FX market is open for trading 24 hours a day, but the futures market has confusing market hours which vary based on the product traded. For example, if you traded gold futures, it is only open for trading between 7:20am and 1:30pm on the COMEX. If you traded crude oil futures on the New York Mercantile Exchange, trading would only be open between 8:30am. and 2:10pm. These varying hours not only create confusion but also makes it difficult to act on breakthrough announcements throughout the reminder of the day.

In addition, if you have a day job and can only trade after hours, futures would be a very inconvenient market product to trade. You would basically be placing orders based on past prices that are not current market prices. This lack of transparency makes trading very cumbersome. In addition, each time zone has its own unique news and developments that could move specific currency pairs, and with futures it can difficult to act on breaking overnight news.

Low to Zero Transaction Costs

In the equity market, traders must pay a spread and/or a commission. With future brokers, average commissions can run close to $160 per trade on positions of $100,000 or greater. The OTC structure of the FX market eliminates exchange and clearing fees, which can in turn lowers transaction costs. Costs are further reduced by the efficiencies created by a purely electronic market place that allows clients to deal directly with the market maker, eliminating both ticket costs and middlemen. Because the currency market offers round-the-clock liquidity, traders receive tight, competitive spreads day and night. Futures traders are more vulnerable to liquidity risk and typically receive wider dealing spreads, especially during after-hours trading.

Low to zero transaction costs make online FX trading the best market to trade for short-term traders. If you are an active futures trader who typically places 20 trades a day, at $100 commission per trade, you would have to pay $2,000 in daily transaction costs. A typical futures trade involves a broker, a future commissions merchant (FCM) order desk, a clerk on the exchange floor, a runner, and a pit trader. All of these parties need to be paid, and their payment comes in the form of commission and clearing fees, whereas the electronic nature of the market minimizes these costs.

No Limit Up or Down Rules/Profit in Both Bull and Bear Markets

Unlike the tight restriction on the futures market, there is no limit down or limit up rule in the FX market. For example, on the S&P index futures, if the contract value falls more than 5% from the previous day's close, limit down rules will come in effect, whereby on a 5% move, the index would only be allowed to trade at or above this level for the next 10 minutes. For a 20% decline, trading would be completely halted. Due to the decentralized nature of the FX market, there are no exchange-enforced restrictions on daily activity, which can help eliminate missed opportunities caused by archaic exchange regulations.

Execution Quality and Speed/Low Error Rates

The futures market is also known for inconsistent execution, both in terms of pricing and execution time. Every futures trader has, at some point in time, experienced a half hour or so wait for a market order to be filled, only to find that the order has been executed at a price far away from where the market was trading when the initial order was placed. Even with electronic trading and limited guarantees of execution speed, the price for fills on market orders is far from certain. The reason for this inefficiency is the number of steps that are involved in placing a futures trade. A futures trade is typically a seven-step process:

1. The client calls his broker and places his trade (or places it online).
2. The trading desk receives the order, processes it, and routes it to the FCM order desk on the exchange floor.
3. The FCM order desk passes the order to the order clerk.
4. The order clerk hands the order to a runner or signals it to the pit.
5. The trading clerk goes to the pit to execute the trade.
6. The trade confirmation goes to the runner or is signaled to the order clerk and processed by the FCM order desk.
7. The broker receives the trade confirmation and passes it on to the client.

An FX trade in comparison is typically only a three-step process. A trader would place an order on the platform, the FX dealing desk would automatically execute it electronically, and the order confirmation would be posted or logged on the trader's trading station. The elimination of the involvement of these additional parties increases the speed of the trade execution and decreases errors.

In addition, the futures market typically operates under a "next best order" system, under which your trades frequently do not get executed at the initial market order price, but rather, at the next best price available. For example, let's say a client is long 5 March Dow Jones futures contracts at 8800. If the client enters a stop order at 8700, when the rate reaches this level, the client will most likely be executed at 8690. This 10-point difference would be attributed to slippage, which is very common in the futures market.

On most FX trading stations, traders execute directly off of real-time streaming prices. Barring any unforeseen circumstances, there is generally no discrepancy between the displayed price and the execution price. This holds true even during volatile times and fast-moving markets. In the futures market, execution is uncertain because all orders must be done on the exchange. This creates a situation where liquidity is limited by the number of participants, which, in turn, limits quantities that can be traded at a given price. Real-time streaming prices ensure that market orders, stops, and limits are executed with minimal slippage and no partial fills.

■ Who Are the Players in the FX Market?

Since the foreign exchange market is an OTC market without a centralized exchange, competition between market makers prohibits monopolistic pricing strategies. If one market maker attempts to drastically skew the price, then traders simply have the option to find another market maker. Moreover, spreads are closely watched to ensure market makers are not whimsically altering the cost of the trade. Many equity markets, on the other hand, operate in a completely different fashion; the New York Stock Exchange, for instance, is the sole place where companies listed on the NYSE can have their stocks traded. Centralized markets are operated by what are referred to as specialists. *Market makers,* on the other hand, is the term used in reference to decentralized marketplaces. Since the NYSE is a centralized market, a stock traded on the NYSE can only have one bid–ask quote at all times. Decentralized markets, such as foreign exchange, can have multiple market makers—all of whom have the right to quote different prices. Here is an illustration of how both centralized and decentralized markets operate.

Centralized Markets

By their very nature, centralized markets tend to be monopolistic: With a single specialist controlling the market, prices can easily be skewed to accommodate the interests of the specialist, not those of the traders (see Figure 1.2). If, for example, the market is filled with sellers that the specialists must buy from but no prospective buyers on the other side, the specialist may simply widen the spread, thereby

FIGURE 1.2 Centralized Market Structure

increasing the cost of the trade and preventing additional participants from entering the market. Or, specialists can drastically alter the quotes they are offering, thus manipulating the price to accommodate their own risk tolerance.

Hierarchy of Participants

While the foreign exchange market is decentralized, and hence employs multiple market makers rather than a single specialist, participants in the FX market are organized into a hierarchy; those with superior credit access, volume transacted, and sophistication receive priority pricing in the market (see Figure 1.3). At the top of the food chain is the interbank market, which trades the highest volume per day in relatively few currencies. In the interbank market, the largest banks can deal with each other directly, via interbank brokers, or through electronic brokering systems like EBS or Reuters. The interbank market is a credit-approved system, where banks trade based solely on the credit relationships they have established with one another. The banks can see the rates everyone is dealing at, but each bank must have a specific credit relationship with that bank in order to trade at the rates being offered. Other institutions such as online FX market makers, hedge funds, and corporations must trade FX through these banks, although some have created their own liquidity pools through the years. Many banks (e.g., small community banks or banks in emerging markets), corporations, and institutional investors do not have access to these rates because they have no established credit lines with big banks. This forces smaller participants to deal through just one bank for their

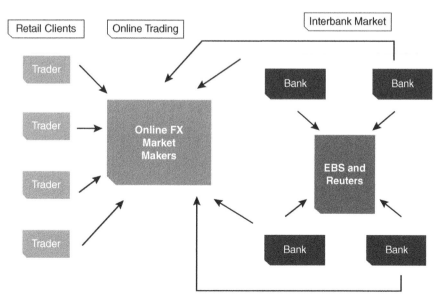

FIGURE 1.3   Decentralized Market Structure

foreign exchange needs, and oftentimes this means much less competitive rates for the participants further down the participant hierarchy. Those receiving the least competitive rates are customers of banks and physical currency exchange companies. Recently, technology has broken down the barriers that used to stand between the end-users of foreign exchange services and the interbank market. The online trading revolution opened its doors to retail clientele by connecting market makers and market participants in an efficient, low-cost manner. In essence, online trading platforms serve as a gateway to the liquid FX market. Average traders can now trade alongside the biggest banks in the world, with virtually similar pricing and execution. What used to be a game dominated and controlled by the "big boys" is slowly becoming a level playing field where individuals can profit and take advantage of the same opportunities as big banks. FX is no longer an old boys club, which means opportunities abound for aspiring online currency traders.

Dealing Stations—Interbank Market

For serious traders who want to know more about the interbank market, the majority of FX volume is actually transacted primarily through the interbank market. The leading banks of the world trade with each other electronically over two platforms—the EBS and Reuters, dealing 3000-spot matching. Both platforms offer trading in the major currency pairs; however, certain currency pairs are more liquid and generally more frequently traded over one versus the other. Some cross-currency pairs are traded over these platforms as well, but others are calculated from the rates of the major currency pairs and are then offset using the "legs." For example, if an interbank trader had a client who wanted to go long NZDCAD, the trader would most likely buy NZDUSD and USDCAD separately. The trader would then multiply these rates and provide the client with the respective NZDCAD rate, creating a synthetic quote and trade.

CHAPTER 2

Historical Events in the FX Markets

Before learning how to trade currencies, it is important for every new and seasoned market participant to have some understanding about the most important historical events that have shaped the currency market. To this day, these events are often referenced by professional traders.

Bretton Woods: Anointing the Dollar as the World Currency (1944)

In July 1944, representatives of 44 nations met in Bretton Woods, New Hampshire, to create a new institutional arrangement for governing the international economy in the years following World War II. Most agreed that international economic instability was one of the principle causes of the war, and that such instability needed to be prevented in the future. The agreement, which was developed by renowned economists John Maynard Keynes and Harry Dexter White, was initially proposed to Great Britain as a part of the Lend Lease Act—an American act designed to assist Great Britain in postwar redevelopment efforts. After various negotiations, the final form of the Bretton Woods Agreement consisted of three key items:

1. The formation of key international authorities designed to promote fair trade and international economic harmony
2. The fixation of exchange rates between currencies
3. The convertibility between gold and the U.S. dollar, thus empowering the U.S. dollar as the reserve currency of choice for the world

Of these three parameters, only the first is still in existence today, but the organizations formed as a direct result of Bretton Woods include the International Monetary Fund (IMF), World Bank, and General Agreement on Tariffs and Trade (GATT); and they all play a crucial role in modern day development and regulation of international economies. Since the demise of Bretton Woods, the IMF has worked closely with the World Bank. Together, the two institutions now regularly lend funds to developing nations, assisting them in the development of a public infrastructure capable of supporting a sound mercantile economy that can contribute in the international arena. In order to ensure that these nations can actually enjoy equal and legitimate access to trade with their industrialized counterparts, the World Bank and IMF must work closely with GATT. While GATT was initially meant to be a temporary organization, it now operates to encourage the dismantling of trade barriers—namely, tariffs and quotas.

The Bretton Woods Agreement existed from 1944 to 1971, after which it was replaced by the Smithsonian Agreement, an international contract pioneered by U.S. President Richard Nixon out the necessity to accommodate for Bretton Woods' shortcomings. Unfortunately, the Smithsonian Agreement possessed the same critical weakness: While it did not include gold/U.S. dollar convertibility, it maintained fixed exchange rates—a facet that did not accommodate the United States' ongoing trade deficit and the international need for a weaker U.S. dollar. As a result, the Smithsonian Agreement was short-lived.

Ultimately, the exchange rates of the world evolved into a free market, where supply and demand were the sole criteria that determined the value of a currency. While this did and still does result in a number of currency crises and greater volatility between currencies, it also allowed the market to become self-regulating, and thus could dictate the appropriate value of a currency without any hindrances.

As for Bretton Woods, perhaps its most memorable contribution to the international economic arena was its role in changing the international perception about the U.S. dollar. While the euro is a revolutionary currency blazing new frontiers in both social behavior and international trade, the U.S. dollar remains the world's reserve currency of choice. This is due, in large part, to the Bretton Woods Agreement: By establishing dollar/gold convertibility, the dollar's role as the world's most accessible and reliable currency was firmly cemented. So while Bretton Woods might be a doctrine of yesteryear, its impact on the U.S. dollar and international economics still resonates today.

■ The End of Bretton Woods: Free Market Capitalism Is Born (1971)

On August 15, 1971, it became official: The Bretton-Woods system was abandoned once and for all. While it had been exorcised before—only to subsequently emerge in a new form—this final eradication of the Bretton Woods system was truly its last stand: No longer would currencies be fixed in value to gold, allowed only to fluctuate in a 1% range, but instead, their fair valuation could be determined by free-market behavior such as trade flows and foreign direct investment.

Although U.S. President Nixon was confident that the end of the Bretton Woods system would bring about better times for the international economy, he was not a believer that the free market could dictate a currency's true valuation in a fair and catastrophe-free manner. Nixon and many well-respected economists at the time reasoned that an entirely unstructured foreign exchange market would result in competing devaluations, which, in turn, would lead to the breakdown of international trade and investment. The end result, Nixon and his board of economic advisors argued, would be global depression.

In response, the Smithsonian Agreement was introduced a few months later. Hailed by President Nixon as the "greatest monetary agreement in the history of the world," the Smithsonian Agreement strived to maintain fixed exchange rates without the backing of gold. Its key difference from the Bretton Woods system was that the value of the dollar could float in a range of 2.25%, compared to just 1% under Bretton Woods.

Ultimately, the Smithsonian Agreement proved to be unfeasible as well. Without exchange rates fixed to gold, the free market gold price shot up to $215 per ounce. Moreover, the U.S. trade deficit continued to grow, and from a fundamental standpoint, the U.S. dollar needed to be devalued beyond the 2.25% parameters established by the Smithsonian Agreement. In light of these problems, the foreign exchange markets were forced to close in February 1972.

The markets reopened in March 1973, and this time, they were not bound by a Smithsonian Agreement: The value of the US dollar was to be determined entirely by the market, as its value was not fixed to any commodity, nor was its exchange rate fluctuation confined to certain parameters. While this did provide the U.S. dollar, and other currencies by default, the agility required to adapt to a new and rapidly evolving international trading environment, it also set the stage for unprecedented inflation. The end of Bretton Woods and the Smithsonian Agreement, as well as conflicts in the Middle East, resulted in substantially higher oil prices and helped to create stagflation—the synthesis of unemployment and inflation—in the U.S. economy. It would not be until later in the decade, when Federal Reserve Chairman Paul Volcker initiated new economic policies and President Reagan introduced a new fiscal agenda, that the U.S. dollar would return to "normal" valuations. By then, the foreign exchange markets had thoroughly developed and were capable of serving a multitude of purposes. In addition to employing a laissez-faire style of regulation on international trade, they also were beginning to attract speculators seeking to participate in a market with unrivaled liquidity and continued growth. Ultimately, the death of Bretton Woods in 1971 marked the beginning of a new economic era, one that liberated international trading while also proliferating speculative opportunities.

Plaza Accord—Devaluation of the U.S. Dollar (1985)

After the demise of all the various exchange rate regulatory mechanisms that characterized the twentieth century—that is, the Gold Standard, the Bretton Woods Standard, and the Smithsonian Agreement—the currency market was left with virtually no regulation other than the mythical "invisible hand" of free market capitalism, one that supposedly strived to create economic balance through supply and demand. Unfortunately, due to a number of unforeseen economic events—such as the OPEC oil crises, stagflation throughout the 1970s, and drastic changes in the U.S. Federal Reserve's fiscal policy—supply and demand, in and of themselves, became insufficient means by which the currency markets could be regulated. A system of sorts was needed, but not one that was inflexible: Fixation of currency values to a commodity, such as gold, proved to be too rigid for economic development, as was also the notion of fixing maximum exchange rate fluctuations. The balance between structure and rigidity was one that had plagued the currency markets throughout the twentieth century, and while advancements had been made, a definitive solution was still greatly needed.

Hence, in 1985, the respective ministers of finance and central bank governors of the world's leading economies—France, Germany, Japan, the United Kingdom, and the United States—convened in New York City, with the hopes of arranging a diplomatic agreement that would work to optimize the economic effectiveness of the foreign exchange markets. Meeting at the Plaza Hotel, the international leaders came to the following agreements regarding specific economies and the international economy as a whole:

- Across the world, inflation was at very low levels. Contrary to the stagflation of the 1970s—where inflation was high and real economic growth was low—the global economy in 1985 had done a complete 180, as inflation was now low and growth was strong.

- While low inflation, even when coupled with robust economic growth, still allowed for low interest rates—a caveat that developing countries particularly enjoyed—there was an imminent danger of protectionist policies such as tariffs entering the economy. The United States was experiencing a large and growing current account deficit, while Japan and Germany were facing large and growing surpluses. An imbalance so fundamental in nature could create serious economic disequilibrium, which, in turn, would result in a distortion of the foreign exchange markets, and thus, the international economy as a whole.

- The results of current account imbalances, and the protectionist policies that ensued, required action. Ultimately, it was believed that the rapid acceleration in the value of the U.S. dollar, which appreciated more than 80% against the currencies of its major trading partners, was the primary culprit. The rising value of the U.S. dollar created enormous trade deficits, hurting many different economies.

At the meeting in the Plaza Hotel, the United States persuaded other attending countries to coordinate a multilateral intervention, and on September 22, 1985, the Plaza Accord was implemented. This agreement was designed to allow for a controlled decline of the dollar and the appreciation of the main anti-dollar currencies. Each country agreed to changes to their economic policies and to intervene in currency markets as necessary to weaken the value of the dollar. The United States agreed to cut its budget deficit and lower interest rates. France, the United Kingdom, Germany, and Japan agreed to raise interest rates. Germany also agreed to tax cuts, while Japan agreed to let the value of the yen "fully reflect the underlying strength of the Japanese economy." However, one major problem was that not every country adhered to their pledges made under the Plaza Accord. The United States, in particular, did not follow through with its initial promise to cut the budget deficit. Japan was severely hurt by the sharp rise in the yen, as its exporters were unable to remain competitive overseas, and it is argued that this eventually triggered a 10-year recession in Japan. The United States, on the other hand, enjoyed considerable growth and price stability as a result of the agreement.

The effects of the multilateral intervention were seen immediately, and within less than two years, the dollar fell 46% and 50% against the German deutschemark and the Japanese yen, respectively, as shown in Figure 2.1. The U.S. economy

FIGURE 2.1 Plaza Accord Price Action

became far more export-oriented as a result, while other industrial countries like Germany and Japan assumed the role of major net importers. This gradually resolved the current account deficits for the time being, and also ensured that protectionist policies were minimal and nonthreatening. But perhaps most importantly, the Plaza Accord cemented the role of the central banks in regulating exchange rate movement—yes, the rates would not be fixed, and hence would be determined primarily by supply and demand; but ultimately, such an invisible hand is insufficient, and it was the right and responsibility of the world's central banks to intervene on behalf of the international economy when necessary.

George Soros—The Man Who Broke the Bank of England

When George Soros placed a $10 billion speculative bet on the UK pound and won, he became universally known as "the man who broke the Bank of England." Whether you love him or hate him, Soros led the charge in one of the most fascinating events in currency trading history. Here are the details.

The UK Joins the Exchange Rate Mechanism

In 1979, a Franco-German initiative set up the European Monetary System (EMS) to stabilize exchange rates, reduce inflation, and prepare for monetary integration. The Exchange Rate Mechanism (ERM), one of the EMS's main components, gave each participatory currency a central exchange rate against a basket of currencies, the European Currency Unit (ECU). Participants (initially France, Germany, Italy, the Netherlands, Belgium, Denmark, Ireland, and Luxemburg) were then required to maintain their exchange rates within a 2.25% fluctuation band above or below each bilateral central rate. The ERM was an adjustable-peg system, and nine realignments would occur between 1979 and 1987. While the United Kingdom was not one of the original members, it would eventually join in 1990 at a rate of DM2.95 to the pound and with a fluctuation band of +/−6%.

Until mid-1992, the ERM appeared to be a success, as a disciplinary effect had reduced inflation throughout Europe under the leadership of the German Bundesbank. The stability wouldn't last, however, as international investors started worrying that the exchange rate values of several currencies within the ERM were inappropriate. Following German reunification in 1989 government spending surged, forcing the Bundesbank to print more money. This led to high inflation and left the German central bank with little choice but to increase interest rates. However, the rate hike came with consequences as it placed upward pressure on the German mark. This forced other central banks to raise their interest rates as well as to maintain their pegged currency exchange rates (a direct application of Irving Fischer's interest parity theory). Realizing that the UK's weak economy and high unemployment rate would not permit the British government to maintain this policy for long, George Soros stepped into action.

Soros Bets Against the Success of UK Involvement in the ERM

The quantum hedge fund manager essentially wanted to bet that the pound would depreciate because the United Kingdom would either devalue the pound or leave the ERM. Thanks to the progressive removal of capital controls during the EMS years, international investors at the time had more freedom than ever to take advantage of perceived disequilibria, so Soros established short positions in pounds and long positions in marks by borrowing pounds and investing in mark-denominated assets. He also made great use of options and futures. In all, his positions accounted for a gargantuan $10 billion. Soros was not the only one; many other investors soon followed suit. Everyone was selling pounds, placing tremendous downward pressure on the currency.

At first, the Bank of England (BoE) tried to defend the pegged rates by buying 15 billion pounds with its large reserve assets, but its sterilized interventions (whereby the monetary base is held constant thanks to open market interventions) were limited in their effectiveness. The pound was trading dangerously close to the lower levels of its fixed band. On September 16, 1992, a day that would later be known as Black Wednesday, the bank announced a 2% rise in interest rates (from 10% to 12%) in an attempt to boost the pound's appeal. A few hours later, it promised to raise rates again to 15%, but international investors such as Soros could not be swayed, knowing that huge profits were right around the corner. Traders kept selling pounds in huge volumes, and the BoE kept buying them until, finally, at 7:00 pm that same day, Chancellor Norman Lamont announced that Britain would leave the ERM and that rates would return to their initial level of 10%. The chaotic Black Wednesday marked the beginning of a steep depreciation in the pound's effective value.

Whether the return to a floating currency was due to the Soros-led attack on the pound or because of simple fundamental analysis is still debated today. What is certain, however, is that the pound's depreciation of almost 15% against the deutschemark and 25% against the dollar over the next five weeks as seen in Figure 2.2 and Figure 2.3 resulted in tremendous profits for Soros and others traders (the pound also weakened by a similar proportion to the dollar). Within a month, the quantum fund cashed in on approximately $2 billion by selling the now more expensive DMs and buying back the now cheaper pounds. "The man who broke the Bank of England" showed how central banks can still be vulnerable to speculative attacks.

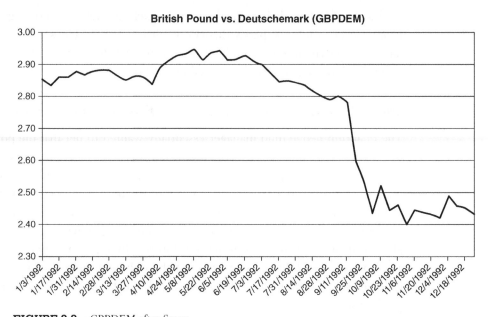

FIGURE 2.2   GBPDEM after Soros

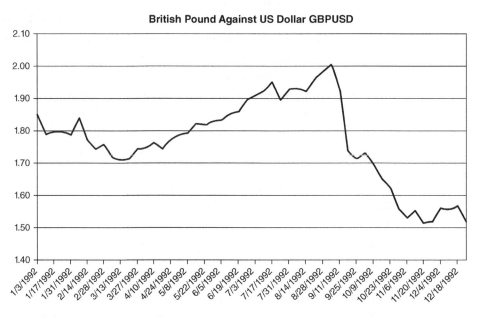

FIGURE 2.3   GBPUSD after Soros

■ Asian Financial Crisis (1997–1998)

Falling like a set of dominos on July 2, 1997, the relatively nascent Asian tiger economies provide the perfect example of the interdependence in global capital markets and their subsequent effects throughout international currency forums. Based on several fundamental breakdowns, the cause of the "contagion" stemmed largely from shrouded lending practices, inflated trade deficits, and immature capital markets. Compiled, these factors contributed to a perfect storm that left major regional markets incapacitated and once-prized currencies devalued to significantly lower levels. With adverse effects easily seen in the equities markets, currency market fluctuations were negatively impacted in much the same manner during this time period.

The Bubble

Leading up to 1997, investors had become increasingly attracted to Asian investment prospects, focusing on real estate development and domestic equities. As a result, foreign investment capital flowed into the region as economic growth rates climbed on improved production in countries like Malaysia, the Philippines, Indonesia, and Korea. Thailand, home of the baht, experienced a 6.5% growth rate in 1996, falling from 13% in 1988. Lending additional support for a stronger economy was the enactment of a fixed currency peg to the U.S. dollar. With a fixed valuation to the greenback, countries like Thailand could ensure financial stability in their own markets and a constant rate for export trading purposes with the world's largest economy. Ultimately, the region's national currencies appreciated, as underlying fundamentals were justified and increased speculative positions of further climbs in price mounted.

Ballooning Current Account Deficits and Nonperforming Loans

However, in early 1997, a shift in sentiment began to occur as international account deficits became increasingly difficult for respective governments to handle and lending practices were revealed to be detrimental to the economic infrastructure. In particular, economists were alerted to the fact that Thailand's current account deficit ballooned in 1996 to $14.7 billion and had been climbing since 1992. Although comparatively smaller than the U.S. deficit, the gap represented 8% of the country's gross domestic product. Shrouded lending practices also contributed heavily to these breakdowns, as close personal relationships with high-ranking banking officials were well rewarded and surprisingly common throughout the region. In particular this affected many of South Korea's highly leveraged conglomerates as total nonperforming loan values skyrocketed to 7.5 percent of gross domestic product. Additional evidence of these practices could be observed in financial institutions throughout Japan. First announcing questionable and nonperforming loans of $136 billion in 1994, Japanese authorities admitted to an alarming $400 billion total a year later. Coupled with a then-crippled stock market, cooling real estate values, and dramatic slowdowns in the economy, investors saw opportunity in a depreciating yen, subsequently adding selling pressure to neighbor currencies. When their own asset bubble collapsed, asset prices fell by $10 trillion, with the fall in real estate prices accounting for nearly 65% of the total decline—the losses were worth two years of national output. This fall in asset prices sparked the banking crisis in Japan. It began in the early 1990s and then developed into a full-blown, systemic crisis in 1997, following the failure of a number of high-profile financial institutions. In response, Japanese monetary authorities issued rhetoric on potentially increasing benchmark interest rates in hopes of defending the domestic currency valuation. Unfortunately, these considerations never materialized and a shortfall ensued. Sparked mainly by an announcement of a managed float of the Thai baht, the slide snowballed as central bank reserves evaporated and currency price levels became unsustainable in light of downside selling pressure.

Currency Crisis

Following mass short speculation and attempted intervention, the aforementioned Asian economies were left ruined and momentarily incapacitated. The Thailand baht, a once-prized possession, was devalued by as much as 48 percent, even slumping closer to a 100% fall at the turn of the new year. The most adversely affected was

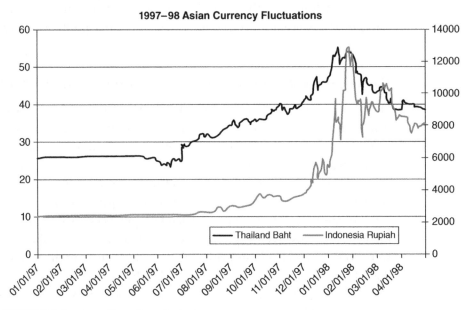

FIGURE 2.4 Asian Crisis Price Action

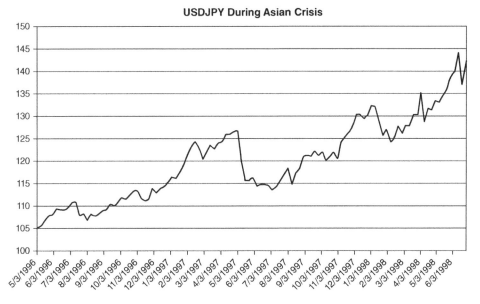

FIGURE 2.5 USDJPY Asian Crisis Price Action

the Indonesian rupiah. Also relatively stable prior to the onset of a "crawling peg" with the Thai baht, the rupiah fell a whopping 228%, worsening previously to a high of 12,950 to the fixed U.S. dollar. These particularly volatile price actions are shown in Figure 2.4. Among the majors, the Japanese yen fell approximately 23% from its high to low against the U.S. dollar between 1997 and 1998, and after having retraced a significant portion of its losses, ended the 8-month debacle down 15%, as shown in Figure 2.5.

Lasting for less than a year, the financial crisis of 1997 revealed the interconnectivity of economies and their effects in the global currency markets. Additionally, it showed the inability of central banks to successfully intervene in currency valuations with the absence of secure economic fundamentals and overwhelming market forces. Today, with the assistance of IMF reparation packages and the implementation of stricter requirements, Asia's four little dragons are healthy once again. With inflationary benchmarks and a revived exporting market, Southeast Asia is building back its once prominent stature among the world's industrialized economic regions. With the experience of evaporating currency reserves under their belt, the Asian tigers now take active initiatives to ensure that there is large pot of reserves on hand in case speculators attempt to attack their currencies once again.

■ Introduction of the Euro (1999)

The introduction of the euro was a monumental achievement, marking the largest monetary changeover ever. The euro was officially launched as an electronic trading currency on January 1, 1999. Euro notes and coins were put into circulation in 2002. The 11 initial member states were: Belgium, Germany, Spain, France, Ireland, Italy, Luxembourg, the Netherlands, Austria, Portugal, and Finland. As of 2015, there are 17 countries in the Eurozone. Each country fixed its currency to a specific conversion rate against the euro, and a common monetary policy governed by the European Central Bank (ECB) was adopted. To many economists, the system would ideally include all of the original 15 EU nations, but the United Kingdom, Sweden, and Denmark decided to keep their own currencies. In deciding whether to adopt the euro, EU members have many important factors to consider.

The 1993 Maastricht Treaty sets out five main convergence criteria for member states to participate in the European Monetary Union (EMU):

Maastricht Treaty: Convergence Criteria

- The country's government budget deficit could not be greater than 3% of GDP.

- The country's government debt could not be larger than 60% of GDP.

- The country's exchange rate had to be maintained within ERM bands without any realignment for two years prior to joining.

- The country's inflation rate could not be higher than 1.5% above the average inflation rate of the three EU countries with the lowest inflation rates.

- The country's long-term interest rate on government bonds could not be higher than 2% above the average of the comparable rates in the three countries with the lowest inflation.

Although the ease of traveling is one of the most attractive reasons to join the euro, being part of the monetary union provides other benefits:

- It eliminates exchange rate fluctuations, providing a more stable environment to trade within the euro area.

- The purging of all exchange rate risk within the zone allows businesses to plan investment decisions with greater certainty.

- Transaction costs also diminish, mainly those relating to foreign exchange operations, hedging operations, cross-border payments, and the management of several currency accounts.

- Prices become more transparent as consumers and businesses can compare prices across countries more easily, which, in turn, increases competition.

- A huge single currency market becomes more attractive for foreign investors.

- The economy's magnitude and stability allow the ECB to control inflation with lower interest rates, thanks to increased credibility.

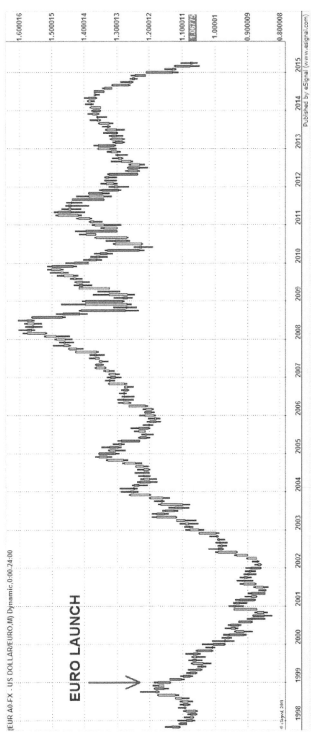

FIGURE 2.6 EURUSD Price Since Launch

Source: eSignal

Yet the euro is not without its limitations. Leaving aside political sovereignty issues, the main problem is that, by adopting the euro, a nation essentially forfeits any independent monetary policy. Since each country's economy is not perfectly correlated to the EMU's economy, a nation might find the ECB hiking interest rates during a domestic recession. This can be particularly true for many of the smaller nations. As a result, countries try to rely more heavily on fiscal policy, but the efficiency of fiscal policy is limited when it is not effectively combined with monetary policy. This inefficiency is further exacerbated by the 3% of GDP limit on budget deficits, as stipulated by the Stability and Growth Pact.

Some concerns also subsist regarding the ECB's effectiveness as a central bank. The central bank strives for a 2% inflation target, but in the past 15 years, it strayed away from this level often. Also, from 1999 to late 2002, a lack of confidence in the union's currency (and in the union itself) led to a 24% depreciation, from approximately $1.15 to the euro in January 1999 to $0.88 in May 2000, forcing the ECB to intervene in foreign exchange markets in the last few months of 2000. Figure 2.6 shows a daily chart of the euro since it was launched in 1999.

Since 2000, things have greatly changed, with the euro trading at a premium to the dollar, but quantitative easing in 2014 put the currency back in a downtrend versus the dollar. Some analysts claim that the euro will one day replace the dollar as the world's dominant international currency, and while we believe it will have a greater share in reserve portfolios, we doubt that this will be likely.

CHAPTER 3

What Moves the Currency Market?

Now that we know a little bit about the history of the forex market, let's take a look at what moves currencies. There are two primary ways to analyze financial markets: fundamental analysis and technical analysis. Fundamental analysis is rooted in understanding underlying economic conditions, while technical analysis uses historical prices to predict future movements. For as long as technical analysis has been around, there has been an ongoing debate as to which methodology is more successful. Short-term traders prefer to use technical analysis, focusing their strategies primarily on price action, while medium-term traders tend to use fundamental analysis to determine a currency's current and future valuation.

Before implementing successful trading strategies, it is important to understand what drives the movements of currencies in the foreign exchange market. The best strategies tend to be the ones that combine both fundamental and technical analysis. Textbook perfect technical formations have failed too often because of major fundamental news and events like U.S. nonfarm payrolls. But trading on fundamentals alone can also be risky. There will oftentimes be sharp gyrations in the price of currency on a day when there are no news or economic reports. This suggests that the price action is driven by nothing more than flows, sentiment, and pattern formations. Therefore, it is very important for technical traders to be aware of the key economic data or events that are scheduled for release, and, in turn, for fundamental traders to be aware of important technical levels that the general market may be focusing on.

■ Fundamental Analysis

Fundamental analysis focuses on the economic, social, and political forces that drive supply and demand. Those using fundamental analysis as a trading tool look at various macroeconomic indicators such as growth rates, interest rates, inflation, and unemployment. We outlined some of the most important economic releases in the first chapter of this book. Fundamental analysts will combine all of this information to assess current and future performance. This requires a lot of work and thorough analysis, as there is no single set of beliefs that guides fundamental analysis. Traders employing fundamental analysis need to continually keep abreast of news and announcements, as they can indicate potential changes to the economic, social, and political environment. All traders should be aware of the broad economic conditions before placing trades. This is especially important for day traders who are trying to make trading decisions based on news events because even though Federal Reserve Monetary Policy decisions are always important, if the rate move is completely priced into the market, then the actual reaction in the EURUSD could be nominal.

Taking a step back, currencies move primarily based on supply and demand. That is, on the most fundamental level, a currency rallies because there is demand for that currency. Regardless of whether the demand is for hedging, speculative, or conversion purposes, true movements are based on the need for the currency. Currency values decrease when there is excess supply. Supply and demand should be the real determinants for predicting future movements. However, how to predict supply and demand is not as simple as many would think. There are many factors that contribute to the net supply and demand for a currency. This includes capital flows, trade flows, speculative, and hedging needs.

For example, the U.S. dollar was very strong (against the euro) between 1999 and the end of 2001. This rally was driven primarily by the dot-com boom and the desire by foreign investors to participate in these elevated returns. This demand for U.S. assets required foreign investors to sell their local currencies and purchase U.S. dollars. Since the end of 2001, geopolitical uncertainty arose, the United States started cutting interest rates, and foreign investors started to sell U.S. assets in search of higher yields elsewhere. This required foreign investors to sell U.S. dollars, increasing supply and lowering the dollar's value against other major currency pairs. The availability of funding or interest in buying a currency is a major factor that can impact the direction that a currency trades. It was one of the primary drivers of the U.S. dollar between 2002 and 2005, making foreign official purchases of U.S. assets (also known as the Treasury International Capital Flow, or TIC data) an important economic indicator.

Capital and Trade Flows

Capital flows and trade flows constitute a country's balance of payments, which quantifies the amount of demand for a currency over a given period of time. Theoretically, a balance of payments equal to zero is required for a currency to maintain its current valuation. A negative balance of payments number, on the other hand, indicates that capital is leaving the economy at a more rapid rate than it is entering, and hence, it should fall in value.

This is particularly important in current conditions (at the time of this book's publication), where the United States is running a consistently large trade deficit without sufficient foreign inflow to fund that deficit. As a result of this very problem, the trade-weighted dollar index fell 22% in value between 2003 and 2005. The Japanese yen is another good example. As one of the world's largest exporters, Japan runs a very high trade surplus. Therefore, despite a zero interest rate policy that prevents capital flows from increasing, the yen has a natural tendency to trade lower based on trade flows, which is the other side of the equation. To be more specific, following is a more detailed explanation of what capital and trade flows encompass.

Capital Flows

Capital flows measure the net amount of a currency that is being purchased or sold due to capital investments. A positive capital flow balance implies that foreign inflows of physical or portfolio investments into a country exceed outflows. A negative capital flow balance indicates that there are more physical or portfolio investments bought by domestic investors than foreign investors. There are generally two types of capital flows—physical flows and portfolio flows (which are further segmented into equity markets and fixed-income markets).

Physical Flows

Physical flows encompass actual foreign direct investments by corporations such as investments in real estate, manufacturing, and local acquisitions. All of these require that a foreign corporation sell its local currency and buy the foreign currency, which leads to movements in the FX market. This is particularly important for global mergers and corporate acquisitions that involve more cash than stock.

Physical flows are important to watch, as they represent the underlying changes in actual physical investment activity. These flows shift in response to changes in each country's financial health and growth opportunities. Changes in local laws that encourage foreign investment also serve to promote physical flows. For example, due to China's entry into the WTO, its foreign investment laws have been relaxed. As a result of China's cheap labor and attractive revenue opportunities (population of over 1 billion), corporations globally have flooded China with investments. From an FX perspective, in order to fund investments in China, foreign corporations need to sell their local currency and buy Chinese renminbi (RMB).

Portfolio Flows in Equity Markets

As technology has enabled greater ease with respect to transportation of capital, investing in global *equity markets* has become far more feasible. Accordingly, a rallying stock market in any part of the world serves as an ideal opportunity for all, regardless of geographic location. The result of this has become a strong correlation between a country's equity markets and its currency: If the equity market is rising, investment dollars generally come in to seize the opportunity. Alternatively, falling equity markets could prompt domestic investors to sell their shares of local publicly traded firms to take advantage of investment opportunities abroad.

The attraction of equity markets over fixed-income markets has increased across the years. Since the early 1990s, the ratio of foreign transactions in U.S. government bonds over U.S. equities has declined from 10 to 1 to 2 to 1. As indicated in Figure 3.1, it is evident that the Dow had a high correlation (of approximately 81%) with the U.S. dollar (against the EUR) between 1994 and 1999. In addition, from 1991–1999, the Dow increased 300%, while the USD index appreciated nearly 30% for the same time period. As a result, currency traders closely followed the global equity markets to predict short and intermediate term equity-based capital flows. However, this relationship shifted after the tech bubble burst in the United States as

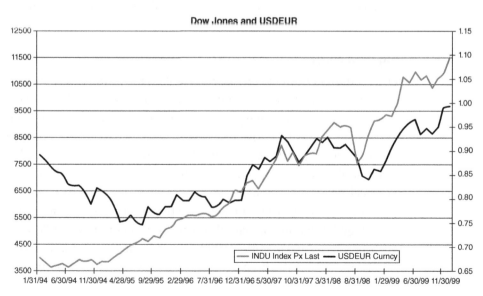

FIGURE 3.1 Dow and USDEUR

foreign investors remained relatively risk averse causing a lower correlation between the performance of the U.S. equity market and the U.S. dollar. Nevertheless, a relationship still exists, making it important for all traders to keep an eye on global market performances in search of intermarket opportunities.

Portfolio Flows in Fixed-Income Markets

Just as the equity market is correlated to exchange rate movement, so too is the fixed-income market. In times of global uncertainty, fixed-income investments can become particularly appealing, due to the inherent safety they possess. As a result, economies boasting the most valuable fixed-income opportunities will be capable of attracting foreign investment—which will naturally first require the purchasing of the country's respective currency.

A good gauge of fixed-income capital flows are the short- and long-term yields of international government bonds. It is important to monitor the spread differential between the 10-year U.S. Treasury yield and the yield on foreign bonds because international investors tend to move money from one country to another in search of the highest yielding assets. When U.S. assets have one of the highest yields, this encourages more investments in U.S. financial instruments, hence benefiting the U.S. dollar. When the United States has the lowest yields, this discourages investments. Investors can also use short-term yields, such as the spreads on 2-year government bonds, to gauge the short-term flow of international funds. Aside from government bond yields, Fed fund futures can also be used to estimate movement of U.S. funds, as they price in the expectation of future Fed interest rate policy. Euribor futures are a barometer for the Euro region's expected future interest rates and can give an indication of EU future policy movements. We will discuss how to use fixed-income products to trade FX further in our strategy section.

Trade Flows: Measuring Exports versus Imports

Trade flows are the basis of all international transactions. Just as the investment environment of a given economy is a key driver of its currency valuation, trade flows represent a country's net trade balance. Countries that are net exporters—meaning they sell more goods abroad than they buy—will experience a net trade surplus. Countries that are net exporters are more likely to have their currency rise in value because from the perspective of international trade, their currency is being bought more than it is sold. This impacts currency flows because international clients buying the exported product/service must first buy the currency of the exporting nation.

Countries who are net importers purchase more goods abroad than they sell, creating a trade deficit. These nations will generally see more downward than upward pressure on their currencies because in order to purchase these foreign goods, importers must sell their own currency and purchase the currency of the country from which they are buying the good or service. This accordingly drives down the value of the currency when all else is equal. This concept is important because it is one of primary reasons why many economists say that certain currencies need to fall to reverse burgeoning trade deficits.

To understand this further, let's imagine that the UK economy is booming, and its stock market is performing well. Meanwhile, in the United States, a lackluster economy is creating a shortage of investment opportunities. In this type of environment U.S. investors will feel more inclined to sell their U.S. dollars and buy British pounds to participate in the outperformance of the UK economy. When they elect to do so, it results in the outflow of capital from the United States and the inflow of capital into the United Kingdom. From an exchange rate perspective, this would induce a fall in the USD coupled with a rise in the GBP, as demand for USD declines and the demand for GBP increases, translating into strength for the GBP/USD currency pair.

Even day and swing traders will find it valuable to keep up with incoming economic reports from the major economies.

Trading Tip: Charting Economic Surprises

One way for traders to stay on top of economic trends is to chart economic data surprises against price action. Figure 3.2 illustrates how this can be done. The chart graphs how much an economic indicator has deviated from its consensus forecast, or the "surprise," and stacks them on the same side and graphs price (blue line) action when the data was release against the surprise, with a simple regression line (white line). This can be done for all of the major currency pairs and provides a visual guide to understanding whether price action has been in line with economic fundamentals and can be used as a guide to future price action. Economic data can be found on the calendars of any major forex website, and price action can generally be downloaded from your trading platforms.

According to Figure 3.2, in November of 2004, there were 14 out of 15 positive economic surprises and yet the dollar sold off against the euro during the month of December, which was the month in which the economic data were released. Although this methodology is not exact, the analysis is simple and past charts have yielded some extremely useful clues to future price action. Figure 3.3 shows how the EURUSD moved the following month. As you can see, the EURUSD quickly corrected itself during the month of January, indicating that the fundamental divergence from price action that occurred in December proved to be quite useful to dollar longs, which harvested almost 600 pips as the euro quickly retracted a large part of its gains in January. This method of analysis, called *variant perception,* was first invented by the legendary hedge fund manager Michael Steinhardt, who produced 24% average rates return for 30 consecutive years.

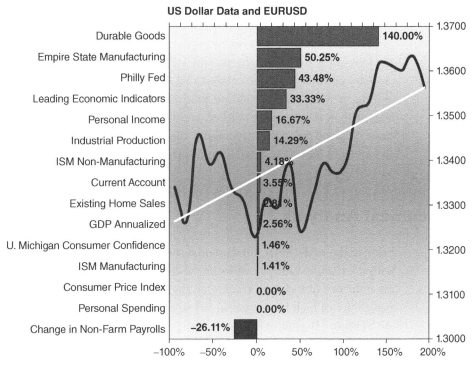

FIGURE 3.2 Charting Economic Surprises

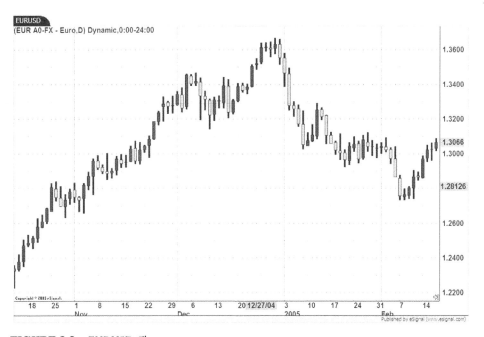

FIGURE 3.3 EURUSD Chart

Source: eSignal

Although these charts will rarely offer such clear-cut signals, their analytical value may also lie in spotting and interpreting the outlier data. Large positive and negative surprises in economic data can often yield clues to future price action. If you go back and look at the EURUSD charts, you will see that the record current account deficits in October 2004 were the catalyst that sent the dollar plunging over the next two months. In many ways, economic fundamentals matter more in the foreign exchange market than in any other market, and charts such as these could provide valuable clues to price direction. Generally, the 15 most important economic indices are chosen from each region, and then a price regression line is superimposed over the past 20 days of price data.

■ Technical Analysis

Prior to the mid-1980s, fundamental traders dominated the FX market. However, with the rising popularity of technical analysis and the advent of new technologies, the influence of technical trading on the FX market has increased significantly. The availability of high leverage also led to an increased number of high frequency and momentum. They have become active participants in the FX market, with the acute ability to influence currency prices.

Unlike fundamental analysis, technical analysis focuses on the study of price movements. Technical analysts use historical currency data to forecast the direction of future prices. The underlying belief behind technical analysis is that all current market information is already reflected in the price of that currency; therefore, studying price action is all that is required to make informed trading decisions. In a nutshell, technical analysis assumes that history will repeat itself.

Technical analysis is an extremely popular tool used by short- and medium-term traders for analyzing the forex market. It works especially well in the currency markets because short-term currency price fluctuations are primarily driven by human emotions or market perceptions. The primary tool in technical analysis is price and charts. Traders will look for trends and patterns to identify trading opportunities. The most basic concept of technical analysis is that markets have a tendency to trend. Being able to identify trends in their earliest stage of development is the key to technical analysis. Range trading is also very popular, and similar tools can be used to identify these setups. Technical analysis integrates price action and momentum to construct a pictorial representation of past currency price action and to use this information to predict future performance. Technical analysis tools such as Fibonacci retracement levels, moving averages, oscillators, candlestick charts, and Bollinger bands provide further information on the value of the emotional extremes of buyers and sellers. It also helps to gauge when greed and fear are the strongest. There are basically two types of markets, trending or range bound, and in the trade parameters section, we outline some rules that can help traders determine the type of market they trading in right now and the sort of trading opportunities they should be looking for.

Is Technical Analysis or Fundamental Analysis Better?

No one will ever win the age-long battle between technical and fundamental analysis. However, most individual traders will start trading with technical analysis because it is easier to understand and does not require hours of study. Technical analysts can also follow many currencies and markets at one time, whereas fundamental analysts tend to focus on a few pairs due to the overwhelming amount of data in the market. Nonetheless, technical analysis works well because the currency market tends to develop strong trends. Once technical analysis is mastered, it can be applied with equal ease to any time frame or currency traded.

However, it is important to take both strategies into consideration, as fundamental analysis can trigger technical movements such as breakouts or reversal in trends. Technical analysis, on the other hand, can also explain moves that fundamentals cannot, especially in quiet markets, causing resistance in trends or unexplainable movements. For example, as shown in Figure 3.4, in the days leading up to September 11, USDJPY had just broken out of a triangle formation and looked poised to head higher. However, as the chart indicates, instead of breaking higher as technicians may have anticipated, USDJPY broke down following the September 11, 2001, terrorist attacks and ended up hitting a low of 115.81 from a high of 121.88 on September 10.

▪ Currency Forecasting—What Bookworms and Economists Look At

For more avid students of foreign exchange who want to learn more about fundamental analysis and valuing currencies, this section examines the different models of currency forecasting used by analysts of the major investment banks. There are seven major models for forecasting currencies, which include the balance of payments theory, purchasing power parity, interest rate parity, the monetary model, the real interest rate differential model, the asset market model, and the currency substitution model.

Balance of Payments Theory

The balance of payments theory states that exchange rates should be at their equilibrium level, which is the rate that produces a stable current account balance. Countries with trade deficits experience a run on their foreign exchange reserves due to the fact that exporters to that nation must sell that nation's currency in order

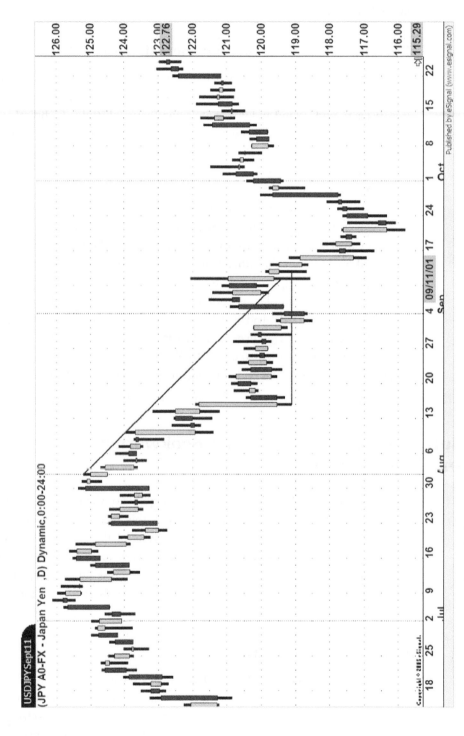

FIGURE 3.4 USDJPY September 11th Chart

Source: eSignal

to receive payment. The cheaper currency makes the nation's exports less expensive abroad, which in turn fuels exports and brings the currency into balance.

What Is the Balance of Payments (BOP)?

The balance of payments account is divided into two parts: the current account and the capital account. The current account measures trade in tangible, visible items such as cars and manufactured goods; the trade balance is the surplus or deficit between exports and imports. The capital account measures flows of money, such as investments for stocks or bonds. Balance of payments data can be found on the website of the Bureau of Economic Analysis.

Trade Flows

The trade balance of a country shows the net difference over a period of time between a nation's exports and imports. When a country imports more than it exports, the trade balance is negative or is in a deficit. If the country exports more than it imports, the trade balance is positive or is in a surplus. The trade balance reflects the redistribution of wealth among countries and is a major channel through which the macroeconomic policies of a country may affect another.

In general, if a country has a trade deficit, it is considered to be unfavorable, since it negatively impacts the value of the nation's currency. For example, if U.S. trade figures show greater imports than exports, more dollars flow out of the United States and the value of the U.S. currency depreciates. A positive trade balance, in comparison, will affect the dollar by causing it to appreciate against the other currencies.

Capital Flows

In addition to trade flows, there are also capital flows that occur among countries. They record a nation's incoming and outgoing investment flows, such as payments for entire or parts of companies, stocks, bonds, bank accounts, real estate, and factories. Capital flows are influenced by many factors, including the financial and economic climate of other countries, and can be in the form of physical or portfolio investments. In general, in developing countries, the composition of capital flows tends to be skewed toward foreign direct investment (FDI) and bank loans. For developed countries, due to the strength of the equity and fixed-income markets, stocks and bonds appear to be more important than bank loans and FDI.

Equity Markets

Equity markets have a significant impact on exchange rate movements because they are a major place for high-volume currency movements. Their importance is considerable for the currencies of countries with developed capital markets, where a great amount of capital inflows and outflows occur, and where foreign investors are major participants. The amount of the foreign investment flows in the equity markets is dependent on the general health and growth of the market, reflecting the well-being of companies and particular sectors. Movements of currencies occur when foreign investors move their money to a particular equity market. Thus, they convert their capital in a domestic currency and push the demand for it higher, making the currency appreciate. When the equity markets are experiencing recessions, however, foreign investors tend to flee, thus converting back to their home currency and pushing the domestic currency down.

Fixed-Income (Bond) Markets

The effect that fixed-income markets have on currencies is similar to that of the equity markets and is a result of capital movements. An investor's interest in the fixed-income market depends on the company's specifics and credit rating, as well as on the general health of the economy and the country's interest rates. The movement of foreign capital into and out of fixed-income markets leads to change in the demand and supply for currencies, hence impacting the currencies' exchange rates.

Summary of Trade and Capital Flows

Determining and understanding a country's balance of payments is perhaps the most important and useful tool for those interested in fundamental analysis. Any international transaction gives rise to two offsetting entries: trade flow balance (current account) and capital flow balance (capital account). If the trade flow balance is a negative outflow, the country is buying more from foreigners than it sells (imports exceed exports). When it is a positive inflow, the country is selling more than it buys (exports exceed imports). The capital flow balance is positive when foreign inflows of physical or portfolio investments into a country exceed that country's outflows. A capital flow is negative when a country buys more physical or portfolio investments than are sold to foreign investors.

These two entries, trade and capital flow, when added together signify a country's balance of payments. In theory, the two entries should balance and add up to zero in order to provide for the maintenance of the status quo in a nation's economy and currency rates.

In general, countries might experience positive or negative trade, as well as positive or negative capital flow balances. In order to minimize the net effect of the two on the exchange rates, a country should try to maintain a balance between the two. For example, in the United States, there is a substantial trade deficit, as more is imported than is exported. When the trade balance is negative, the country is buying more from foreigners than it sells, and therefore it needs to finance its deficit. This negative trade flow might be offset by a positive capital flow into the country, as foreigners buy either physical or portfolio investments. Therefore, the United States seeks to minimize its trade deficit and maximize its capital inflows, with hopes that the two will balance out.

A change in this balance is extremely significant and carries ramifications that run deep into economic policy and currency exchange levels. The net result of the difference between the trade and capital flows, positive or negative, will impact the direction in which the nation's currency will move. If the overall trade and capital balance is negative, it will result in a depreciation of the nation's currency, and if positive, it will lead to an appreciation of the currency.

Clearly, a change in the balance of payments carries a direct effect for currency levels. It is therefore possible for any investor to observe economic data relating to this balance and interpret the results that will occur. Data relating to capital and trade flows should be followed most closely. For instance, if an analyst observes an increase in the U.S. trade deficit and a decrease in the capital flows, a balance of payments deficit would occur, and as a result, an investor may anticipate a depreciation of the dollar.

Limitations of BOP Model

The BOP model mainly focuses on traded goods and services, while ignoring international capital flows. Indeed, international capital flows often dwarfed trade flows in the currency markets toward the end of the 1990s, and this oftentimes balanced out the current account of debtor nations like the United States.

For example, in 1999, 2000, and 2001, the United States maintained a large current account deficit while the Japanese ran a large current account surplus. However, during this same period in time the U.S. dollar rose against the yen even though trade flows were running against the dollar. The reason was that capital flows balanced out trade flows, thus defying the BOP's forecasting model for a period of time. Indeed, the increase in capital flows has given rise to the *asset market model*.

Note: It is probably a misnomer to call this theory the *balance of payments* theory since it only takes into account the current account balance, not the actual balance of payments. However, until the 1990s capital flows played a very small role in the world economy, so the main statistic viewed was the trade balance, which made up the bulk of the balance of payments for most nations.

Purchasing Power Parity

The *purchasing power parity* (PPP) theory is based on the belief that foreign exchange rates should be determined by the relative prices of a similar basket of goods between two countries. Any change in a nation's inflation rate should be balanced by an opposite change in that nation's exchange rate. Therefore, according to this theory, when a country's prices are rising due to inflation, that country's exchange rate should depreciate in order to return to parity.

PPP's Basket of Goods

The basket of goods and services priced for the PPP exercise is a sample of all goods and services covered by GDP. It includes consumer goods and services, government services, equipment goods, and construction projects. More specifically, consumer items include food, beverages, tobacco, clothing, footwear, rents, water supply, gas, electricity, medical goods and services, furniture and furnishings, household appliances, personal transport equipment, fuel, transport services, recreational equipment, recreational and cultural services, telephone services, education services, goods and services for personal care and household operation, and repair and maintenance services.

Big Mac Index

One of the most well-known examples of PPP is *The Economist*'s Big Mac Index. The Big Mac PPP calculates the exchange rate that would leave hamburgers costing the same in America as elsewhere. Comparing these with actual rates helps to signal if a currency is under- or overvalued. As described by *The Economist,* the index is a lightheartedly guide to currency valuation. It was never intended as a precise gauge of currency misalignment, but merely a tool to make exchange-rate theory more digestible.

For example, in January 2015, the exchange rate between the U.S. dollar and Chinese yuan was approximately 6.20. At the time, a Big Mac cost $4.79 in the United States. In China, the same burger cost 17.15 yuan, or approximately $2.77 at market exchange. This means that based on the comparison between the two burger prices, the Chinese yuan was undervalued by 42%.

OECD Purchasing Power Parity Index

The Organization of Economic Cooperation and Development (OECD) releases a more formal index. Under a joint OECD-Eurostat PPP Program, the OECD and Eurostat share the responsibility for calculating PPPs. Their latest information on which currencies are under- or overvalued against the U.S. dollar can be found on the OECD website at www.oecd.org. The OECD publishes a table that shows the price levels for the major industrialized countries. Each column shows the number of specified monetary units needed in each of the countries listed to buy the same representative basket of consumer goods and services. In each case, the representative basket costs a hundred units in the country whose currency is specified. The chart that is then created compares the PPP of a currency with its actual exchange rate. The chart is updated weekly to reflect the current exchange rate. It is also updated about twice a year to reflect new estimates of PPP. The PPP estimates are taken from studies carried out by the OECD; however, it should not be taken as definitive. Different methods of calculation will arrive at different PPP rates.

According to the OECD's data as of April 17, 2015, the PPP value of the Australian dollar versus the U.S. dollar based on GDP is 0.6712. At the time, the AUD/USD exchange rate was 0.7812. Using this model of valuation, this indicates that the Australian dollar was 14% overvalued.

Limitations to Using Purchasing Power Parity

PPP theory should only be used for long-term fundamental analysis. While the economic forces behind PPP will eventually equalize the purchasing power of currencies, this can take many years. A time horizon of 5–10 years is typical.

PPP's major weakness is that it assumes goods can be traded easily, without regard to such things as tariffs, quotas, or taxes. For example, when the U.S. government announces new tariffs on imported steel, the cost of domestic manufactured goods goes up; but those increases will not be reflected in the U.S. PPP tables.

There are other factors that must also be considered when weighing PPP: inflation, interest rate differentials, economic releases/reports, asset markets, trade flows, and political developments. Indeed, PPP is just one of several theories traders should use when determining exchange rates.

Interest Rate Parity

The interest rate parity theory states that if two different currencies have different interest rates, then that difference should be reflected in the premium or discount for the forward exchange rate to prevent riskless arbitrage.

For example, if U.S. interest rates are 3% and Japanese interest rates are 1%, then the U.S. dollar should depreciate against the Japanese yen by 2% in order to prevent riskless arbitrage. This future exchange rate is reflected in the forward exchange rate stated today. In our example, the forward exchange rate of the dollar is said to be at discount because it buys fewer Japanese yen in the forward rate than it does in the spot rate. The yen is said to be at a premium.

Interest rate parity has shown very little proof of effectiveness in recent years. Oftentimes, currencies with higher interest rates rise and attract incoming investment, while currencies with low and falling interest rates decline as outflows slow.

The Monetary Model

According to the monetary model, exchange rates are determined by a nation's monetary policy. The premise is that countries that follow a stable monetary policy over time should have appreciating currencies. Countries that have erratic monetary policies or excessively expansionist policies should see the value of their currency depreciate.

How to Use the Monetary Model

Three factors influence exchange rates under this theory:

1. A nation's money supply
2. Expected future levels of a nation's money supply
3. The growth rate of a nation's money supply

All of these factors are key to understanding and spotting a monetary trend that may force a change in exchange rates. For example, let's assume that the Japanese economy has been slipping in and out of recession for over a decade. Interest rates are near zero and annual budget deficits prevent the Japanese from spending their way out of recession, which leaves only one tool left at the disposal of Japanese officials determined to revive Japan's economy: printing more money. By buying stocks and bonds, the Bank of Japan (BoJ) is increasing the nation's money supply, which produces inflation, and this forces a change in the exchange rate. The example in Figure 3.5 illustrates the effect of money supply changes to the Japanese yen using the monetary model.

Indeed, it is in the area of excessive expansionary monetary policy that the monetary model is most successful. One of the only ways a country can keep its currency from sharply devaluing is by pursuing a tight monetary policy. For example, during the Asian Currency Crisis, the Hong Kong dollar came under attack from speculators. Hong Kong officials raised interest rates to 300% to halt the Hong Kong dollar from being dislodged from its peg to the U.S. dollar. The tactic worked perfectly, as speculators were cleared out by such sky-high interest rates. The downside was that the Hong Kong economy would slide into recession. But in the end, the peg held and the monetary model worked.

Limitations of the Monetary Model

Very few economists rely solely on this model because it does not take into account trade flows and capital flows. For example, throughout 2014 Australia had higher interest rates, growth rates, and inflation rates than both the United States and the European Union, yet, the AUD appreciated in value against both the dollar and the euro. Indeed, the monetary model has greatly struggled since the dawn of freely

FIGURE 3.5 Monetary Model

floating currencies. The model holds that high interest rates signal growing inflation, which it often does, followed by a depreciating currency. But this does not take into account the capital inflows that would take effect as a result of higher interest yields or of an equity market that may be thriving in a booming economy—thus causing the currency to possibly appreciate.

In any case, the monetary model is one of several valuation tools that can be employed in tandem with other models to determine the direction an exchange rate is heading.

Real Interest Rate Differential Model

According to the real interest rate differential theory, exchange rate movements are determined by a country's interest rate. The idea is that countries with high interest rates should see their currency appreciate in value, while countries with low interest rates should see their currency depreciate in value.

Basics of the Model

The basic premise of the model is that when a country raises its interest rates, international investors will buy that currency because they find its yield more attractive. When a country lowers interest rates, they sell the currency. Figure 3.6

Interest Rates vs. United States	Eurozone	Japan	UK	Canada	Australia	New Zealand
Central Bank Rate End of 2003	100	−100	275	175	425	400
% Change 2003 vs. USD	20%	12%	11%	21%	34%	27%

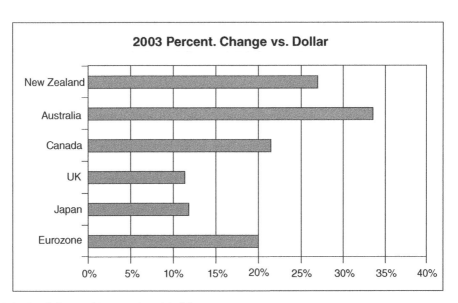

FIGURE 3.6 Real Interest Rate Model

shows how well this theory held up in 2003, when interest spreads were near their widest levels in years.

The data from this graph show a mixed result. The Australian dollar had the largest basis point spread and also had the highest return against the U.S. dollar, which seems to vindicate the model, as investors bought up higher-yielding Aussie. The same can be said for the New Zealand dollar, which also had a higher yield than the U.S. dollar and gained 27% against USD. Yet the model becomes less convincing when comparing the euro, which gained 20% against the dollar (more than every currency except NZD), even though its basis point differential was only 100 points. The model then comes under serious question when comparing the British pound and the Japanese yen. The yen differential is −100, and yet it appreciated almost 12% against the dollar. Meanwhile, the British pound gained only 11% against the dollar even though it had a whopping 275 point interest rate differential.

This model also stresses that one of the key factors in determining the severity of an exchange rate's response to a shift in interest rates is the expected persistence of that shift. Simply put, a rise in interest rates that is expected to last for five years will have a much larger impact on the exchange rate than if that rise were expected to last for only one year.

Limitations to the Interest Rate Model

There is a great deal of debate among international economists over whether there is a strong and statistically significant link between changes in a nation's interest rate and currency price. The main weakness of this model is that it does not take into account a nation's current account balance, relying on capital flows instead. Indeed, the model tends to overemphasize capital flows at the expense of numerous other factors, such as political stability, inflation, and poor economic growth. Absent these types of factors, the model can be very useful, since it is quite logical to conclude that an investor will naturally gravitate toward the investment vehicle that pays a higher reward.

The Asset Market Model

The basic premise of the asset market model theory is that the flow of funds into the financial assets of a country such as equities and bonds increases the demand for that country's currency (and vice versa). As proof, advocates point out that the amount of funds that are placed in investment products such as stocks and bonds now dwarf the amount of funds that is exchanged as a result of the transactions in goods and services for import and export purposes. The asset market theory is basically the opposite of the balance of payments theory since it takes into account a nation's capital account instead of its current account.

A Dollar-Driven Theory

Throughout 1999, many experts argued that the dollar would fall against the euro on the grounds of the expanding U.S. current account deficit and an overvalued Wall Street. That was based on the rationale that non-U.S. investors would begin withdrawing their funds from U.S. stocks and bonds into more economically sound markets, which would weigh significantly on the dollar. Yet, such fears have lingered since the early 1980s when the U.S. current account soared to a record high 3.5% of GDP.

In the two decades that followed, the balance of payments approach in assessing the dollar's behavior has given way to the asset market approach. This theory continues to hold the most sway over pundits due to the enormity of U.S. capital markets. In May and June of 2002, the dollar plummeted over 1000 points versus the yen at the same time equity investors fled U.S. equity markets due to the accounting scandals that were plaguing Wall Street. As the scandals subsided toward the end of 2002, the dollar rose 500 points from a low of 115.43 to close at 120.00 against the yen, even though the current account balance remained in massive deficit the entire time.

Limitations to the Asset Market Theory

It is frequently argued that over the long run, there is no relationship between a nation's equity market performance and the performance of its currency. See Figure 3.7 for a comparison. Between April 2014 and April 2015, the German DAX and EURUSD have a very weak correlation.

Also, what happens to a nation's currency when the stock market is trading sideways—stuck between bullish and bearish sentiments? That was the scenario in

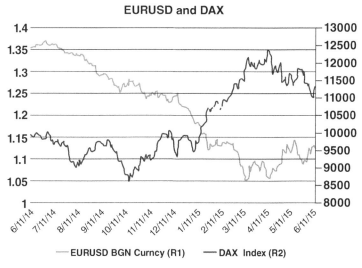

FIGURE 3.7 The DAX Index and the EURUSD

Germany for much of 2014, and currency traders found themselves going back to older money making models, such as interest rate arbitrage, as a result. Only time will tell whether the asset market model will hold up or merely be a short-term blip on the currency forecasting radar.

The Currency Substitution Model

The currency substitution model is an enhanced version of the monetary model because it takes into account investor flows. It posits that the shifting of private and public portfolios from one nation to another can have a significant effect on exchange rates. The ability of individuals to change their assets from domestic and foreign currencies is known as currency substitution. When this model is added to the monetary model, evidence shows that shifts in expectations of a nation's money supply can have a decided impact on that nation's exchange rates. Simply put, investors are looking at monetary model data and coming to the conclusion that a change in money flow is about to occur, thus affecting the exchange rate, so they are investing accordingly, which turns the monetary model into a self-fulfilling prophecy. Investors who subscribe to this theory are merely jumping on the currency substitution model bandwagon on the way to the monetary model party.

The Yen Example

In the monetary model we talked about how the Japanese government was basically printing yen and increasing the money supply when it bought stocks and bonds. Monetary model theorists would say that this monetary growth would spark inflation (more yen chasing fewer products), decrease demand for the yen, and finally cause the yen to depreciate. A currency substitution theorist would agree with this scenario and look to take advantage of this view by shorting the yen, or if they were long the yen promptly getting out of the position. By taking this action, our yen trader is helping to drive the market precisely in that direction, thus making the monetary model theory a fate accompli. The step-by-step process is illustrated in Figure 3.8.

A. Japan announces new stock and bond buyback plan. Economists are now predicting Japan's money supply will dramatically increase.
B. Economists are also predicting a rise in inflation with the introduction of this new policy. Speculators expect a change in the exchange rate as a result.
C. Economists expect interest rates to rise and inflation takes hold in the economy. Speculators start selling short the yen in anticipation of a change in the exchange rate.
D. Demand for the yen plummets as money flows easily through the Japanese economy and speculators dump yen in the markets.
E. The exchange rate for the Japanese yen changes dramatically as the yen falls in value to foreign currencies, especially those that are easily substituted by investors (read: liquid yen crosses).

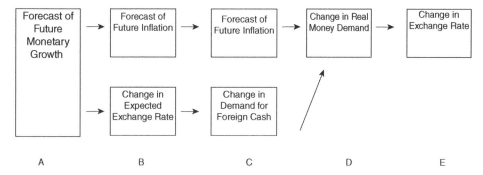

FIGURE 3.8 Currency Substitution Model

Limitations of the Currency Substitution Model

Among the major, actively traded currencies, this model has not yet shown itself to be a convincing, single determinant for exchange rate movements. While this theory can be used with more confidence in underdeveloped countries where "hot money" rushes in and out of emerging markets with enormous effect, there are still too many variables not accounted for by the currency substitution model. For example, using the yen illustration in Figure 3.8, even though Japan may try to spark inflation with its securities' buyback plan, it still has an enormous current account surplus that will continually prop up the yen. Also, Japan has numerous political landmines it must avoid in its own neighborhood, and should Japan make it clear that it is trying to devalue its currency, there will be enormous repercussions. These are just two of many factors the substitution model does not take into consideration. However, this model (like numerous other currency models) should be considered part of an overall, balanced, FX forecasting diet.

CHAPTER 4

A Deeper Look at the FX Market

The next three chapters cover some of the unique studies that I have done on the FX market that provide some telling details for both the novice and advanced trader. This includes the following:

1. What are the best times to trade for individual currency pairs?
2. What are the most market moving economic data?
3. What are currency correlations, and how can we use them?

▉ What Are the Best Times to Trade for Individual Currency Pairs?

The Foreign Exchange market operates 24 hours a day, making it nearly impossible for a single trader to track every market movement and respond immediately at all times. Timing is everything in currency trading. In order to devise an effective and time-efficient investment strategy, it is important to understand how much liquidity there is around the clock to maximize the number of trading opportunities during a trader's own market hours. Besides liquidity, a currency pair's trading range is also heavily dependent on geographical location and macroeconomic factors. Knowing what time of day a currency pair has the widest or narrowest trading range will undoubtedly help traders improve their investment utility due to better capital allocation. This section outlines the typical trading activity of major currency pairs in different time zones to see when they are the most volatile. Figure 4.1 tabulates

Currency Pairs	Asian Session 7pm–4am	European Session 2am–12pm	U.S. Session 8am–5pm	Europe 3am–12pm	U.S.-Europe Overlap 8am–12pm	Europe-Asian Overlap 2am–4am
EURUSD	51	87	78	84	65	32
USDJPY	78	79	69	77	58	29
GBPUSD	65	112	94	109	78	43
USDCHF	68	117	107	114	88	43
EURCHF	53	53	49	52	40	24
AUDUSD	38	53	47	51	39	20
USDCAD	47	94	84	93	74	28
NZDUSD	42	52	46	50	38	20
EURGBP	25	40	34	39	27	16
GBPJPY	112	145	119	140	99	60
GBPCHF	96	150	129	146	105	62
AUDJPY	55	63	56	62	47	26

FIGURE 4.1 Currency Pair Ranges

the average pip range for the different currency pairs during various time frames between 2013 and 2014.

The FX market is broken into three primary trading sessions.

Asian Session (Tokyo): 7pm to 4am EST

Trading begins on Sunday in Asia at 5pm NY Time, but the Tokyo session begins around 7pm NY Time. During the Asian trading session, the largest volume is transacted in Tokyo, followed by Hong Kong and Singapore. Trading in Tokyo can be thin from time to time; but large investment banks and hedge funds are known to try to use the Asian session to run important stop and option barrier levels, especially during Sunday trade. Figure 4.2 provides a ranking of the different currency pairs and their ranges during the Asian trading session.

More risk-tolerant traders may choose to trade USDJPY, GBPCHF, and GBPJPY because their broad ranges provide short-term traders with lucrative profit potentials, with an average daily range of 90 pips. Foreign investment banks and institutional investors who hold mostly dollar-dominated assets also contribute to the daily flow in USDJPY through their Japanese equity and bond markets transactions. The Bank of Japan, who holds over $1.2 trillion of U.S. Treasury debt, is an active player with their open market operations impacting the value of the currency. Last but not least, large Japanese exporters may choose to repatriate their foreign earnings during the Tokyo trading session, adding to the fluctuations of the currency pair. A pair like GBPJPY is especially volatile because large market participants may start to scale into or out of positions ahead of the European market open.

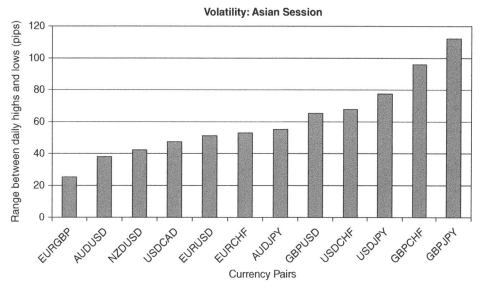

Volatility: Asian Session

FIGURE 4.2 Asian Session Volatility

More risk-averse participants may prefer to trade EURGBP, AUDUSD or NZDUSD because they generally have less volatility, which can help to shield traders and their investment strategies from irregular market movements caused by aggressive intraday speculation.

U.S. Session (New York): 8am to 5pm EST

According to the Bank of International Settlements' 2013 Triennial Central Bank Survey of Foreign Exchange and Derivatives Market Activity, New York is the second largest FX marketplace, accounting for 19% of total forex market volume. The majority of the transactions during the U.S. session are executed between 8am to 12pm NY Time, a period with high liquidity because the European and U.S. markets overlap. After 12pm, trading starts to wind down with ranges narrowing until the open of the Tokyo session. There can be some range expansions right before the U.S. equity market closes but generally speaking the volatility is far less than in the 8am to 12pm time period.

More risk-tolerant traders will find GBPUSD, USDCHF, GBPJPY, and GBPCHF attractive currency pairs to day trade because their daily ranges average around 120 pips (Figure 4.3). Trading in these currency pairs is particularly active because they involve the U.S. dollar. When the U.S. equity and bond markets are open during the U.S. session, foreign investors have to convert their domestic currency, such as the euro, Japanese yen, and the Swiss franc into dollar-dominated assets in order to carry out their transactions. With the market overlap, GBPJPY and GBPCHF have the widest daily ranges. Most currencies in the FX market are quoted with U.S. dollar

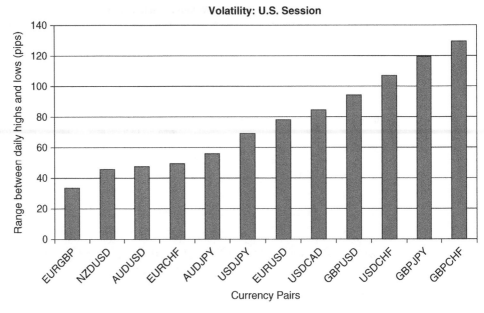

Volatility: U.S. Session

FIGURE 4.3   U.S. Session Volatility

as the base and the primary instrument traded before a cross. In AUDCAD for example, for an Australian dollar to be converted into Canadian dollars, it usually has to be traded against the USD first, then CAD. This means an AUDCAD trade typically involves two different currency transactions, AUDUSD and USDCAD, and its volatility is ultimately determined by the correlations of the two derived currency pairs. Since AUDUSD and USDCAD are negatively correlated, which means they tend to move in opposite directions, the volatility of AUDCAD is amplified. Trading currency pairs with high volatility can be very lucrative, but in doing it is also important to bear in mind that the risk involved can also be high. Traders should continuously evaluate their strategies as market conditions change because big moves in exchange rates can easily nullify their long-term strategies.

For the more risk-averse traders, USDJPY, EURUSD, and USDCAD can be attractive pairs because they offer a decent trading range with lower risk. The highly liquid nature of these currency pairs can also allow investor to secure profits or cut losses promptly and efficiently. The modest volatility of these pairs provides a favorable environment for traders who want to pursue long-term strategies.

European Session (London): 3am to 12pm EST

London is the largest and most important dealing center in the world, with a market share of more than 40% according to the BIS survey. Most of the dealing desks of large banks are located in London, and the majority of major FX transactions are

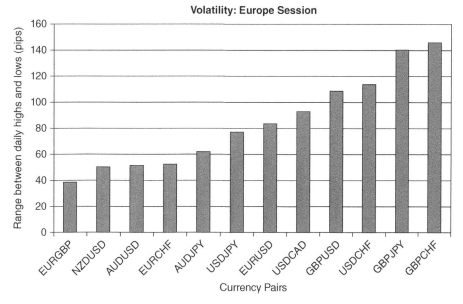

Volatility: Europe Session

FIGURE 4.4 European Session Volatility

completed during London hours due to the market's high liquidity and efficiency. The vast number of market participants and their high transaction value makes London the most volatile FX trading session. Half of the 12 major pairs surpass the 80 pips line, the benchmark that we used to identify volatile pairs from the rest, with GBPJPY and GBPCHF reaching as high as 140 pips and 146 pips, respectively, during this time period (Figure 4.4).

With an average daily range of more than 140 pips, GBPJPY and GBPCHF are two currency pairs that risk-tolerant traders love to trade. While such high volatility can create much in the way of opportunity, it is important to realize that the peak of daily trade activity in these two pairs generally happens during the London session. With the London trading session overlapping both the New York and Tokyo sessions, it is the perfect market for banks and institutional investors to reposition their portfolios, and these adjustments contribute to the volatility in the market.

Traders with moderate risk profiles will also find plenty of pairs to choose from. EURUSD, USDCAD, GBPUSD, and USDCHF have an average range of 100 pips. As mentioned earlier, trading in these pairs is active because large market participants like to adjust their portfolios before the U.S. session opens.

For the more risk-averse, the NZDUSD, AUDUSD, EURCHF, and AUDJPY, with an average of 50 pips range, are good choices as these pairs provide traders with high interest income and profit potential. These pairs allow investors to determine their direction of movements based on fundamental economic factors and tend to be less prone to losses caused by intraday speculative trades.

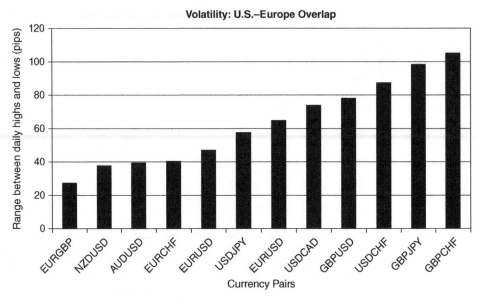

FIGURE 4.5 U.S.–Europe Overlap

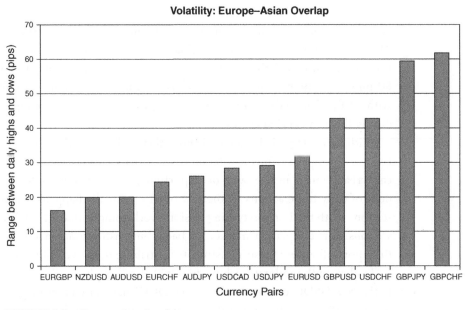

FIGURE 4.6 Europe–Asia Overlap

US–Europe Overlap: 8am to 12pm EST

The FX markets tend to be most active when the hours of the world's two largest trading centers overlap. The range of trading between 8am and 12pm EST constitutes on average 70% of the total average range of trading for all of the currency pairs during the European trading hours and 80% of the total average range of trading for all of the currency pairs during U.S. trading hours. Just these percentages alone tell day traders that if they are looking for high volatility and they don't want to sit in front of the screen all day, then the best time to trade is the U.S. and European overlap (see Figure 4.5).

European–Asian Overlap: 2am to 4am EST

In contrast, there is far less volatility during the European and Asian market overlap because of the slow trading during the Asian morning (see Figure 4.6). Of course, the two-hour gap is also a relatively short time period. What is interesting about this period, however, is that it usually precedes a breakout at the European market open between 4am and 5am.

CHAPTER 5

What Are the Most Market Moving Economic Data?

For any type of trader, fundamental or technical, the importance of economic data cannot be underestimated. Having worked in the FX markets for many years, I have learned that even though there are many traders who claim to be pure technicians who do not factor fundamentals into their trading strategies, these same traders have also frequently stayed out of the markets ahead of key economic releases. In fact, many system traders will turn off their trading systems ahead of big releases like the nonfarm payrolls reports. Of course, there are technicians who factor fundamentals into their trading strategies, and some will even utilize key economic releases to trade breakouts. All traders, fundamental, technical, or both, will find it valuable to know when important economic data are scheduled for release, particularly those that will affect the U.S. dollar. This is because 90% of all currency trades are against the greenback, making currencies naturally sensitive to U.S. economic releases.

Based on a study that I conducted in 2004, the most significant movements in the dollar (against the euro) on the back of an economic release occurred in the first 20 minutes of trading following the release. Although more than 10 years have passed, the results are still relevant, as the nonfarm payrolls report is, hands down, the most important piece of U.S. data. On average, EURUSD would move 124 pips in the first 20 minutes following the release. Excluding any release that came in within 10% of estimates, the average move was 133 pips. On a daily basis, the EURUSD moved an average of 193 and 208 pips, excluding its response to data that met expectations. On average, the EURUSD moves 111 pips throughout the course of the trading day. In contrast, the GDP reports result in an average move of only 43 pips for the EURUSD in the first 20 minutes and 110 pips on a daily basis. The GDP ranking on the 20-minute table is higher than the daily table because prices do retrace throughout the course of the day. Interestingly enough, the biggest 20-minute mover for the dollar may not be the most significant market mover for the rest of the trading day. Based on our own analysis of 20-minute and daily ranges, we have created the following rankings for economic data.

Top Market Moving Indicators for the Dollar in the First 20 Minutes
1. Unemployment (nonfarm payrolls)
2. Interest rates (FOMC rate decisions)
3. Trade balance
4. Inflation (Consumer Price Index)
5. Retail sales
6. GDP
7. Current account
8. Durable goods
9. Foreign purchases of U.S. Treasuries (TIC data)

Top Market Moving Indicators for the Dollar on a Daily Basis
1. Unemployment (nonfarm payrolls)
2. Interest rates (FOMC rate decisions)
3. Foreign purchases of U.S. Treasuries (TIC data)
4. Trade balance
5. Current account
6. Durable goods
7. Retail sales
8. Inflation (Consumer Price Index)
9. GDP

The breakdowns of the average pip ranges for the EURUSD are shown in Figure 5.1. You can compare that to the average daily range for the EURUSD, which was approximately 110 pips.

■ Relative Importance of Data Changes over Time

With a dynamic market, one caveat is that the significance of economic data releases changes with time. According to a paper written by the National Bureau

| For 2004: | | | |
For 20 min	Avg. Range (pips)	Total Daily Range	Avg. Range (pips)
Nonfarm Payrolls	124	Nonfarm Payrolls	193
FOMC Decision	74	FOM C Decision	140
Trade Balance	64	TICS	132
Inflation - CPI	44	Trade Balance	129
Retail Sales	43	Current Account	127
GDP	43	Durable Goods	126
Current Account	43	Retail Sales	125
Durable Goods	39	Inflation—CPI	123
TICS	33	GDP	110

FIGURE 5.1 Range of EURUSD Following Economic Releases

of Economic Research (NBER), in 1992, the trade balance was the number-one market moving US economic release on a 20-minute basis, while nonfarm payrolls (and unemployment data) was the third. In 1997, unemployment took the top place while the trade balance fell to the fourth. As indicated in Figure 5.1, the trade balance and inflation report switched places while the significance of labor market data held steady. Intuitively, this makes sense since the market shifts its attention to different economic sectors and data based on the conditions of the domestic economy—for example, trade balances may be more important when a country is running unsustainable deficits, while an economy that has difficulty creating jobs will see unemployment data as more important. However in 2014, employment, monetary policy decisions, and inflation data remain the most market-moving releases.

FX Dealer Ranking of Importance of Economic Data: Changes over Time

As of 1997:	As of 1992:
1. Unemployment	1. Trade balance
2. Interest rates	2. Interest rates
3. Inflation	3. Unemployment
4. Trade balance	4. Inflation
5. GDP	5. GDP

**Calculated based on minute reactions

GDP Is No Longer a Big Deal

GDP report has also become one of least important economic indicators on the U.S. calendar, as it has led to some of the smallest relative movements in the EURUSD.

FIGURE 5.2   EURUSD Daily Chart

Source: eSignal

One possible explanation is that GDP is released less frequently than other data in our study (it comes out quarterly versus monthly), but in general, the GDP report is more prone to ambiguity and misinterpretation. For example, surging GDP brought about by rising exports will be positive for the home currency; however, if GDP growth is a result of inventory buildup, the effect on the currency may actually be negative. Also, a large number of the components that comprise the GDP report are known in advance of the release.

How Can You Use This to Your Benefit?

For breakout traders, knowing which data have the potential of creating the largest average range for a currency can be useful in determining how to weight positions accordingly. For example, in Figure 5.2, which shows the daily EURUSD chart, there is a triangle forming as prices consolidate significantly. A breakout trader could overweight positions ahead of the August 6 nonfarm payrolls release the day before in the anticipation of a large breakout move following this release. In contrast, the third bar of the consolidation was the day of the GDP release. As you can see, the range was still comparatively tight, and given the knowledge that the average instantaneous 20-minute move off of the GDP release is only a third of the nonfarm payrolls move, the same breakout players hoping for a large move off of that economic release should probably only put on half of the same position that they would have put on for an NFP-based breakout. These same guidelines apply for range traders or system traders. Nonfarm payrolls day would be a perfect day to stand on the sidelines and wait for prices to settle, while the day that GDP is released could still provide an opportunity for solid range or systems-based trading.

Overall, knowing which economic indicator moves the market the most is very important for all traders. Being aware of the 20-minute versus daily range can also be helpful because the exchange rate adjustment to economic news tends to be very swift; any reaction beyond a 15–30 minute window after the data are released might be the result of investor overreaction or trading related to customer flow rather than news alone. The GDP report is a perfect example—the 20-minute reaction ranking is higher than the daily ranking.

■ Resources

Yin-Wong Cheung and Menzie D. Chinn, *Macroeconomic Implications of the Beliefs and Behavior of Foreign Exchange Traders*, Working Paper 7417, National Bureau of Economic Research, www.georgetown.edu/faculty/evansm1/New%20Micro/chinn.pdf.

CHAPTER 6

What Are Currency Correlations, and How Can We Use Them?

When it comes to forex, one of the most important things to know is that currencies do not trade in a vacuum. In many cases, foreign economic conditions, interest rates, and price changes affect much more than just a single currency pair. Everything is interrelated in the forex market to some extent and knowing the direction and how strong this relationship is can be an advantage; it has the potential to be a great trading tool. The bottom line is that unless you only want to trade one pair at a time, it can be very profitable to take into account how pairs move relative to one another. To do this, we use correlation analysis. Correlations are calculations based on pricing data, and these numbers can help gauge the relationships that exist between different currency pairs. The information that the numbers provide can be a good aid for any traders who want to diversify their portfolio, double up on positions without investing in the same currency pair, or just get an idea of how much risk their trades are opening them up to. If used correctly, this method has the potential to maximize gains, gauge exposure, and help prevent counterproductive trading.

■ Positive/Negative Correlations—What They Mean and How to Use Them

Knowing how closely correlated the currency pairs are in your portfolio is a great way to measure your exposure and risk. You might think that you're diversifying your portfolio by investing in different pairs, but many of them have a tendency to move in the same or opposite direction from one another. The correlations between pairs can be strong or weak and last for weeks, months, or even years. Basically, what a correlation number measures is an estimate of how often these pairs move together or how opposite their actions are over a specified period of time. Any correlation calculation will be in decimal form; the closer the number is to 1, the stronger the connection between the two currencies. For example, by looking at the sample data in Table 6.1, we can see a +0.94 correlation between the EURUSD and the NZDUSD over the last month. If you are not a fan of decimals, you can also think of the number as a percentage by multiplying it by 100% (in this case, getting a 94% correlation between the EURUSD and the NZDUSD). High decimals reflect currency pairs that closely mirror one another, while lower numbers tell us that the pairs do not usually move in a parallel fashion. Therefore, because there is a high correlation in this particular pair, we can see that by investing in both the EURUSD and the NZDUSD at the same time, you are virtually doubling up on a position. Likewise, it might not be the best idea to go long one of the pairs and short the other because a rally in one has a high likelihood of also setting off a rally in the other currency pair. While this would not make your profit and losses exactly zero because they have different pip values, the two do move in such a similar fashion that taking opposing positions could take a bite out of profits or even cause losses.

Positive correlations aren't the only way to measure similarities between pairings; negative correlations can be just as useful. In this case, instead of a very positive number, we are looking for a highly negative one. The closer the number is to −1, the increasingly connected the two currencies movements are, but this time in the opposite direction. Again, we can use the EURUSD as an example. While we just saw a strong positive correlation with the NZDUSD, the EURUSD has a very negative relationship with the USDCHF. Between these two currency pairs, the correlation has been −0.98 over the last year and −0.99 over the past month. This number indicates that these two pairs have a strong propensity to move in opposite directions. Therefore, buying both currency pairs at the same time will often lead to gains in one and losses in the other. Buying one pair and selling the other would be an intensification of risk that can be viewed as doubling up on the same or similar position.

Important Fact about Correlations: They Change

Anyone who has ever traded the FX market knows that currencies are very dynamic; economic conditions, both sentiment and pricing, change every day. Because of this, the most important aspect to remember when analyzing currency correlations is that they can also change overtime. The strong correlations that are calculated today might not be the same this time next year, or even next month. Due to the constant reshaping of the forex environment, it is imperative to keep current if you decide to use this method for trading. For example, over a one-month period that we observed, the correlation between USDCAD and USDJPY was 0.06. This is a very low number and would indicate that the pairs do not really share any definitive trend in their movements. However, if we look at the three-month data for the same time period, the number increases to 0.12 and then to 0.59 for six months, and finally to 0.80 for a year. In this particular example, we can see that there was a recent breakdown in the relationship between these two pairs. What was once a strongly positive association over time has deteriorated completely in the short term. On the other hand, the correlation between USDCHF and AUDUSD strengthened in more recent reports. The correlation between these two pairs started at –0.78 for the year and edged up to –0.94 for the last month. This suggests that there is an increasing probability that if one of the trades became profitable, the other would as well. The opposite is also true that if one of the trades incurs significant losses, the other has a very high likelihood of also ending up unprofitable.

An even more dramatic example of the extent to which these numbers can change can be found in the GBPUSD and AUDUSD pairs; there was a –0.79 correlation between the two for the yearlong data. However, while these two tended to move in reasonably opposite directions in the long term, over the month of February 2005, for example, they were positively correlated with a +0.76 reading. The major events that change the amount and even direction that pairs are correlated are usually associated with major economic developments, such as interest rate changes or quantitative easing.

Calculating Correlations Yourself

Because correlations have the tendency to shift overtime and the data in the table could be stale by the time you read it, the best way to keep current on the direction and strength of your pairings is to calculate them yourself. Although it might seem like a tricky concept, the actual process can be made quite easy. The simplest way to calculate the numbers is to use Microsoft Excel. In Excel, you can take the currency pairs that you want to derive a correlation from over a specific time period

EURUSD	AUDUSD	USDJPY	GBPUSD	NZDUSD	USDCHF	USDCAD
1 Month	0.94	−0.92	0.92	0.94	−0.99	−0.32
3 Month	0.47	−0.37	0.83	0.57	−0.98	−0.61
6 Month	0.74	−0.83	0.94	0.78	−0.96	−0.57
1 Year	0.85	−0 86	0.91	0.93	−0 98	−0.89

AUDUSD	EURUSD	USDJPY	GBPUSD	NZDUSD	USDCHF	USDCAD
1 Month	0.94	−0.91	0.95	0.96	−0 94	−0.17
3 Month	0.47	0.24	0.81	0.90	−0 44	−0.14
6 Month	0.74	−0.70	0.75	0.89	−0.70	−0.54
1 Year	0.85	−0.87	0.79	0.90	−0.78	−0.81

USDJPY	EURUSD	AUDUSD	GBPUSD	NZDUSD	USDCHF	USDCAD
1 Month	−0.92	−0.91	−0.88	−0.91	0.94	0.06
3 Month	−0.37	0.24	−0.08	0.15	0.40	0.12
6 Month	−0.83	−0.70	−0.75	−0.61	0.83	0.59
1 Year	−0.86	−0.87	−0.82	−0.84	0.83	0.80

GBPUSD	EURUSD	AUDUSD	USDJPY	NZDUSD	USDCHF	USDCAD
1 Month	0.92	0.95	−0.88	0.87	−0.95	−0.03
3 Month	0.83	0.81	−0.08	0.83	−0.82	−0.36
6 Month	0.94	0.75	−0.75	0.84	−0.88	−0.42
1 Year	0.91	0.79	−0.82	0.82	−0.90	−0.70

NZDUSD	EURUSD	AUDUSD	USDJPY	GBPUSD	USDCHF	USDCAD
1 Month	0.94	0.96	−0.91	0.87	−0.92	−0.29
3 Month	0.57	0.90	0.15	0.83	−0.53	−0.35
6 Month	0.78	0.89	−0.61	0.84	−0.69	−0.38
1 Year	0.93	0.90	−0.84	0.82	−0.88	−0.94

USDCHF	EURUSD	AUDUSD	USDJPY	GBPUSD	NZDUSD	USDCAD
1 Month	−0.99	−0.94	0.94	−0.95	−0.92	0.21
3 Month	−0.98	−0 44	0.40	−0.82	−0.53	0.55
6 Month	−0.96	−0 70	0.83	−0.88	−0.69	0.70
1 Year	−0.98	−0 78	0.83	−0.90	−0.88	0.87

USDCAD	EURUSD	AUDUSD	USDJPY	GBPUSD	NZDUSD	USDCHF
1 Month	−0.32	−0.17	0.06	−0.03	−0.29	0.21
3 Month	−0.61	−0.14	0.12	−0.36	−0.35	0.55
6 Month	−0.57	−0.54	0.59	−0 42	−0.38	0.70
1 Year	−0.89	−0.81	0.80	−0 70	−0.94	0.87

Date		EURUSD	AUDUSD	USDJPY	GBPUSD	NZDUSD	USDCHF	USDCAD
03/29/2004 - 09/29/2004	6 Month Trailing	0.10	−0.28	0.69	0.68	−0.88	−0.60	
04/29/2004 - 10/28/2004	6 Month Trailing	0.77	−0.67	0.47	0.84	−0.90	−0.78	
05/31/2004 - 11/29/2004	6 Month Trailing	0.96	−0.88	0.61	0.88	−0.97	−0.89	
06/30/2004 - 12/29/2004	6 Month Trailing	0.93	−0.94	0.87	0.94	−0.98	−0.85	
07/30/2004 - 01/28/2005	6 Month Trailing	0.93	−0.93	0.92	0.95	−0.99	−0.86	
08/31/2004 - 03/01/2005	6 Month Trailing	0.88	−0.91	0.96	0.91	−0.98	−0.80	
09/30/2004 - 03/31/2005	6 Month Trailing	0.74	−0.83	0.95	0.79	−0.96	−0.58	
	Average	0.76	−0.78	0.78	0.86	−0.95	−0.77	

FIGURE 6.1 March Correlation Table

and just use the correlation function. Calculating this on a one-year, six-month, three-month, and then on a one-month and six-month trailing basis provides the most comprehensive view of the positive and negative correlation between different currency pairs; however, you can decide which or how many of these readings you want to analyze.

Breaking the process down step by step, let's take a look at how a simple correlation between the USDGBP and USDCHF can be calculated. First, you'll need to get the pricing data for the two pairs. To keep organized, label one column GBP and the other CHF and then put in the daily or weekly values of these currencies using the last price and pairing them with the USD for whatever time period you want to use. At the bottom of the two columns, go to an empty slot and type in =CORREL. Highlight all of the data in one of the pricing columns, type in a comma, and then do the same thing for the other currency; the number produced is your correlation. Although it is not necessary to update your numbers every day, updating them every few weeks or at the very least once a month is generally a good idea.

Sample Correlations Results

Figure 6.1 presents a sample of the output results.

CHAPTER 7

Trade Parameters for Various Market Conditions

After learning about the emergence of the foreign exchange market, who the major players are, significant historical milestones, and what moves the markets, it is time to move on and discuss some of my favorite strategies for trading currencies. However, before I even begin going over these strategies, the most important first step for any trader, regardless of the market that you are trading in, is to create a trading journal.

■ Keep a Trading Journal

Through my experience, I have learned that being a successful trader is not about finding the holy grail of indicators that can perfectly forecast movements 100% of the time, but instead, to develop discipline. I cannot undermine the importance of "the journal" as the primary first step to becoming a successful and professional trader. While working on the Inter-bank FX trading desk at J.P. Morgan and then on the Cross-Markets trading desk after the merger with Chase, the trading journal mentality was engrained into the minds of every dealer and proprietary trader on the trading floors, regardless of rank. The reason was simple—the bank was providing the capital for trading and we needed to be held accountable, especially since each transaction involved millions of dollars. For every trade that was executed, we needed to have a solid rationale as well as justification for the choice of entry and exit levels. More specifically, you had to know where to place your exit points before you placed the trade to approximate worst case losses and to manage risk.

With this sort of accountability, the leading banks of the world are able to breed successful and professional traders. For individual traders, this practice is even more important because you are trading with your own money and not someone else's. Bank traders are trading with someone else's money so regardless of how poorly they perform over a one- or two-week basis, they will receive their paycheck twice a month. At a bank, traders have plenty of time to make the money back without any disruptions to their daily way of life—unless of course they lose $1 million in one day. As an individual trader—you do not have this luxury. When you are trading with your own money, each dollar lost is a dollar less that you own. So even though you should only be trading with risk capital, or money that would not otherwise be used for rent or groceries, one way or the other, the pain is felt. To avoid repeating the same mistakes and taking large losses, I cannot stress enough the importance of keeping a trading journal. The journal is designed to ensure that as a trader, you only take calculated losses and learn from each mistake. The trading journal setup that I recommend should be broken up into three parts:

1. Currency pair checklist
2. Trades that I am waiting for
3. Existing or completed trades

Currency Pair Checklist

The first section of your trading journal should consist of a spreadsheet that can be printed out and completed every day. This purpose of this checklist is to get a feel of the market and to identify trades. It should list of all of the currency pairs that are offered for trading on the left column, followed by three columns for the current, high, and low prices, and then a series of triggers laid out as a row on the right hand side. Newer traders should start with following only the four major currency pairs, which are the EURUSD, USDJPY, USDCHF, and the GBPUSD, and then gradually add the AUDUSD, USDCAD, and NZDUSD, followed by the nondollar pairs. Although the checklist that I have created is fairly detailed, I find that it is a very useful daily exercise and should take no more than 20 minutes to complete once the appropriate indicators are saved on the charts. The purpose of this checklist is to get a clear visual of which currencies are trending and which are range trading. Comprehending the big picture is the first step to trading successfully. Too often have I seen traders fail because they lose sight of the overall environment that they are trading in. The worst thing to do is to trade blindly. Trying to pick tops or bottoms in a strong trend or buying breakouts in a range-bound environment can lead to significant losses. Just take a look at Figure 7.1 of the EURUSD. If you tried

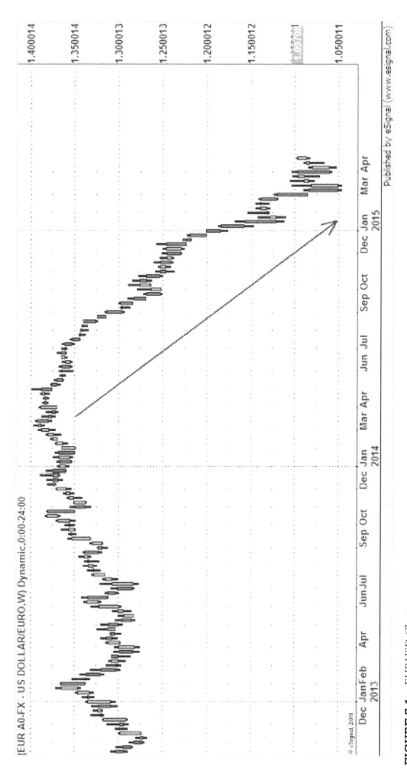

FIGURE 7.1 EURUSD Chart

Source: eSignal

to pick bottoms in this pair, it would have led to an entire year of frustrating and unsuccessful trading. In trending environments, traders will find a higher success rate by buying on retracements in an uptrend or selling on rallies in a downtrend. Picking tops and bottoms should only be a strategy that is used in clear range trading environments and even with that, traders need to be careful of contracting ranges that can lead to breakout scenarios.

A simplified version of the daily market overview sheet that I use is shown in Figure 7.2.

As you can see in Figure 7.2, the first two columns after the daily high and low prices are the levels of the 10-day high or low. Recording this price helps to identify where current prices are within previous price action. This helps traders get a gauge of whether we are pressing toward a 10-day high or low or if we are simply trapped in the middle of the range. Yet the prices alone do not provide enough information to determine if we are in a trending or a range-bound environment. The next five indicators is a checklist for determining a trending environment. The more X marks in this section, the stronger the trend.

The first column in the trending indicator group is the "ADX (14) above 25." ADX is the Accumulation Distribution Index, which is the most popular used indicator for determining the strength of a trend. If the index reading is above 25, it indicates that a trend has developed. Generally speaking, the greater the number, the stronger the trend. The next column is Bollinger Bands. When strong trends develop, the pair will frequently tag and cross either the upper or lower Bollinger Band. The next three trend indicators are the longer term moving averages. A break above or below these moving averages may also be indicative of a trending environment. With moving averages, crossovers in the direction of the trend can be used as a further confirmation. If there are two or more Xs in this section, traders should be looking for opportunities to buy on dips in an uptrend or sell on rallies in a downtrend rather than selling at the top and buying back at the bottom of the range.

The last section of the trading journal is indications of range. The first indicator is also ADX, but this time, we are looking for ADX below 25, which signals that the currency pair's trend is weak. Next, we look at the traditional oscillators, RSI and stochastics. If the ADX is weak and there is significant technical resistance above, provided by indicators such as moving averages or Fibonacci retracement levels, and RSI and/or stochastics are at overbought or oversold levels, we identify an environment that is highly conducive to range trading.

Of course, the market overview sheet is not foolproof, and just because you have a lot of X marks in either the trend or range group doesn't mean that a trend will not fade or a breakout will not occur. Yet, what this spreadsheet will do is prevent traders from trading blindly and ignoring the broader market conditions. It provides traders with a launching pad from which to identify the day's trading opportunities.

Date – Time								Trending							Range		
Currency Pair	Current Price	Daily High	Daily Low	10-day High	10-day Low	Bollinger Band Up	Bollinger Band Down	(14) above 25	Crosses 50-Day	Crosses 100-day	Crosses 200-day	Bollinger Band Range	ADX (14) below 25	RSI (14) Greater than 80	(14) Less than 80	Stochastics > 70	Stochastics < 30
EURUSD	1.105	1.1144	1.0923				X	X							X		X
GBPUSD																	
USDJPY																	
USDCHF																	
AUDUSD																	
NZDUSD																	
USDCAD																	
EURJPY																	
EURGBP																	
EURCHF																	
AUDJPY																	
CHFJPY																	
GBPJPY																	
GBPCHF																	
AUDCAD																	
EURCAD																	
AUDNZD																	

FIGURE 7.2   Currency Checklist

Trades That I Am Waiting For

The next section in the trading journal lists out the possible trades for the day. Based on an initial overview of the charts, this section is where you should list the trades for which you are waiting. A sample entry would look like the following:

April 5, 2015
Buy AUDUSD on a break of 0.7850 (previous day high)
Stop at 0.7800 (50-day SMA)
Target 1—0.7925 (38.2% Fibonacci retracement of Nov-Mar bull wave)
Target 2—0.8075 (Upper Bollinger)
Target 3—10-day Trailing Low

As soon as your entry level is reached, you know exactly how to take action and where to place your stops and limits. Of course, it is also important to take a quick glance at the market to make sure that the trading conditions that you were waiting for are still intact. For example, if you were looking for a strong breakout with no retracement to occur at the entry level, when it does break, you want to make sure that the break has decent momentum. This exercise will help you develop a plan of action to approach your trading day. Before every battle, warriors will regroup to go over the plan of attack—in trading, you want to have the same mentality. Plan and prepare for the worst-case scenario and know your plan of attack for the day!

Existing or Completed Trades

This section is developed and used to enforce discipline and to learn from your mistakes. At the end of each trading day, it is important to review this section to understand why certain trades resulted in losses and others in profits. The purpose of this section is to identify trends. To understand why this is important, let's look at an example that is completely unrelated to trading. On a normal given day, most people will subconsciously inject a lot of "ums" or "uhs" into their daily conversation. However, most of these people do not even realize that they are even doing so until someone records their conversation and replays it back to them. This is one of the ways that professional presenters and newscasters train to kick the habit of using placeholder words. Having worked with over 65,000 traders, too often have I seen these traders make the same mistakes repeatedly. This includes taking profits too early, letting losses run, getting emotional about trading, ignoring economic releases, or entering a trade prematurely. Keeping a record of previous trades is like keeping a recording of your conversations. When you flip back to the trades that you have completed, you may have a perfect map of what strategies have or have not been profitable for you. The reason why a journal is so important is because it minimizes the emotional intervention of trades. I frequently see novice traders take profits early but let losses run. The following are two samples of trade journal entries that could have provided learning opportunities:

February 12, 2015

Trade: Short 3 lots of EURUSD @ 1.1045

Stop: 1.1195 (former all-time high)

Target: 1.0800

Result: Trade closed on Feb 13, 2015—stopped out of the 3 lots @ 1.1195 (−150 pips)

Comments: Got margin call! It broke the all-time high, I thought it was going to reverse, did not stick to stop—kept letting losses run, eventually margin call closed out all positions. Note to self: MAKE SURE STICK TO STOPS!

April 3, 2015

Trade: Long 2 lots of USDCAD @ 1.2135

Stop: 1.2000 (strong technical support—confluence of 50-day moving average and 68% Fibonacci retracement of Feb—March rally)

Target: First lot @ 1.2295 (upper Bollinger and 5 pips shy of 1.2300 psychological resistance)

Second lot @ 1.2450 (Former head and shoulders support turned resistance, 100-day SMA)

Result: Trade closed on April 5, 2015—stopped out of the 2 lots at 1.2000 (−135 pips)

Comments: USDCAD did not continue uptrend and was becoming overbought, I didn't see that ADX was weakening and falling from higher levels, there was also a divergence in Stochastics. Note to self: MAKE SURE TO LOOK FOR DIVERGENCES NEXT TIME!

Unlike many traders, the best trades in my opinion are the trades where both technicals and fundamentals support the trade. In general, I prefer to stay out of trades that contradict my fundamental outlook. For example, if there is a bullish formation in both the GBPUSD and the AUDUSD due to U.S. dollar weakness, but the Bank of England has finished raising interest rates, while the Reserve Bank of Australia has full intentions of tightening to tame the strength of the Australian economy, I would most likely choose to express my bearish dollar view in the AUDUSD rather than the GBPUSD. My bias for choosing the AUDUSD over the GBPUSD would be even stronger if the AUDUSD already offered a higher interest rate differential than the GBPUSD. I seen technicals thwarted by fundamentals so often that now I always incorporate both into my trading strategy. I use a combination of technical, fundamental, and positioning, and am generally also a trend follower. I also typically use a top-down approach that involves the following:

1. I will start by taking an overall technical survey of the market and pick the currency pairs that have retraced to attractive levels for entry in order to participate in a medium term fundamentally supportive trend.

2. For currencies with a dollar component (i.e., not the crosses), I determine if my initial technical view for that pair coincides with my fundamental view on the dollar, as well as my view on how upcoming U.S. releases may impact trading for the day. The reason why I look at the dollar specifically is because 80% of all currency trades involve the dollar, which makes U.S. fundamentals particularly important.

3. If it is a cross, I will proceed by determining if the technical view coincides with the fundamental outlook using Fibonacci retracements, ADX, moving averages, oscillators, and other technical tools.

4. Then I like to look at positioning using the Commitment of Traders Report or the FXCM Speculative Sentiment index to see if it supports the trade.

5. If I am left with two equally compelling trade ideas, I will choose the one with a positive interest rate differential.

Have a Toolbox—Use What Works for the Current Market Environment

Once you have created a trading journal, it is time to figure out which indicators to lay on your charts. The reason why a lot of traders fail is because they neglect to realize that their favorite indicators are not foolproof. Buying when stochastics are in oversold territory and selling when it is in overbought territory is a strategy that is used quite often by range traders, to a great deal of success, but once the market stops range trading and begins to trend, then relying on stochastics could lead to tremendous amount of losses. In order to become consistently profitable, successful traders need to learn to be adaptable.

One of the most important practices that every trader must understand is to be conscious of the environment that they are trading in. Every trader needs to have some sort of checklist that will help to classify the trading environment so that they can determine whether the market is trending or range bound. Defining trade parameters is one of the most important disciplines of trading. Too many traders have tried to pick the top within a trend, only to wind up with consistently unprofitable trades.

Although defining trade parameters is important to traders in any market (currencies, futures, equities), it is particularly important in the currency market since over 80% of the volume is speculative in nature. This means that currencies can spend a very long period of time in a certain trading environment. Also, the currency market obeys technical analysis particularly well, given its large scale and number of participants.

There are basically two types of trading environments, which means that at any point in time an instrument is either range trading or trending. The first step every trader needs to take is to define the current trading environment. The shortest time frame that traders should start looking at when their trading day starts are daily charts, even if you are trading on a 5-minute time frame.

Step #1: Determine the Trading Environment

Rules to Determining Trading Environment

There are many different ways that traders can determine whether a currency pair is range trading or trending. Of course, many people do it visually, but having set rules will help to keep traders out of trends that may be fading or to prevent traders from getting into a range trade in the midst of a possible breakout. In Figure 7.3, I have outlined some of the rules that I look for in order to classify a currency pair's trading environment.

Profiling a Range Environment

Look for:

1. *ADX (Average Directional Index) less than 20*—The Average Directional Index is one of the primary technical indicators used to determine the strength of a trend. When ADX is less than 20, this suggests that the trend is weak, which is generally characteristic of range-bound market. If ADX is less than 20 and trending downward, it provides a further confirmation that the trend is not only weak but will probably stay in a range-trading environment for a while longer.
2. *Decreasing implied volatility*—There are many ways to analyze volatility. What I like to do is actually track short-term versus long-term volatility. When short-term volatility is falling, especially after a burst above long-term volatility, it is usually indicative of a reversion to range trading scenarios. Volatility usually

Trade	Rules	Indicators
Range	■ ADX < 20 ■ Decreasing implied volatility ■ Risk reversals near choice or flipping between favoring calls and puts	Bollinger, Bands, ADX, Options
Trend	■ ADX > 25 ■ Momentum consistent with trend direction ■ Risk reversals strongly bid for put or call	Moving averages, ADX, Options, Momentum

FIGURE 7.3 Trend/Range Trading Rules

blows out when a currency pair experiences sharp, quick moves. It contracts when ranges are narrow and the trading is very quiet in the markets. The lazy man's version of the way I track volatility is Bollinger Bands, which is actually also a fairly decent measure for determining volatility conditions. A narrow Bollinger Band suggests that ranges are small and there is low volatility in the markets, while wide Bollinger Bands are reflective of large ranges and a highly volatile environment. In a range-trading environment, we are looking for fairly narrow Bollinger Bands, ideally in a horizontal formation similar to the USDJPY chart in Figure 7.4.

3. *Risk reversals flipping between calls and puts*: A risk reversal consists of a pair of options, a call and a put, on the same currency. Risk reversals have both the same expiration (1 month) and sensitivity to the underlying spot rate. They are quoted in terms of the difference in volatility between the two options. While in theory these options should have the same implied volatility in practice, these volatilities often differ in the market. Risk reversals can be seen as having a market polling function. A number strongly in favor of calls or puts indicates that the market prefers calls over puts. The reverse is true if the number is strongly in favor of puts versus calls. Thus, risk reversals can be used as a substitute for gauging positions in the FX market. In an ideal environment, far out of the money calls and puts should have the same volatility. However, this is rarely the case, since there is generally a sentiment bias in the markets that is reflected in risk reversals. In range-bound environments, risk reversals tend

FIGURE 7.4 USDJPY Bollinger Band Chart

to flip between favoring calls and puts at nearly zero (or equal). This indicates that there is indecision among bulls and bears, and there is no strong bias in the markets.

What Does a Risk Reversal Table Look Like?

According to the risk reversals in Figure 7.5, we can see that the market is strongly favoring yen calls (JC) and dollar puts over the long term. EURUSD short-term risk reversals are near choice, which is what you are looking for when profiling a range-bound environment. Risk reversal information used to be readily available but is more difficult to find these days. Currently, the only place we know of that provides this information is the Bloomberg Professional Terminal, which costs over US$1500 a month.

Identifying a Trending Environment

Look for three things:

1. *ADX (Average Directional Index) greater than 20*—As mentioned earlier when we talked about range-trading conditions, the Average Directional Index is one of the primary technical indicators used to determine the strength of a trend. In a trending environment, we look for ADX to be greater than 25 and rising. If ADX is greater than 25 but sloping downward, especially off of the extreme 40 level, you have to be careful of aggressive trend positioning since it may indicate that the trend is waning.

2. *Momentum consistent with trend direction*—In addition to using ADX, I also recommend looking for confirmation of a trending environment through momentum indicators. Traders should look for momentum to be consistent

14:40 GMT April 19th

1 Month To 1 Year Risk Reversal

Currency	1M R/R	3M R/R	6M R/R	1YR R/R
USDJPY	0.3/0.6 JC	0.7/1.0 JC	**1.1/1.3 JC**	1.3/1.6 JC
EURUSD	**0.1/0.3 EC**	0.0/0.3 EC	0.0/0.3 EC	0.1/0.4 EC
GBPUSD	0.0/0.3 SP	0.0/0.3 SC	0.0/0.3 SC	0.0/0.3 SC
USDCHF	0.2/0.2 CC	0.0/0.3 CC	0.0/0.4 CC	0.1/0.5 CC

* JC = Japanese yen call   * SC = Sterling call
* EC = Euro call   * CC = Swiss call
* SP = Sterling put

FIGURE 7.5 Risk Reversals

with the direction of the trend. Most currency traders will look for oscillators to point strongly in the direction of the trend. For example, in an uptrend, trend traders will look for the moving averages, RSI, stochastics, and MACD to all point strongly upward. In a downtrend, they will look for these same indicators to point downward. Some currency traders use the momentum index, but in my experience, it is less popular and reliable. Instead, one of the strongest momentum indicators is a perfect order of moving averages. A perfect order is when we have the moving averages line up perfectly: that is, for an uptrend, the 10 day SMA is greater than the 20-day SMA, which is greater 50-day SMA. The 100-day SMA and the 200-day SMA are below the shorter-term moving averages. In a downtrend, a perfect order would be when the shorter-term moving averages stack up below the longer-term moving averages.

3. *Options (risk reversals)*—With a trending environment, we are looking for risk reversals to strongly favor calls or puts. When one side of the market is laden with interest, it is usually indicative of a strong trending environment or that a contra-trend move may be brewing if risk reversals are at extreme levels.

■ Step #2: Determine the Time Frame for Trade

Once you have determined that a currency pair is either range-bound or trending, it is time to determine how long you plan on holding the trade. The following is a set of guidelines and indicators that I use for trading different time frames. Not all of the guidelines need to be met, but the more guidelines that are met, the more solid the trading opportunity.

Intraday Trade (Range)

Rules:

1. Use hourly charts to determine entry points and daily charts to confirm that a range trade exists on a longer-time frame.
2. Use oscillators to determine entry point within range.
3. Look for short-dated risk reversals to be near choice.
4. Look for reversal in oscillators (RSI or stochastics at extreme point).
5. Trade stronger when prices fail at key resistance or hold key support levels (use Fibonacci retracement points and moving averages).

Indicators Used:
Stochastics, MACD, RSI, Bollinger Bands, options, Fibonacci retracement levels

Medium-Term Range Trade

Rules:

1. Use daily charts.
2. There are two ways to range trade medium term—position for upcoming range trading opportunities or get involved in existing ranges.
3. *Upcoming range opportunities*: Look for high-volatility environments, where short-term implied volatilities are significantly higher than longer-term volatilities. Seek reversion back to the mean environments.
4. *Existing ranges*: Use Bollinger Bands to identify existing ranges.
5. Look for reversals in oscillators such as RSI and stochastics.
6. Make sure ADX is below 25 and ideally falling.
7. Look for medium-term risk reversals near choice.
8. Confirm with price action—failure at key range resistances and bounces on key range supports (using traditional technical indicators).

Indicators:

Options, Bollinger Bands, stochastics, MACD, RSI, Fibonacci retracement levels

Medium-Term Trend Trade

Rules:

1. Look for ranges on daily charts and use weekly charts for confirmation.
2. Refer back to the characteristics of a trending environment—look for those parameters to be met.
3. Buy breakout/retracement scenarios on key Fibonacci levels or moving averages.
4. Look for no major resistance levels in front of trade.
5. Look for candlestick pattern confirmation.
6. Look for moving average confluence to be on same side of trade.
7. Enter on a break of significant high or low.
8. The ideal is to wait for volatilities to contract before getting in.
9. Look for fundamentals to also be supportive of trade—growth and interest rates. You want to see a string of economic surprises or disappointments depending on directional bias.

Indicators

ADX, Parabolic SAR, RSI, Ichimoku Clouds, Elliot waves, Fibonacci

Medium-Term Breakout Trade

Rules:

1. Use daily charts.
2. Look for contraction in short-term volatility to a point where it is sharply below long-term volatility.
3. Use pivot points to determine whether a break is a true break or a false break.
4. Look for moving average confluences to be supportive of trade.

Indicators

Bollinger Bands, moving averages, Fibonacci

■ Risk Management

Although risk management is one of the more simple topics to grasp, it is also one of the most important. Too often we have seen traders turn winning positions into losing positions and solid strategies result in losses instead of profits. The fact of the matter is that regardless of how intelligent and knowledgeable a trader may be about the markets, their own psychology will cause them to lose money. Why does this happen? Are the markets really so enigmatic that few can profit? Or is there simply a common mistake that virtually all traders are prone to making? The answer is the latter. And the good news is that the problem, while it can be an emotionally and psychologically challenging, is ultimately fairly easy to grasp and solve.

Most traders lose money simply because they have no understanding or place no importance in *risk management*. Risk management involves essentially knowing how much you are willing to risk and how much you are looking to gain. Without a sense of risk management, most traders simply hold on to losing positions for an extremely long amount of time, but take profits on winning positions prematurely. The result is a seemingly paradoxical scenario that in reality is all too common: The trader ends up having more winning positions than losing ones, but ends up with a negative P/L. So, what can traders do to ensure they have solid risk management habits? There are a few key guidelines that every trader, regardless of their strategy or what they are trading, should keep in mind:

- *Risk-reward ratio.* Traders should look to establish a risk-reward ratio for every trade they place. In other words, they should have an idea of how much they are willing to lose, and how much they are looking to gain. Generally, the risk-reward ratio should be at least 1:2, if not more. Having a solid risk-reward ratio can prevent traders from entering positions that ultimately are not worth the risk.

- *Stop-loss orders.* Traders should also employ stop-loss orders as a way of specifying the maximum loss they are willing to accept. By using stop-loss orders, traders can avoid the common predicament of being in a scenario where they have many winning trades but a single loss large enough to eliminate any trace of profitability in the account. Trailing stops to lock in profits are particularly useful. A good habit of more successful traders is to employ the rule of moving your stop to break even as soon as your position has profited by the same amount that you initially risked through the stop order. At the same time, some traders may also choose to close a portion of their position.

For those looking to add to a winning position or go with trend, the best strategy is to treat it as if it were a new trade of its own, independent of the winning position. If you are going to add to a winning position, perform the same analysis of the chart that you would if you had no position at all. If a trade continues to go in your favor, you can also close out part of the position while trailing your stop higher on the remaining lots that you are holding. Try thinking about your risk and reward on each separate lot that you have bought if they are at different entry points as well. If you buy a second lot 50 pips above your first entry point, don't use the same stop price on both, but manage the risk on the second lot independently from the first.

Using Stop-Loss Orders to Manage Risk

Given the importance of money management to successful trading, using the stop-loss order is imperative for any trader looking to succeed in the currency market. Stop-loss orders allow traders to specify the maximum loss they are willing to accept on any given trade. If the market reaches the rate the trader specifies in his/her stop-loss order, then the trade will be closed immediately. As a result, using stop-loss orders allows you to know how much you are risking at the time you enter the trade.

There are two parts to successfully using a stop-loss order: (1) initially placing the stop at a reasonable level and (2) trailing the stop—or moving it forward toward profitability—as the trade progresses in your favor.

Placing the Stop Loss

We recommend two ways of placing a trailing stop-loss order:

- *The first is a two-day low method.* These volatility-based stops involve placing your stop-loss order approximately 10 to 20 pips below the *two-day low* of the pair. For example, if the low on the EURUSD's most recent candle was 1.1200, and the previous candle's low was 1.1100, then the stop should be placed around 1.1090—10 pips below the two-day low—if a trader is looking to get long. This type of trailing stop allows you to keep tight control of the position and minimizes the time in trade. The downside is that it can be closed prematurely during a brief period of consolidation.

- *Parabolic SAR.* Another form of volatility-based stop is the parabolic SAR, an indicator that is found on many currency trading charting applications. This indicator graphically displays a small dot at the point on the chart where the stop should be placed. The benefit of parabolic SAR is that it is dynamic and generally further away from the current price.

There is no magic formula for what works best in every situation, but the following is an example of how these stops could be used.

Upon entering a long position, determine where support is and place a stop 20 pips below support. For example, let's say this is 60 pips below the entry point. If the trade earns a profit of 60 pips, close half of my position using a market order, then move the stop up to the entry point. At this point, trail the stop 60 pips behind the moving market price. If the parabolic SAR moves up so that it is above the entry point, you could switch to using parabolic SAR as the stop level. Of course, during the day, there can be other signals that could prompt you to move your stop. If the price breaks through a new resistance level, that resistance then becomes support. You can place a stop 20 pips below that support level, even if it is only 30–40 pips away from the current price. The underlying principle you have to use is to find a point to place your stop where you would no longer want to be in the trade once the price reaches that level. Usually it falls at a point where the price goes below support.

Aside from employing proper risk management strategies, one of the other more crucial yet overlooked elements of successful trading is maintaining a healthy psychological outlook. At the end of the day, a trader who is unable to cope with the stress of market fluctuations will not stand the test of time—no matter how skilled they may be at the more scientific elements of trading. Here are some tips:

- *Practice emotional detachment.* That is, traders must make trading decisions based on strategies independent of fear and greed. One of the premiere attributes a good trader has is emotional detachment: While these traders are dedicated and fully involved in their trades, they are not emotionally married to them; they accept losing, and make their investment decisions on an intellectual level. Traders who are emotionally involved in trading often make substantial errors, as they tend to whimsically change their strategy after a few losing trades, or become overly carefree after a few winning trades. A good trader must be emotionally balanced, and must base all trading decisions on strategy—not fear or greed.

- *Know when to take a break.* In the midst of a losing streak, consider taking a break from trading before fear and greed dominate your strategy.

  Not every trade can be a winning one. As a result, traders must be psychologically capable of coping with losses. Most traders, even successful ones, will go through a stretch of losing trades. The key to being a successful trader, though, is being able to go through a losing stretch unfazed and undeterred. If you are experiencing a string of losing trades, it may be time to take a break from trading. Often, taking a few days off from watching the market to clear your mind can be the best remedy for a losing streak. Continuing to trade relentlessly during a tough market condition can breed greater losses and ruin your psychological trading capacity. Ultimately, it's always better to acknowledge your losses rather than continue to fight through them and pretend they don't exist. Make no mistake about it: Regardless of how much you study, practice, or trade, there will be losing trades throughout your entire career. The key is to make them small enough that you can live to trade another day and allow your winning trades room to breathe and flourish. You can overcome a lot of bad luck with proper money management techniques. This is why we have stressed a 2:1 reward to risk ratio, and why we recommend not risking more than 2% of your equity on any single trade.

Whether you are trading forex, equities, or futures, there are 10 trading rules that successful traders should live by:

1. Limit your losses.
2. Let your profits run.
3. Keep position sizes within reason.
4. Know your risk versus reward ratio.
5. Be adequately capitalized.
6. Don't fight the trend.
7. Never add to losing positions.
8. Know market expectations.
9. Learn from your mistake—keep a trade log.
10. Have a maximum drawdown.

CHAPTER 8

Technical Trading Strategy: Multiple Time Frame Analysis

To trade successfully on an intraday basis, it is important to be selective. Trend trading is one of the most popular strategies employed by global macro hedge funds. Although many traders prefer to range trade, the big profit potentials tend to lie in trades that capture and participate in big market moves. It was once said by Mark Boucher, a hedge fund manager of Midas Trust Fund and a former number-one money manager as ranked by Nelson's World Best Money Managers, that 70% of a market's moves occurs 20% of the time. This makes multiple time frame analysis particularly important, because no trader wants to lose sight of the big picture. A great comparison would be to imagine taking a road trip from Chicago to Florida. There are going to be a lot of left and right turns along the way, but the most important thing to be aware of during the trip is that you should be headed south. The same approach should be taken in trading. Looking for opportunities to buy in an uptrend or sell in a downtrend can be far much more profitable than trying to pick tops and bottoms.

The most common form of multiple time frame analysis is to use daily charts to identify the overall trend and then use the hourly charts to determine specific entry levels.

FIGURE 8.1 USDJPY Monthly Chart

Source: eSignal

Take a look at the USDJPY chart in Figure 8.1. This is a daily chart of the U.S. dollar against the Japanese yen (USDJPY). As you can see, USDJPY has been trending higher since late 2012. During this period, range or contrarian traders looking to pick tops would have been faced with at least two years of difficult and most likely unprofitable trading—particularly when the currency pair was hitting three- or four-year highs in late 2013 and early 2014. This area would have certainly attracted a good deal of traders looking to pick a top or to fade the trend. Despite a dip in mid-2013, USDJPY remained strong going into 2105, making life very difficult for medium-term range players.

Instead, the more effective trading strategy would have been to take a position in the direction of the trend. In USDJPY, this would have involved looking for opportunities to buy on dips. Figure 8.2 shows one way to do so on a 15-minute chart using the Relative Strength Index (RSI). Rather than looking for opportunities to sell when RSI rose above 70, it was smarter to buy when it dipped to 30. The first horizontal line in Figure 8.2 shows the point at which RSI rose above 70. If you sold at that level, USDJPY would have moved against you by 40 pips before reversing. The second horizontal line shows the point at which RSI dipped to 30. If you bought at that level, you would have picked the bottom on this short term USDJPY chart for a move of at least 50 pips.

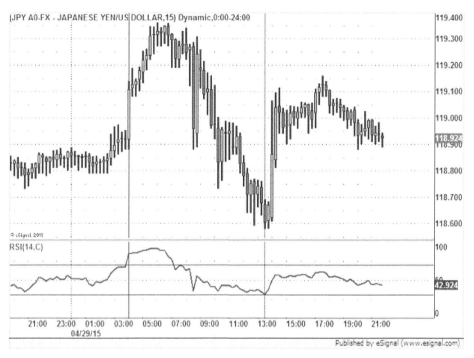

FIGURE 8.2 USDJPY 15-Minute Chart

Source: eSignal

Now let's take a look at another example of the British pound. Figure 8.3 shows the monthly chart of the USDCAD from January 2013 to January 2015. Like USDJPY, traders trying to pick tops in the USDCAD would have faced at least two straight years of difficult trading—particularly when the USDCAD was climbing to fresh five-year highs in late 2014 early 2015. This level would have certainly attracted a number of top pickers. To the frustration of those who tried to fade the move, USDCAD rallied 9% beyond its five-year highs, which means those top pickers would have incurred significant losses. Taking a look at the hourly chart for the USDCAD, we want to look for opportunities to buy on dips rather than sell on rallies. Figure 8.4 shows Fibonacci retracement levels drawn from the 2002 to 2008 bear wave. Those levels held pretty well with declines finding support at the 38.2% Fibonacci retracements between January 2008, January 2009, and January 2015.

Multiple time frame analysis can also be employed on a shorter-term basis. Let us take a look at an example using CHFJPY. First we start with the hourly chart of CHFJPY, shown in Figure 8.5. Using Fibonacci retracements, we can see on the hourly charts that prices have failed at the 38.2% retracement of the December 30, 2004, to February 9, 2005, bear wave numerous times. This indicates that the pair is contained within a weeklong downtrend below those levels. In this case, we want to use our 15-minute charts to look for entry levels to participate in the

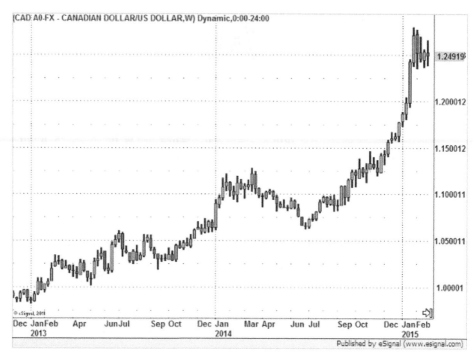

FIGURE 8.3 USDCAD Weekly Chart

Source: eSignal

overall downtrend. However, in order to increase the successfulness of this trade, we want to make sure that CHFJPY is also in a downtrend on a daily basis. Taking a look at Figure 8.6, we can see that CHFJPY is indeed trading below the 200-day simple moving average, with the 20-day SMA crossing below the 100-day SMA. This confirms the bearish momentum in the currency pair. So as a day trader, we move to the 15-minute chart to identify entry levels. Figure 8.7 is the 15-minute chart; the horizontal line is the 38.2% Fibonacci retracement of the earlier downtrend. We see that CHFJPY broke above the horizontal line on May 11, 2005; however, rather than buying into a potential breakout trade, the bearish big picture reflected on the hourly and daily charts point to a contrarian trade. In fact, there were two instances shown in Figure 8.7 where the currency pair broke above the Fibonacci level only to trade significantly lower. Disciplined day traders would use those opportunities to fade the breakout.

The importance of multiple time frame analysis cannot be underestimated. Looking at the big picture first can help to keep traders out of a lot of dangerous trades. The majority of new traders in the market are range traders for the simple fact that buying at the low and selling at the high is an easy concept to grasp.

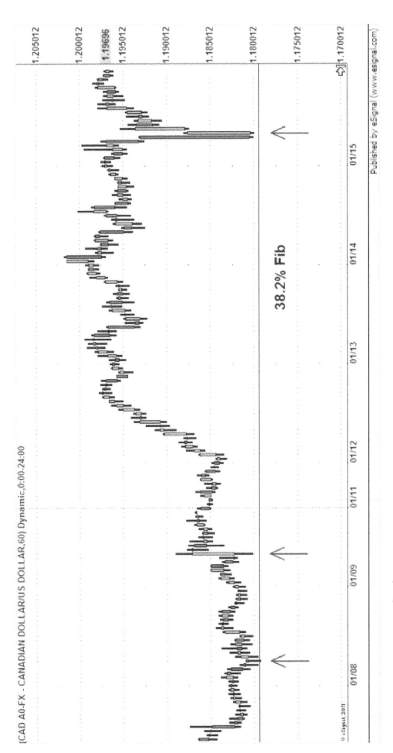

FIGURE 8.4 USDCAD Hourly Chart

Source: eSignal

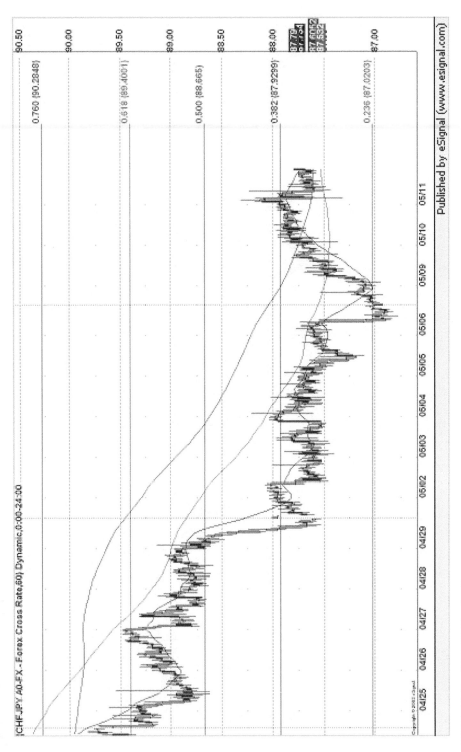

FIGURE 8.5 CHFJPY Hourly Chart

Source: eSignal

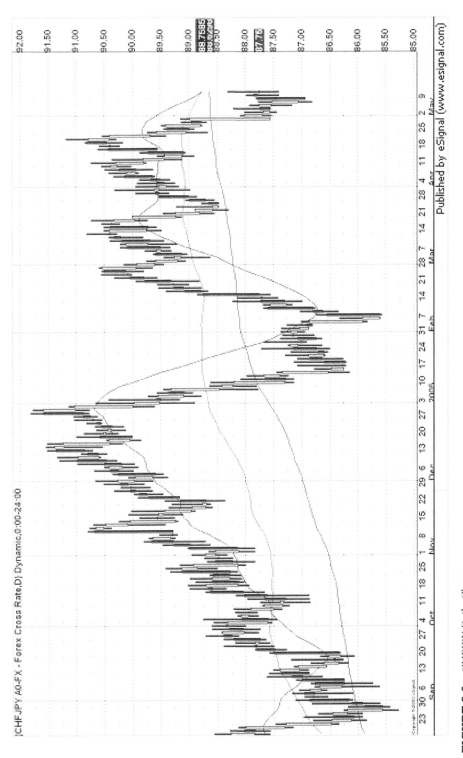

FIGURE 8.6 CHFJPY Daily Chart

Source: eSignal

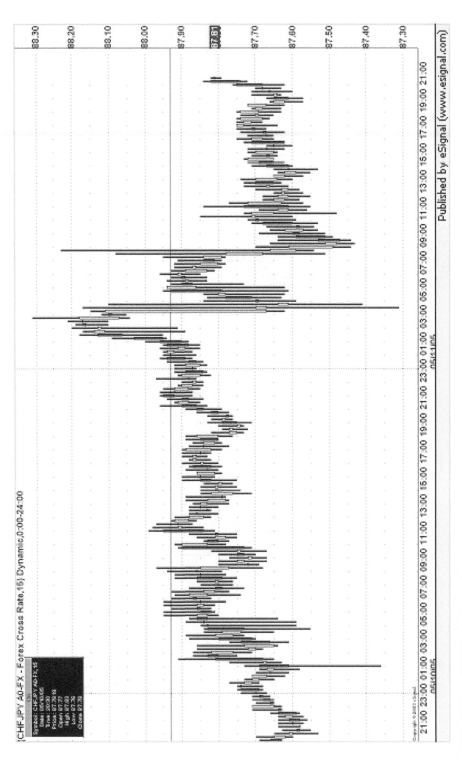

FIGURE 8.7   CHF JPY 15-Minute Chart

Source: eSignal

Of course, this strategy will work from time to time, but traders need to be mindful of the overall trading environment if they want to be consistently profitable. Referencing back to Chapter 7, range traders should only try to play the trade when the conditions for a range bound market are met. One useful way to identify this type of market is to look for ADX to be less than 25 and ideally trending downward.

CHAPTER 9

Technical Strategy: Trading with Double Bollinger Bands

One of the most useful technical indicators in my experience is Bollinger Bands. Traditionally, Bollinger Bands are used as overbought and oversold indicators, but given the trending nature of currencies, there are more efficient ways to use the bands. Traditionally, Bollinger Bands consists of three lines—the 20-period moving average and the two standard deviation bands above and below the moving average. If the currency pair rises to the upper Bollinger Band, it is considered overbought because the move extended to an extreme level and should therefore be faded. The same is true if it drops to the lower Bollinger Band. Unfortunately, currencies are trending, and using the 20-period two standard deviation bands may not be the best way to trade. Take a look at Figure 9.1. In this daily chart of EURUSD, the arrows highlight the points where the currency pair "hugs" the second standard deviation band. If you bought each time EURUSD touched the lower band or sold each time it touched the upper band, there would be significant losses before the currency pair finally turned around.

The better technique would be to add another set of Bollinger Bands—the 20-period, one-standard deviation. This would put four bands on the chart if the basis

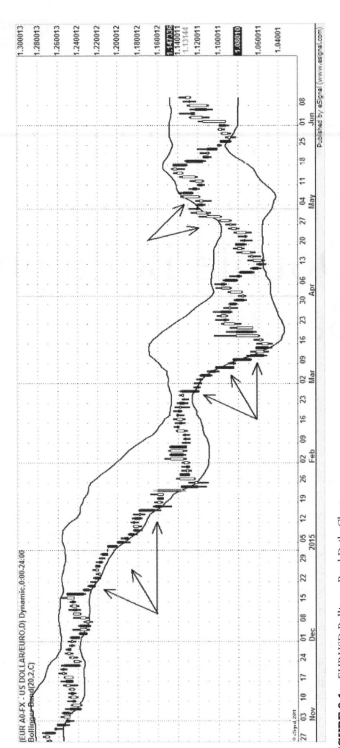

FIGURE 9.1 EURUSD Bollinger Band Daily Chart

Source: eSignal

or the 20-period moving average is removed, and most charting packages will allow you to do that. Figure 9.2 shows how the same EURUSD daily chart with look with two sets of Bollinger Bands. The outer lines are the two-standard-deviation Bollinger Bands, and the two inner lines are the one-standard-deviation Bollinger Bands.

■ Using Double Bollinger Bands to Pick Tops and Bottoms

Having two sets of Bollinger Bands on your chart is a much more effective way to pick a top or bottom in currencies. The general rule of thumb is that we don't buy a bottom until the currency pair has traded above the first standard deviation Bollinger Band. Along the same lines, we do not sell a top until the pair trades below the first standard deviation Bollinger Band. While this technique may not pick the perfect bottom, it can help avoid prematurely picking a top or bottom which can mean major losses in a trending environment. Here are the rules for the long and short trades on a daily chart for picking tops and bottoms using the double Bollinger Bands.

Strategy Rules for Long Trade

1. Look for the currency pair to be trading between the lower first and second standard deviation Bollinger Bands.
2. Look for a close above the first standard deviation Bollinger Band.
3. If so, BUY at close of candle or 5pm NY Time.
4. Stop 50 pips below first standard deviation Bollinger Band.
5. Close half of position when it moves by amount risked; move stop on rest to initial entry price (breakeven).
6. Close remainder of position at two times risk or trail the stop.

Strategy Rules for Short Trade

1. Look for the currency pair to be trading between the upper first and second standard deviation Bollinger Bands.
2. Look for a close below the first standard deviation Bollinger Band.
3. If so, *sell* at close of candle or 5pm NY Time.
4. Stop 30 pips above first standard deviation Bollinger Band.
5. Close half of position when it moves by amount risked; move stop on rest to initial entry price (breakeven).
6. Close remainder of position at two times risk or trail the stop.

Lets take a look at the same EURUSD chart. Figure 9.3 shows the points at which a trade would have been entered, and in most cases, it was a more effective way to pick a top or bottom in the currency pair.

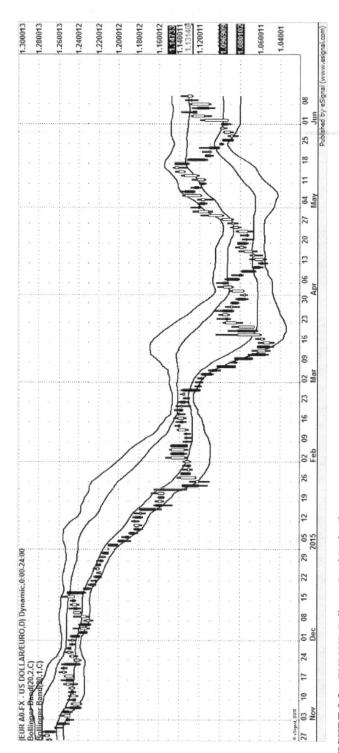

FIGURE 9.2 EURUSD Bollinger Band Daily Chart

Source: eSignal

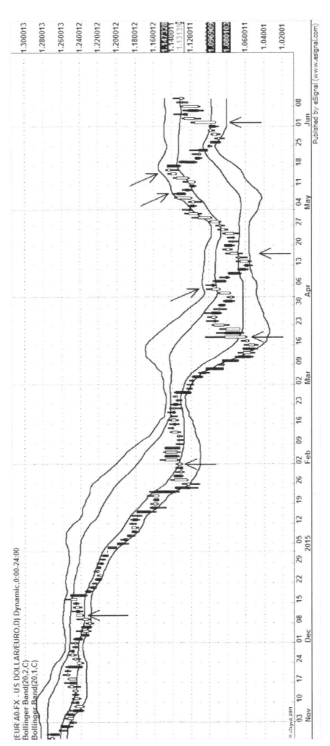

FIGURE 9.3 EURUSD Bollinger Band Daily Chart

Source: eSignal

TECHNICAL STRATEGY: TRADING WITH DOUBLE BOLLINGER BANDS

FIGURE 9.4 EURUSD Short Trade

Source: eSignal

Now let's take a look at some examples in more detail. In Figure 9.4, we see that on May 18, the EURUSD, which had been trading between the two upper bands, fell strongly to break out of the zone and close below the first standard deviation Bollinger Band. We sell at the NY close (there's usually a leeway of two hours). A two-lot trade is established at 1.1313 with a stop 30 pips above the first standard deviation Bollinger Band (1.1341) at 1.1371. The risk is 58 pips, which means that the first exit is 1.1313 minus 58 pips or 1.1255. The second profit target is 1.1197, which is two times risk or 116 pips. The first and second profit targets are reached on the very next day when the currency pair drops to a low of 1.1119, for a profit of 58 pips on the first half of the position and another 116 pips on the second half. If the stop was trailed using a moving average or percentage, a trader may have been able to capitalize on the selloff that ensued.

Figure 9.5 shows that on June 2, the EURUSD, which had been trading between the two lower bands, rose strongly to break out of the zone and close firmly above the first standard deviation Bollinger Band. We buy at the NY close (there's usually a leeway of two hours). A two-lot trade is established at 1.1151, with a stop 30 pips below the first standard deviation Bollinger Band (1.0970) at 1.0940. The risk is 211 pips, which means that the first exit is 1.1151 plus 211 pips, or 1.1361. This profit target is reached two days later, when the currency pair races to a high of 1.1380. At the time, the stop is moved to 1.1151, and the following day the breakeven stop

14:40 GMT April 19th 1 Month To 1 Year Risk Reversal				
Currency	1M R/R	3M R/R	6M R/R	1YR R/R
USDJPY	0.3/0.6 :IC	0.7/1.0 JC	**1.1/1.3 JC**	1.3/1.6 JC
EURUSD	**0.1/0.3 EC**	0.0/0.3 EC	0.0/0.3 EC	0.1/0.4 EC
GBPUSD	0.0/0.3 SP	0.0/0.3 SC	0.0/0.3 SC	0.0/0.3 SC
USDCHF	0.2/0.2 CC	0.0/0.3 CC.	0.0/0.4 CC	0.1/0.5 CC

* JC = Japanese Yen Call   * SC = Sterling Call

* EC = Euro Call   * CC = Swiss Call

* SP = Sterling Put

FIGURE 9.5   EURUSD Long Trade

Source: eSignal

is hit, and we end up banking only +211 on the first half of the trade with no losses or gains on the second half.

Using Double Bollinger Bands to Determine Trend versus Range

In addition to identifying levels to pick tops and bottoms, the double Bollinger Bands can also be very helpful in determining the market environment. One of the most commonly asked questions in forex is whether a currency pair is in trend or range. When the pair is trading between the two lower or upper Bollinger Bands, it is in trend, and when it is trading between the first standard deviation Bollinger Bands, it is in range, as shown in Figure 9.6. When the currency pair is in trend mode, it is best to look for opportunities to join the trend. When it is in the range zone, picking tops and bottoms is preferred.

Using Double Bollinger Bands to Join a New Trend

Another way to use the double Bollinger Bands is to join a new uptrend or downtrend using a daily chart. Here are the trading rules:

Strategy Rules for Long Trade

1. Look for the currency pair to close above the first standard deviation Bollinger Band.
2. Check to see if the last two candles were below the first standard deviation Bollinger Band.
3. If so, *buy* at close of candle or 5pm NY Time.
4. Initial stop at +65 pips.

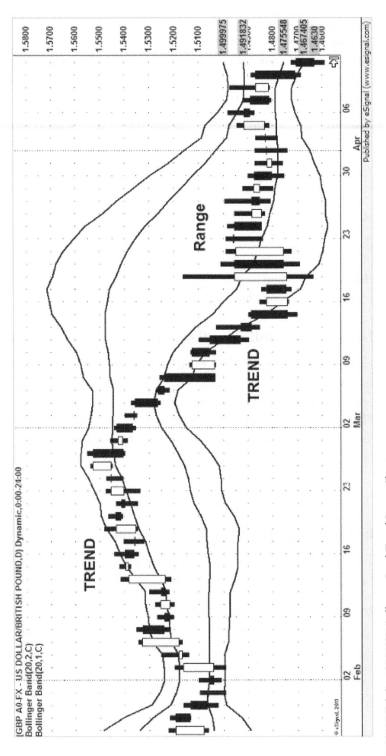

FIGURE 9.6 GBPUSD Bollinger Band Trend Range Chart

Source: eSignal

FIGURE 9.7 USDJPY Long Trade

Source: eSignal

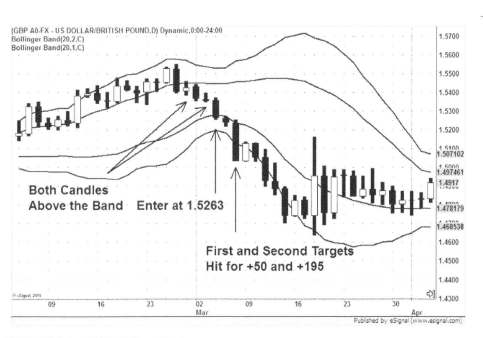

FIGURE 9.8 GBPUSD Short Trade

Source: eSignal

5. Close half of position at +50 pips; move stop on rest to initial entry price (breakeven).
6. Close remainder of position at +195 pips.

Strategy Rules for Short Trade

1. Look for the currency pair to close below the first standard deviation Bollinger Band.
2. Check to see if the last two candles were above the first standard deviation Bollinger Band.
3. If so, *sell* at close of candle or 5pm NY Time.
4. Initial stop at +65 pips.
5. Close half of position at +50 pips; move stop on rest to initial entry price (breakeven).
6. Close remainder of position at +195 pips.

Here are some examples:

In Figure 9.7, we see that USDJPY closed above the first standard deviation Bollinger Band on May 18. We check to see if the last two candles were below the band and the rules are satisfied, allowing us to initiate a long trade at 119.97. The stop is placed 65 pips below at 119.32. The target for the first half of the position is 50 pips, or 120.47, and the target for the second half is 195 pips, or 121.92. The first profit target is reached 24 hours later (which is generally the case). When that happens, the stop is raised to 119.97, which is the initial entry or breakeven price. The trade is left on and the second profit target of +195 pips is reached six trading days after the trade was first initiated.

In Figure 9.8, we see GBPUSD close below the first standard deviation Bollinger Band on March 1, so we check to see if the last two candles were above the band and the rules are satisfied, allowing us to initiate a short trade at 5pm when the currency pair is trading at 1.5263. The stop is placed 65 pips above at 1.5328. The target for the first half of the position is 50 pips, or 1.5213, and the target for the second half is 195 pips, or 1.5068. The trade floats for 24 hours, then GBPUSD drops sharply, hitting our first and second profit target on the very same day.

We encourage you to lay the Bollinger Bands on your charts and look for more examples of these strategies in action. There are many ways to use the double Bollinger Bands for forex trading. Both of these strategies are for daily charts, but different strategies and rules can be used for intraday trading using the bands.

CHAPTER 10

Technical Trading Strategy: Fading the Double Zeros

O ne of the most widely overlooked areas of trading is market structure. Developing a keen understanding of market structure and its dynamics can help day traders to gain an unbelievable advantage. Developing a feel and understanding for market dynamics is key to profitably taking advantage of short-term fluctuations. In foreign exchange trading this is especially critical as the primary influence of intraday price action is order flow. Given the fact that most individual traders are not privy to sell-side bank order flow, day traders looking to profit from short-term fluctuations need to learn how to identify and anticipate price zones where large order flows should be triggered. This technique is very efficient for intraday traders as it allows them to get on the same side as the market maker.

When trading intraday, it is impossible to look for bounces off every support or resistance level and expect to be profitable. The key to successful intraday trading requires more selectivity and only entering at those levels where a reaction is more likely. Trading off psychologically important levels such as the *double zeros* or round numbers is one good way of identifying such opportunities. Double zeros represent numbers where the last two digits are zeros. Examples of double zeros would be 118.**00** in USDJPY or 1.11**00** in the EURUSD. After noticing how many times a currency pair would bounce off double zero support or resistance levels intraday despite the underlying trend, we have observed that these bounces are usually much larger and more relevant that rallies off other price levels. This type of reaction is perfect for intraday FX traders because it gives them the opportunity to make 30 to 50 pips while risking only 15–20 pips.

This trading technique is not difficult, but it requires individual traders to develop a solid feel for dealing room and market participant psychology. The idea behind this double zero methodology is simple. Large banks with access to conditional order flow have a distinct advantage over other market participants. The bank's order book gives them direct insight into potential reactions at different price levels. Dealers will often use this strategic information to put on short-term positions in their own accounts.

Market participants as a whole tend to put conditional orders near or around the same levels. While stop-loss orders are usually placed just beyond the round numbers, traders will cluster their take profit orders at the round number. The reason why this occurs is because traders are humans, and humans tend to think in round numbers. As a result, take profit orders have a very high tendency of being placed at the double zero level. Since the FX market is a 24-hour continuous market, speculators also use stop and limit orders more frequently than in other markets. Large banks with access to conditional order flow, like stops and limits, actively seek to exploit this clustering of positions to basically gun stops. The *fading the double zero strategy* attempts to put traders on the same side as market makers by positioning traders for a quick contra-trend move at the double zero level.

This trade is most profitable when there are other technical indicators that will confirm the significance of the double zero level. Here are some guidelines for fading the double zeros or "round numbers."

■ Strategy Rules

Long:

1. Identify a currency pair that is trading below its intraday 20-period simple moving average on a 15-minute chart.
2. Enter a long position 10 to 15 pips above the figure.
3. Place an initial protective stop 20 pips below the figure.

   a. When the position is profitable by the amount risked, close half of the position and move your stop on the remaining portion of the trade to breakeven.
   b. Trail your stop as the price moves in your favor.

Short:

1. Identify a currency pair that is trading above its intraday 20-period simple moving average on a 15-minute chart.
2. Short the currency pair 10 to 15 pips below the figure.

3. Place an initial protective stop 20 pips above the round number.
4. When the position is profitable by the amount that you risked, close half of the position and move your stop on the remaining portion of the trade to breakeven. Trail your stop as the price moves in your favor.

Market Conditions

This strategy works best when the move happens in quieter market conditions without the influence of major reports. It is more successful for currency pairs with tighter trading ranges, crosses, and commodity currencies. This strategy also works in the majors but under quieter market conditions since the stop loss is relatively tight.

Further Optimization

Round numbers are important because they are significant levels but if the price coincides with a key technical level, a reversal becomes more likely. This means the strategy has an even higher probability of success when other important support or resistance levels converge at the figure. This can be caused by moving averages, key Fibonacci levels or Bollinger Bands, or other technical indicators.

Examples

Now let's take a look at some of the examples of this strategy in action. The first example that we will go over is a 15-minute chart of USDJPY shown in Figure 10.1. According to the rules of the strategy, we can see that on April 24, USDJPY was trading above its 20-period moving. Prices continued to move higher with the currency pair drifting toward 120.00, our double zero level. In accordance with the rules, we place an entry order a few pips below the round number at 1110.85. Our order is triggered, and we put our stop 20 above the figure at 120.20. USDJPY climbs to a high of 120.08 before turning lower. We close half of the position when it moves by the amount risked or 35 pips at 1110.50. Notice that USDJPY falls and then rallies again before hitting our initial profit target. When the first profit target is reached, the stop on the remaining half of the position is moved to breakeven or our initial entry price of 1110.85.

We then proceed to trail stop. The trailing stop can be done using a variety of methods including a monetary or percentage basis. We choose to trail the stop by two-bar low for a really short-term trade and end up getting out of the other half of the position at 1110.50 as well, earning us 35 pips on the first and second half of the positions.

The next chart that we want to look at is GBPUSD. What's interesting about Figure 10.2 is that there are a number of examples. In the first example, labeled "1,"

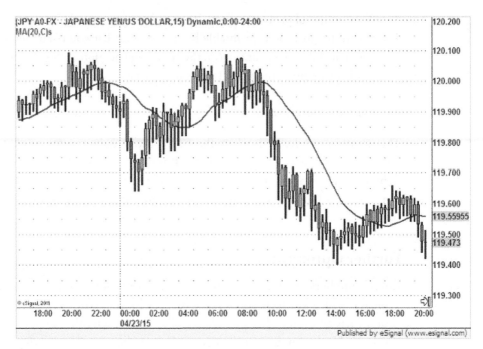

FIGURE 10.1 USDJPY 15-Minute Chart

Source: eSignal

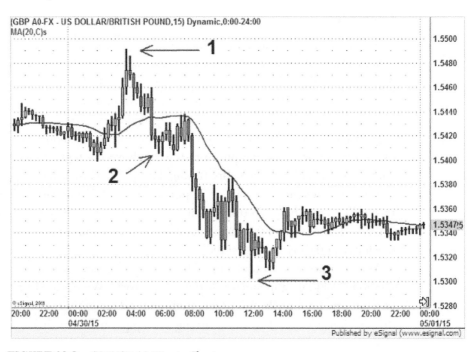

FIGURE 10.2 GBPUSD 15-Minute Chart

Source: eSignal

we can see that GBP/USD was trading above its 20-period moving average on a 15-minute chart and headed for 1.55. According to our rules, we place an order to sell at 1.5485 (the high on this move was 1.5492) with a stop at 1.5520 for 35-pip risk. GBPUSD moves in our favor, and our first profit target is hit at (1.5485 − .0035) at 1.5450. We then move our stop to breakeven, or our initial entry price of 1.5485, and proceed to trail it by the 20-day SMA + 10 pips. If we manage our trade using this type of trailing stop, the second half of the position would have been exited at 1.5350 for 35 pips on the first half of the position and 135 pips on the second. Part of the reason why this trade was so successful is because the 1.5500 is also a significant technical level. Example "2" is a long trail that reversed but not by enough to hit the profit target. Example "3" is a successful long trade that hit the first profit target.

Making sure that the double zero level is a significant level is a key element of filtering for good trades. The last example shown in Figure 10.3 is USDCAD on a 15-minute chart. The great thing about this trade is that it is triple zero level rather than just a double zero level. Triple zero levels hold even more significance than a double zero level because of their less frequent occurrence. In Figure 10.3, we see that USDCAD is also trading well below its 20-period moving average and heading toward 1.2000. We look to go long 15 pips above the double zero level at 1.2015.

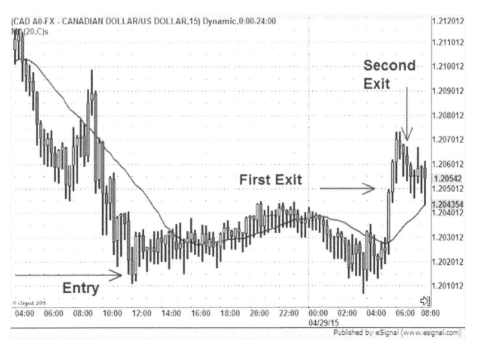

FIGURE 10.3   USDCAD 15-Minute Chart

Source: eSignal

We place our stop 20 pips below the round number at 1.1980. The currency pair hits a low of 1.2011 before moving higher. We then sell half of our positions when the currency pair rallies by the amount that we risked at 1.2050. The stop on the remaining half of the position is then moved to breakeven at 1.2015. We proceed to trail the stop once again by the two-bar low and end up exiting the second half of the position at 1.2055. As a result, we earned 35 pips on the first position and 40 pips on the second position.

CHAPTER 11

Technical Trading Strategy: Waiting for the Deal

The lack of volume data in the FX market has forced day traders to develop different strategies that rely less on the level of demand and more on the micro structure of the market. One of the most common characteristics that day traders try to exploit is the market's 24-hour round-the-clock nature. Although the market is open for trading throughout the course of the day, the extent of market activity during each trading session can vary significantly. Traditionally, trading tends to be the quietest during the Asian market hours as we indicated in Chapter 4. This means that currencies such as the EURUSD and GBPUSD tend to trade within a very tight range during these hours. According to the Bank of International Settlement's Triennial FX Survey published in September of 2014, the United Kingdom is the most active trading center, capturing 41% of total volume. Adding in Germany, France, Italy, and Switzerland, European trading as a whole accounts for 50% of total FX trading. The United States, on the other hand, is only second to the United Kingdom for the title of most active trading center, but that amounts to only approximately 19% of total turnover. This makes the London open exceptionally important because it gives the majority of traders in the market an opportunity to take advantage of events or announcements that may have occurred during late U.S. trading or overnight Asian sessions. This becomes even more critical on days when the FOMC meets to discuss and announce monetary policy because the announcement occurs at 2:15pm NY Time, after the London close.

The British pound trades most actively against the U.S. dollar during the European and London trading hours. There is also active trading during the U.S./European overlap, but outside those time frames, the pair tends to trade relatively lightly because the majority of GBPUSD trading is done through UK and European market makers. This provides a great opportunity for day traders to capture the initial directional intraday real move that occurs within the first few hours of London trading. This strategy exploits the common perception that UK traders are notorious stop hunters. This means that the initial movement at the London open may not always be the real one. Since UK and European dealers are the primary market makers for the GBPUSD, they have tremendous insight into the extent of actual supply and demand for the pair. The "waiting for the real deal" trading strategy first sets up when interbank dealing desks survey their books at the onset of trading and use their client data to trigger close stops on both sides of the markets to gain the pip differential. Once these stops are taken out and the books are cleared, the real directional move in the GBPUSD will begin to occur, at which point we look for the rules of this strategy to be met before entering into a long or short position. This strategy works best following the U.S. open or after a major economic release. With this strategy, you are looking for the noise in the markets to settle before trading the real trend of the day.

Strategy Rules

Longs:

1. Early European trading in GBPUSD begins around 1am NY Time, and we look for the pair to make new range low of at least 25 pips above the opening price (the range is defined as the price action between the Frankfurt and London power hour of 6 GMT to 7 GMT NY Time).
2. Look for the pair to reverse and penetrate the high.
3. Place an entry order to buy 10 pips above the high of the range.
4. Place a protective stop no more than 25 pips away from your range high, or 35 pips.
5. If the position moves lower by 50 pips, close half of the position, move stop on rest to breakeven, and target three times risk, or 105 pips on the remainder.

Shorts:

1. GBPUSD opens in Europe and trades more than 25 pips above the high established during the Frankfurt to London power hour.
2. Wait for the pair to reverse and penetrate the low.

3. When that occurs, place an entry order to sell 10 pips below the low of the range.
4. Place a protective stop no more than 25 pips away from your range low, or 35 pips.
5. If the position moves lower by 50 pips, close half of the position, move stop on rest to breakeven, and target three times risk, or 105 pips on the remainder.

Examples

Now let's take a look at some examples of this strategy in action. Figure 11.1 is a textbook example of the "waiting for the real deal" strategy. Between 6 and 7 GMT, the range high and low for GBPUSD are 1.5359 and 1.5234, respectively. At the start of the London trading session, we see GBPUSD squeeze upwards, taking out the range high of 1.5359. At the time, we place an order to sell GBPUSD 10 pips below the range low at 1.5324. The entry is triggered about an hour and a half later. The protective stop is placed 25 pips above the range low (35 pips total) at 1.5359. A take profit on half of the position is placed at 1.5274, or 50 pips below the entry price. The stop on the remainder of the position is moved to breakeven or 1.5324. The second half of the position is exited at three times risk at 1.5219 shortly after the NY open.

FIGURE 11.1 GBPUSD 5-Minute Chart
Source: eSignal

FIGURE 11.2　GBPUSD 10-Minute Chart

Source: eSignal

FIGURE 11.3　GBPUSD 15-Minute Chart

Source: eSignal

The next example is shown in Figure 11.2. In this example, the range high and low established between 6 and 7 GMT are 1.5433 and 1.5399, respectively. At the start of the London trading session, we see GBPUSD squeeze upward, taking out the range high of 1.5433 and racing all the way to 1.5492. At the time, we place an order to sell GBPUSD 10 pips below the range low at 1.5389. The entry is triggered around the NY open. The protective stop is placed 25 pips above the range low (35 pips total) at 1.5424. A take profit on half of the position is placed at 1.5339, or 50 pips below the entry price. The stop on the remainder of the position is moved to breakeven or 1.5389. The second half of the position is exited at three times risk at 1.5284 after the London open on the following trading day.

The third example is shown in Figure 11.3. In this example, the range during the Frankfurt London power hour is 1.5187 and 1.5139. At the start of the London trading session, GBPUSD drips lower, breaking below the range low and trading down to 1.5105. When the range low is broken, we place an order to buy GBPUSD 10 pips below the range high at 1.5197. The entry is triggered around the NY open. The protective stop is placed 25 pips below the range high (35 pips total) at 1.5172. A take profit on half of the position is placed at 1.5247, or 50 pips below the entry price. The stop on the remainder of the position is moved to breakeven or 1.5197. The second exit is not shown in the chart in Figure 11.3, but the breakeven stop is triggered.

CHAPTER 12

Technical Trading Strategy: Inside Days Breakout Play

Throughout this book, volatility trading has been discussed as one of the most popular strategies employed by professional traders. There are many ways to interpret changes in volatilities, but one of the simplest strategies is actually a visual one that requires nothing more than a keen eye. Although this is a strategy that is very popular in the world of professional trading, new traders are frequently amazed by its ease, accuracy, and reliability. Breakout traders can identify inside days with nothing more than a basic candlestick chart.

An inside day is defined as a day where the daily range has been contained within the prior day's trading range, or in other words, the day's high and low do not exceed the previous day's high and low. There needs to be at least two inside days before the volatility play can be implemented. The more inside days, the higher the likelihood of an upside surge in volatility, or a breakout. This type of strategy is best employed on daily charts, but the longer the time frame, the more significant the breakout opportunity. Some traders use the inside day strategy on hourly charts, which works to some success, but identifying inside days on daily charts tends to lead to an even greater probability of success. For day traders looking for inside days on hourly charts, chances of a solid breakout increases if the contraction precedes the London or U.S. market opens. The key is to predict a valid breakout and not get caught in a false breakout move. Traders using the daily charts could look for breakouts ahead of major economic releases for the specific currency pair. This strategy works with all currencies pairs, but has less frequent instances of false breakouts in the tighter range pairs such as the EURGBP, USDCAD, EURCHF, EURCAD, and AUDCAD.

■ Strategy Rules

Long:

1. Identify a currency pair where the daily range has been contained within the prior day's range for at least two days (we are looking for multiple inside days).
2. Buy 10 pips above the high of the previous inside day.
3. Place stop and reverse order for two lots at least 10 pips below the low of the nearest inside day.
4. Take profit when prices reach double the amount risked or begin to trail stop at that level.

Protect against false breakouts: If the stop and reverse order is triggered, place a stop at least 10 pips above the high of the nearest inside day and protect any profits larger than what you risked with a trailing stop.

Short:

1. Identify a currency pair where the daily range has been contained within the prior day's range for at least two days (we are looking for multiple inside days).
2. Sell 10 pips below the low of the previous inside day.
3. Place stop and reverse order for two lots at least 10 pips above the high of the nearest inside day.
4. Take profit when prices reach double the amount risked or begin to trail stop at that level.

Protect against false breakouts: If the stop and reverse order is triggered, place a stop at least 10 pips below the low of the nearest inside day and protect any profits larger than what you risked with a trailing stop.

Further Optimization

For higher-probability trades, technical formations can be used in conjunction with the visual identification to place a higher weight on a specific direction of the breakout. For example, if the inside days are building and contracting toward the top of a recent range such as a bullish ascending triangle formation, the breakout has a higher likelihood of occurring to the upside. The opposite scenario is also true; if inside days are building and contracting toward the bottom of a recent range and we begin to see that a bearish descending triangle is forming, the breakout has a higher likelihood of occurring to the downside. Aside from triangles, other technical factors that can be considered include significant support and resistance levels. For example, if there are significant Fibonacci and moving average support zones resting below the inside day levels, this either supports a higher likelihood of an upside breakout or at least a higher probability of a false breakout to the downside.

Examples

Let us take a look at a few examples. Figure 12.1 is a daily chart of euro against the British pound, or the EURGBP. The two inside days are identified on the chart, and it is clear visually that each of those days' ranges, which includes the high and low, is contained within the previous day's range. In accordance with our rules, we place an order to go long 10 pips above the high on the previous inside at 0.6634 and an order to sell 10 pips below the low of the previous inside day at 0.6579. Our long order gets triggered two bars after the most recent inside day. We then proceed to place a stop and reverse order 10 pips below the low of the most recent inside day at 0.6579. So basically, we went long at 0.6634 with a stop at 0.6579, which means that we are risking 45 pips. When prices reached our target level of double the amount risked (90 pips), or 0.6724, we have two choices: to either close out the entire trade or begin trailing the stop. More conservative traders should probably square positions at this point, while more aggressive traders could look for more

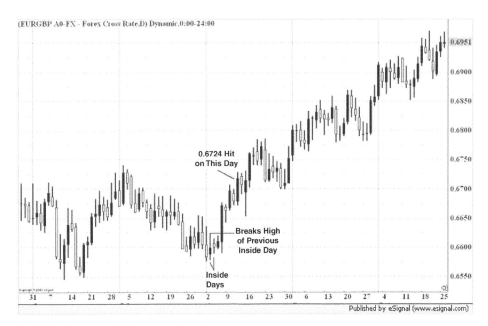

FIGURE 12.1 EURGBP Inside Day Chart

Source: eSignal

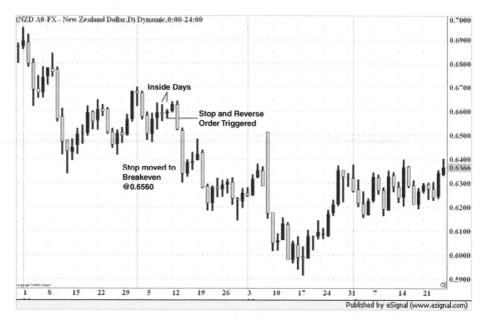

FIGURE 12.2   NZDUSD Inside Day Chart

Source: eSignal

profit potential. We choose to close out the trade for a 90-pip profit, but those who stayed in and weathered a bit of volatility could have taken advantage of another 100 pips of profits three weeks later.

Figure 12.2 is another example of inside day trading using the daily chart of the New Zealand dollar against the U.S. dollar (or the NZDUSD). The difference between this example and the previous one is that our stop and reverse order actually gets triggered, indicating that the first move was a false breakout. The two inside days are labeled on the chart. In accordance with our rules, after identifying the inside days, we place an order to buy on the break of the high of the previous inside day and an order to sell on the break of the low of the previous inside day. The high on the first or previous inside day is 0.6628. This means we place an order to go long at 0.6638 or to go short at 0.6618. Our long order gets triggered on the first day of the break at 0.6638, and we place a stop and reverse order 10 pips below the low of most recent inside day (or the daily candle before the breakout), which is 0.6560. However, instead of continuing the breakout, the pair reverses and we close our first position at 0.6560 with a 78 pips loss. We then enter into a new short position with the reverse order at 0.6560. The new stop is then 10 pips above the high of the most recent inside day at 0.6619. When NZDUSD moves by double the initial amount risked, conservative traders can take profit on the entire position while aggressive traders can trail the stop using various methods that might depend on how wide the trading range is. In this example, since the daily trading

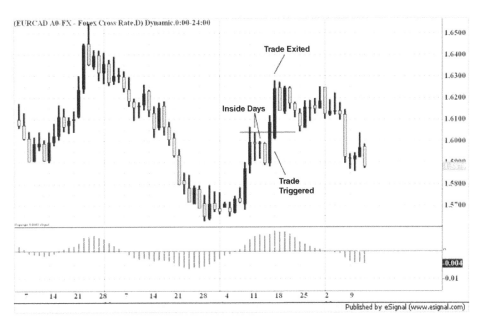

FIGURE 12.3 EURCAD Inside Day Chart

Source: eSignal

range is fairly wide, we choose to close the position once the price reaches our limit of 0.6404 for a profit of 156 pips and a total profit on the entire trade of 78 pips.

The last example uses technicals to help determine a directional bias of the inside day breakout. Figure 12.3 is a daily chart of EURCAD. The inside days are once again identified directly on the chart. The presence of higher lows suggests that the breakout could very well be to the upside. Adding in the MACD histogram to the bottom of the chart, we see that the histogram is also in positive territory right when the inside days are forming. As such, we choose to opt for an upside breakout trade. In accordance with the rules, we go long 10 pips above the high of the previous inside day at 1.6008. Our long trade is triggered, and we place our stop and reverse order 10 pips below the low of the most recent inside day at 1.5905. When prices move by double the amount that we risked to 1.6208, we exit the entire position for a 200-pip profit.

With the inside day breakout strategy, the risk is generally pretty high if done on daily charts, but the profit potentials following the breakout are usually fairly large as well. More aggressive traders can also trade more than one position, which would allow them to lock in profits on the first half of the position when prices move by double the amount risked and then trail the stop on the remaining position. Generally these breakout trades are a precursor to big trends, and using trailing stops would allow traders to participate in the trend move while also banking some profits.

CHAPTER 13

Technical Trading Strategy: Fader

More often than not, traders will find themselves faced with a potential breakout scenario, position for it, and then only end up seeing the trade fail miserably and have prices revert back to range trading. In fact, even if prices manage to break above a significant level, a continuation move is not guaranteed. If this level is very significant, we frequently see interbank dealers or other traders try to push prices beyond those levels momentarily in order to run stops. Breakout levels are very significant levels and for this very reason, there is no hard fast rule as to how much force is needed to carry prices beyond levels into a sustainable trend. Trading breakouts at key levels can involve a lot of risk and as a result, false breakouts appear more frequently than real breakouts. Sometimes prices will test the resistance level once, twice, or even three times before breaking out. This has fostered the development of a large degree of contra-trend traders who look only to fade breakouts in the currency markets. Yet fading every breakout can also result in some significant losses because once a real breakout occurs, the trend is generally strong and long-lasting. So what this boils down to is that traders need a methodology for screening out consolidation patterns for trades that have a higher potential of resulting in a false breakout. The following rules provide a good basis for screening such trades. The fader strategy is a variation of the "waiting for the real deal" strategy. It uses the daily charts to identify the range-bound environment and the hourly charts to pinpoint entry levels.

■ Strategy Rules

Longs:

1. Locate a currency pair whose 14-day ADX is less than 20. Ideally, the ADX should also be trending downward, indicating that the trend is weakening further
2. Wait for the market to break below the previous day's low by at least 15 pips.
3. Place an entry order to buy a few ticks above the previous day's high.
4. After getting filled, place your initial stop no more than 20 pips away.
5. Take profit on half of position when prices increase by the amount you risked; move stop on remaining position to breakeven.
6. Trail the stop on the remaining position.

Shorts:

1. Locate a currency pair whose 14-day ADX is less than 20. Ideally the ADX should also be trending downward, indicating that the trend is weakening further
2. Look for a move above the previous day's high by at least 15 pips.
3. Place an entry order to sell a few ticks below the previous day's low.
4. Once filled, place the initial protective stop no more than 20-pips below your entry.
5. Protect any profits by selling half of the position when it runs 20 pips in your favor.
6. Place a trailing stop on the remainder of the position.

Examples

Let's start by taking a look at an example to the short side. Figure 13.1 shows a daily chart of USDJPY with the ADX below 20 and pointing downward. This is the first signal that a trade setup is in place. In this example, the previous day's high is 120.27. We first look for a move above the previous day's high by at least 15 pips, or 120.42. As shown in Figure 13.2 the hourly chart, that move occurs at the start of the European session after which we place an order to sell 5 pips below the previous day's low of 120.00. The order is filled a few hours later at 119.95. At the time, we place our stop at 120.15 and a first target of 119.75. The first target is reached, and the stop on the rest of the position is moved to breakeven or 119.95. In this example, the second half of the trade remains live and will either be closed at breakeven, or the stop will be trailed.

Now let's take a look at an example to the long side. Figure 13.3 shows a daily chart of EURUSD with the ADX below 20 and pointing downward. This is the first signal that a trade setup is in place. In this example, the previous day's high is

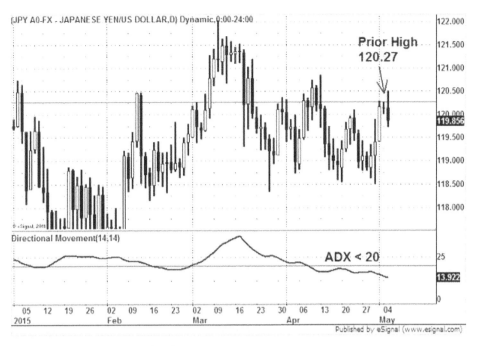

FIGURE 13.1   USDJPY Daily Chart

Source: eSignal

FIGURE 13.2   USDJPY 60-Minute Chart

Source: eSignal

FIGURE 13.3   EURUSD Daily Chart

Source: eSignal

FIGURE 13.4   EURUSD 60-Minute Chart

Source: eSignal

1.0801, and the low is 1.0708. We see that the low is broken first, and when that happens we place an order to buy 5 pips above the previous days high at 1.0806. As shown in Figure 13.4, the order is triggered about 7 hours later. At the time, we place our stop at 1.0786 and a first target of 1.0826. The first target is reached shortly after, and the stop on the rest of the position is moved to breakeven, or 1.0806. In this example, if we trail the stop on the position using a two-bar low, the second half of the trade is closed at 1.0818.

Further Optimization

The false breakout strategy works best when there are no significant economic reports scheduled for release that could trigger sharp unexpected movements. For example, prices often consolidate ahead of the U.S. nonfarm payrolls release. Generally speaking, they are consolidating for a reason, and that reason is because the market is undecided and is either positioned already or wants to wait to react following that release. Either way, there is a higher likelihood that any breakout on the back of those releases would be a real one and not one that you want to fade. This strategy works best with currency pairs that are less volatile and have narrower trading ranges.

CHAPTER 14

Technical Trading Strategy: 20-Day Breakout Trade

Trading breakouts can be both a rewarding and frustrating endeavor as breakouts have a tendency to fail. A major reason why this can occur frequently in the foreign exchange market is because it is more technically driven than others and as a result, there are many market participants who intentionally look to break pairs out in order to "suck" in other nonsuspecting traders. In an effort to filter out potential false breakouts, a price action screener should be used to identify breakouts that have a higher probability of success. The rules behind this strategy are specifically developed to take advantage of strong trending markets that make new highs that then proceed to "fail" by taking out a recent low and then reverse again to make another new high. This type of setup tends to have a very high success rate as it allows traders to enter strong trending markets after weaker players have been flushed out, only to have real money players reenter the market and push the pair up to new highs.

Strategy Rules

Longs:

1. Look for a currency pair that is making a 20-day high.
2. Look for the pair to reverse the same day or next to make a two-day low.

3. Buy the pair if it takes out the 20-day high within three days of making the two-day low.
4. Place the initial stop a few pips below the two-day low.
5. Take profit on half of the position when it moves by the amount risked; move stop on rest to breakeven.
6. Trail stop on the remainder of the position.

Shorts:

1. Look for a currency pair that is making a 20-day low.
2. That day or the next the pair rallies to make a two-day high.
3. Sell the pair if it trades below the 20-day low within three days of making the two-day high.
4. Risk up to a few ticks above the two-day high.
5. Take profit on half of the position when it moves by the amount risked; move stop on rest to breakeven.
6. Trail stop on the remainder of the position.

Examples

Now take a look at our first example in Figure 14.1. The daily chart of GBPUSD shows the currency pair making a new 20-day high on February 5. At this point, the currency pair is on our radar, and we watch for a new two-day low to be made

FIGURE 14.1 GBPUSD Daily Chart

Source: eSignal

within the next three days. This occurs right on schedule after which we wait for the currency pair to make a new 20-day high, which occurs on February 12. At the time, we buy GBPUSD a few pips above the previous 20-day high of 1.5352. We enter at 1.5360. The stop is placed a few pips below the original two-day low of 1.5197 (or 1.5190). As the currency pair moves in our favor, we look to exit half of the position when it moves by the amount that we risked, which is 155 pips or 1.5507. The stop on the remainder of the position is moved to breakeven or the initial entry price of 1.5352. This rest of the trade is exited 24 hours later.

Figure 14.2 provides an example of how the strategy can work in the EURUSD to the short side. On December 23, the currency pair makes a new 20-day low of 1.2165. It goes on radar and we start looking for the currency pair to rebound within the next three days. The recovery occurs the following day, and a new two-day high is made. Then we look for the previous 20-day low to be broken within the following three days and that occurs shortly thereafter. At which point we enter a short EURUSD trade at 1.2155 with a stop at 1.2260, or a few pips above the two-day high of 1.2254. Our risk on the trade is 105 pips. When the currency pair drops to 1.2050, we exit the first half of the position and move the stop on the rest to breakeven. Then we trail the stop using a 2-bar high and end up exiting the remainder of the position at 1.1846.

The final example shown in Figure 14.3 is in AUDUSD. The currency starts by making a new 20-day low on January 26. It goes on radar and we start looking for the currency pair to rebound within the next three days. The recovery occurs

FIGURE 14.2 EURUSD Daily Chart

Source: eSignal

FIGURE 14.3   AUDUSD Daily Chart

Source: eSignal

intraday, and a new two-day high is made right on schedule. Then we look for the previous 20-day low to be broken within the following three days it occurs 24 hours after the two-day high is made. At which point we enter a short AUDUSD trade a few pips below the 20-day low at 0.7850 with a stop at 0.8032, or a few pips above the two-day high of 0.8025. Our risk on the trade is 182 pips. When the currency pair drops to 0.7668, we exit the first half of the position and move the stop on the rest to breakeven. The breakeven stop is triggered the very same day that the first target is reached.

CHAPTER 15

Technical Trading Strategy: Channels

Channel trading is a less exotic but popular trading technique for currencies. The reason why it can work is because currencies rarely spend much time in tight trading ranges and have the tendency to develop strong trends. By reviewing a few charts, traders can see that channels can easily be identified and occur frequently. A common scenario would be channel trading during the Asian session and a breakout in either the London or U.S. session. There are many instances where economic releases are one of the most common triggers for a break of the channel. Therefore, it is imperative that traders keep on top of economic releases. If a channel has formed and a big U.S. number (per say) is expected to be released, and the currency pair is at the top of a channel, the probability of a break is high, so traders should be looking to buy the break out, not fade it.

Channels are created when we draw a trendline, and then draw a line that is parallel to that trendline. Most if not all of the price activity of the currency pair should fall between the two channel lines. We will seek to identify situations where the price is trading within a narrow channel, and then trade in the direction of a breakout from the channel. This strategy can be particularly effective when used prior to a fundamental market event such as the release of major economic news, or prior to the "open" of a major financial market.

Here are some rules for using this technique to find long trades:

1. First, identify a channel on either an intraday or daily chart. The price should be contained within a narrow range.
2. Enter long as the price breaks above the upper channel line by 10 pips.

3. Place a stop at the lower channel line.
4. Exit the position when it moves by double the amount risked.

The short rules are the reverse.

■ Examples

Let examine a few examples. The first example is a USDCAD 15-minute chart shown in Figure 15.1. The total range of the channel is approximately 30 pips with the low being 1.2028 and the high 1.2056. In accordance with our strategy, we place entry orders 10 pips above and below the channel at 1.2018 and 1.2066. The order to buy gets triggered first, and almost immediately we place a stop order at the low of the channel or 1.2028, which means we are risking 38 pips on the trade. USDCAD then proceeds to rally and reaches our target of double the range at 1.2142. More conservative traders could exit half of the position when it moves by the amount risked, or 38 pips, and trail the stop on the remainder of the position.

The next example shown in Figure 15.2 is a 15-minute chart of EURGBP. The total range between the two lines is 12 pips with the low being 0.7148 and the high 0.7160. In accordance with our strategy, we place entry orders 10 pips above and below the channel at 0.7138 and 0.7170. The order to buy gets triggered first and almost immediately we place a stop at the low of the channel or 0.7160 for 10-pip risk. EURGBP then proceeds to rally and reaches our target of 20 pips or double the amount risked.

FIGURE 15.1   USDCAD 15-Minute Chart

Source: eSignal

FIGURE 15.2 EURGBP 15-Minute Chart

Source: eSignal

FIGURE 15.3 EURUSD 15-Minute Chart

Source: eSignal

Figure 15.3 is a 15-minute chart of the EURUSD. The total range during this four-hour period is 18 pips with a high of 1.1206 and a low of 1.1188. In accordance with our strategy, we place entry orders 10 pips above and below the channel at 1.1216 and 1.1178. The order to sell gets triggered first and almost immediately, we place a stop order at the channel high of 1.1206 for a risk of 28 pips. The

EURUSD then proceeds to sell off significantly but only makes it to a low of 1.1132 before stopping us out a few days later. We chose to show this example because it explains why the more conservative approach of exiting half of the position when it moves by the amount risk is more desirable, even though it has worse risk reward. A move of 58 pips is sizable on an intraday basis and may be difficult to achieve. Whenever the risk is greater than 20 pips, it may be more prudent to exit half and trail the stop.

CHAPTER 16

Technical Trading Strategy: Perfect Order

A perfect order in moving averages is defined as a set of moving averages that is in sequential order. For an uptrend, a perfect order would be a situation in which the 10-day simple moving average (SMA) is at a higher price level than the 20-day SMA, which is higher than the 50-day SMA. Meanwhile, the 100-day SMA would be below the 50-day SMA, while the 200-day SMA would be below the 100-day SMA. In a downtrend, the opposite is true, where the 200-day SMA is at the highest level and the 10-day SMA is at the lowest level. Having the moving averages stacked up in sequential order are generally a strong indicator of a trending environment. Not only does it indicate that the momentum is on the side of trend, but the moving averages also serve as multiple levels of support. To optimize the perfect order strategy, traders should also look for ADX to be greater than 20 and trending upward. This represents a strong trend. Entry and exit levels are difficult to determine with this strategy, but generally speaking, we want to stay in the trade for as long as the perfect order remains in place and exit once the perfect order no longer holds. Perfect orders do not happen often, and the premise of this strategy is to capture the perfect order when it first happens.

The perfect order seeks to take advantage of a trending environment near the beginning of the trend:

1. Look for a currency pair with moving averages in perfect order.
2. Look for ADX pointing upwards, ideally greater than 20.
3. Buy five candles after the initial formation of the perfect order (if it still holds).
4. Initial stop is the low on the day of the initial crossover for longs and the high for shorts.
5. Exit the position when the perfect order no longer holds.

■ Examples

Figure 16.1 is a daily chart of the EURUSD. In August 2014, the moving averages in the EURUSD formed a sequential perfect order. We check and see that ADX is greater than 20, and we look to enter into a short trade five candles after the initial formation at 1.3390. Our initial stop is placed at the August 8 high of 1.3432. The pair continues to move lower in the days and weeks that follow, and we remain in the trade until the moving averages are no longer in perfect and the 10-day SMA moves above the 20-day SMA, which occurs on October 17 when EURUSD settles the day at 1.2758. The total profit on this trade is 632 pips. We risked 42 pips on the trade.

The next example is USDSGD. In Figure 16.2, the perfect order forms on November 6. We check and see that ADX is greater than 20, and we look to enter into a long trade five candles after the initial formation at 1.2916. Our stop should be at the November 6 low of 1.2911 but that is below our entry price so we put our stop at the 20-day SMA of 1.2822. The pair continues to move higher in the months that follow, and we remain in the trade until the moving averages are no longer in perfect and the 10-day SMA moves below the 20-day SMA, which occurs on March 27, when USD/SGD closes the day at 1.3685. The total move on this trade is 770 pips for a risk of 89 pips.

Figure 16.3 shows a perfect-order formation on a daily chart in USDJPY. The perfect order formed in October and when that occurred, we entered the trade five days afterward at 116.20. Our stop was placed at 108.75, and we remained in the trade until the 10-day SMA crossed below the 20-day SMA on December 19 at

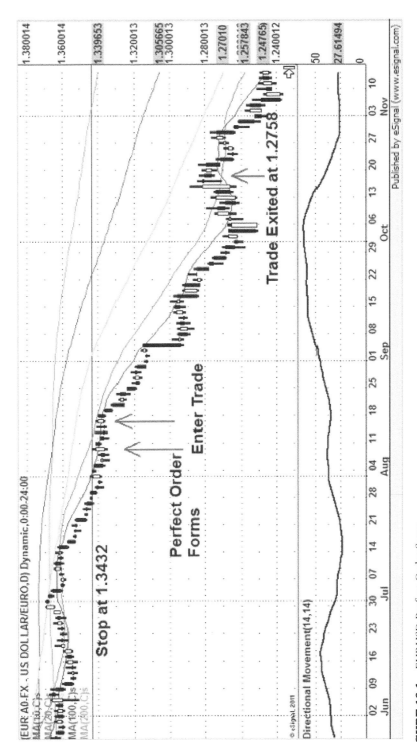

FIGURE 16.1 EURUSD Perfect Order Setup

Source: eSignal

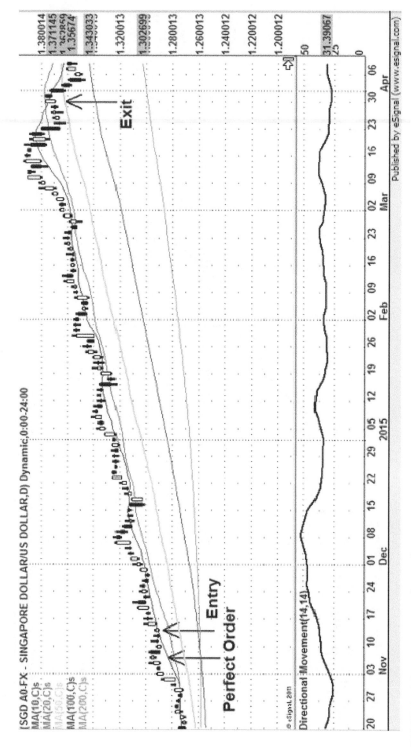

FIGURE 16.2 USDSGD Perfect Order Setup

Source: eSignal

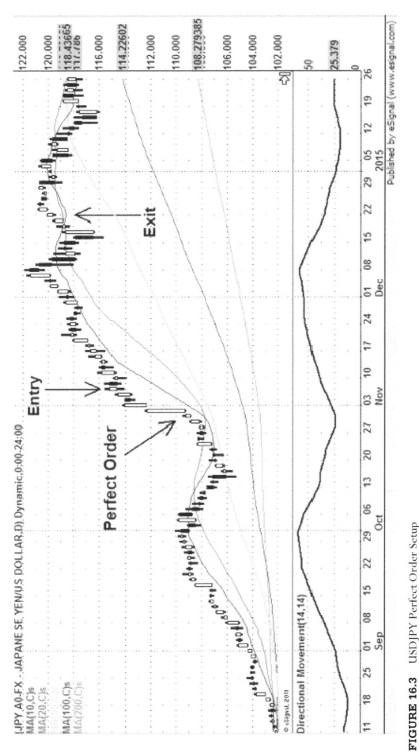

FIGURE 16.3 USDJPY Perfect Order Setup

Source: eSignal

119.45. In this example, the profit was 425 pips for a risk of 645 pips, which was far from ideal.

The perfect order is a strategy that can be high profit but low probability and low frequency. This means there could be numerous stop outs before a long trend emerges. Also, when the currency pair moves more than 250 to 300 pips in profit, you may want to consider taking profit on part of the positions.

CHAPTER 17

Fundamental Trading Strategy: Pairing Strong with Weak

One of the best ways to approach currency trading on a fundamental basis is to pair the strongest currency with the weakest. Of course finding that pairing is rarely simple because it is not just about which countries are the strongest or weakest right now but instead which ones will become strong or weak going forward. Finding these currencies can also be challenging because we live in a global economy where the health of one major economy will affect the outlook of another. Yet buying a weak currency and selling a strong one unknowingly can be a big mistake that translates into large losses, so it is extremely important for forex traders to learn how to pair strong with weak to maximize returns. After doing so you can use technical analysis to help identify points of entry in the direction of the trend.

In 2015, for example, the European Central Bank introduced quantitative easing (QE) as a last ditch effort to boost inflation and stimulate growth. We know that QE lowers interest rates and erodes the value of a currency but selling euros blindly on March 9, 2015, when the central bank started buying bonds for the very first time, yielded only a short-lived decline in the currency. Instead it would have been smarter to look for opportunities to sell the currency against a strong one on rallies.

FIGURE 17.1   EURGBP Daily Chart—Quantitative Easing

Source: eSignal

FIGURE 17.2   NZDCAD Daily Chart—Oil

Source: eSignal

One good candidate at the time was the British pound, which was benefiting from economic improvements and had a central bank that was moving closer to raising rates. Figure 17.1 shows how there was a lot of consolidation in EURGBP near 74 cents prior to the launch of Eurozone quantitative easing. This level proved to be resistance when the pair rallied in late March. Traders could have sold them, assuming that resistance would hold, or waited for the pair to revisit that level in April and May.

Another way to pair strong with weak is to follow the direction of commodity prices. Oil prices bottomed at $43.46 in early 2015, having traded above $100 a barrel only 8 months earlier and started to turn higher in March. As a major oil producer, Canada would stand to benefit from stabilization in crude prices. At the time U.S. policy makers were talking about raising interest rates, the Australian dollar was benefitting from improving domestic conditions, and sterling soared on positive data and a victory by the incumbent during the 2015 general election. Selling any of these currencies and buying the Canadian dollar would have been a risky endeavor. Instead the best bet at the time was to sell the New Zealand dollar and buy the Canadian dollar or the NZDCAD pair because New Zealand reported extremely weak labor data that prompted policy makers to talk about easing. As you can see in Figure 17.2, NZDCAD started to turn lower just as oil prices moved higher in March.

FIGURE 17.3   EURUSD Daily Chart

Source: eSignal

The best way to gauge strong versus weak is to monitor economic data surprises. While the ECB was buying bonds and implementing quantitative easing, Eurozone data started to improve and U.S. data started to weaken. The market had not anticipated this shift in dynamic as they had been looking for weak Eurozone data to reinforce QE and stronger U.S. data to push the Fed to tighten. This unexpected change drove EURUSD sharply higher, and buying breakouts in April and May as shown in Figure 17.3 would have been good bets.

CHAPTER 18

Fundamental Trading Strategy: The Leveraged Carry Trade

The leverage carry trade strategy is the quintessential global macro trade that has long been one of the favorite strategies of hedge funds and investment banks. On its most fundamental level, the carry trade strategy involves buying a high-yielding currency and funding it with the sale of a low-yielding currency. Aggressive speculators will leave the trade unhedged with the hope that the high yielding currency will appreciate in value relative to the lower yielding currency, allowing them to earn the interest rate differential on top of the capital appreciation. More conservative investors may choose to hedge the exchange rate component, earning only the interest rate differential. Although the differentials tend to be small, usually 1 to 3 percent if the position is leveraged 5 to 10 times, the profits from interest rates alone can be substantial. Of course it is important to remember that while leverage can magnify profits, it can also exacerbate losses. Capital appreciation generally occurs when a number of traders identify profit opportunities and pile into the same trade, driving up the value of the currency pair.

In foreign exchange trading, the carry trade is a popular way to take advantage of the notion that money flows in and out of different markets, driven by the law of supply and demand: with markets offering higher rates of return on investment attracting the most capital. Countries are no different—in the world of international capital flows, nations that offer the highest interest rates will generally attract more investment creating greater demand for their currencies. This helps to fuel the carry trade. The carry trade strategy is simple to master, but like all strategies, it contains risk. Carry trades performed extremely well between 2000 and 2007, failed miserably between 2008 and 2009, and recovered between late 2012 into 2015. The chance of loss can be great if you do not understand how, why, and when carry trades work best.

How Do Carry Trades Work?

To understand carry trading, it is important to first understand that currencies are always traded in pairs, so taking a carry trade involves buying a currency that offers a high interest rate and simultaneously selling a currency that offers a low interest rate. Carry trades are profitable when the exchange rate remains unchanged in value and investors are able to earn the difference in interest—or spread—between the two currencies, or when it appreciates in value, allowing the investor to earn the spread along with capital appreciation. If the exchange rate falls by more than the spread on the interest rate, it becomes a net loss for the investor.

Let's take a look at an example: Assume that the Australian dollar offers an interest rate of 4.75%, while the Swiss franc offers an interest rate of 0.25%. To execute the carry trade, an investor buys the Australian dollar and sells the Swiss franc. In doing so, he or she can earn a profit of 4.50% (2.75% in interest earned minus 0.25% in interest paid), as long as the exchange rate between Australian dollars and Swiss francs do not change. Figure 18.1 shows exactly how an investor would execute the carry trade.

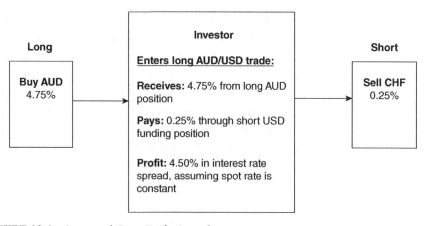

FIGURE 18.1 Leveraged Carry Trade Example

To summarize: A carry trade involves buying a currency that offers a high interest rate while selling a currency that offers a low interest rate.

■ Why Do Carry Trades Work?

Interest rates are very important: Carry trades work because of the constant movement of capital into and out of different countries in search of the highest yield. Interest rates are the main reason why some countries attract more investment than others. There are three reasons why a country can pay a higher interest rate. First, if a country's economy is doing well (high growth, high productivity, low unemployment, rising incomes, etc.), it will be able to offer those who invest in the country a higher rate of return. Second, central banks can raise interest rates on fast growing economies with rising inflation. Third, countries with high debt to GDP ratios, low credit ratings, and/or inherent growth problems may also need to pay a higher interest rate to attract investment.

Investors prefer to earn higher interest rates: Investors who are interested in maximizing their profits will naturally look for investments that offer them the highest rate of return. When making a decision to invest in a particular currency, an investor is more likely to choose one that offers the highest rate of return, or in this case, interest rate. If several investors make this exact same decision, the country will experience an inflow of capital from those seeking to earn a high rate of return, and the currency should appreciate.

What about countries that are not doing well economically? Countries that have low growth and low productivity will not be able to offer investors a high rate of return unless they have a very poor credit rating and are forced to offer a higher rate to compensate for the risk of holding the country's bond or currency. With major economies, however, there will be times where growth is so weak that interest rates are brought to zero, providing investors with no meaningful return. The difference between countries that offer high interest rates versus countries that offer low interest rates is what makes carry trades possible.

Let's take another look at the carry trade example above in more detail.

Imagine an investor in Switzerland who is earning an interest rate of 0.25% per year on her bank deposit in Swiss francs. At the time, a bank in Australia is offering 4.75% per year on a deposit of Australian dollars. Seeing that interest rates are much higher with the Australian bank, this investor would like to find a way to earn this higher rate of interest on her money.

Now imagine that the investor could somehow trade her deposit of Swiss francs by paying 0.25% for a deposit of Australian dollars paying 4.75%. What she has effectively done is to "sell" her Swiss franc deposit and use those funds to "buy" an Australian dollar deposit. With this transaction, she now owns an Australian dollar

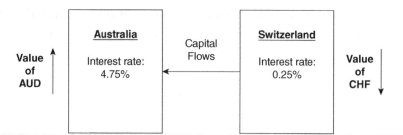

FIGURE 18.2 AUDCHF Carry Trade Example 1

deposit that pays her 4.75% in interest per year, 4.50% more than she was earning with her Swiss franc deposit.

This investor has essentially just done a carry trade by "buying" an Australian dollar deposit, and "selling" a Swiss franc deposit.

The net effect of millions of people doing this transaction is that capital flows out of Switzerland and into Australia, as investors take their Swiss francs and convert them into Australian dollars. Australia attracts more capital because of the higher rates it offers. This inflow of capital increases the value of the currency (see Figure 18.2).

To summarize: Carry trades are made possible by the differences in interest rates between countries. Because they prefer to earn higher interest rates, investors will look to buy and hold high interest rate paying currencies.

When Will Carry Trades Work Best?

There will be times when carry trades work better than others. In fact, carry trades are the most profitable when there is a very specific attitude toward risk.

How Much Risk Are You Willing to Take?

The moods of people in general change over time—sometimes they may feel more daring and willing to take chances; other times they may be more timid and prone to conservativeness. Investors, as a group, are no different. Sometimes they are willing to make investments that involve a good amount of risk; other times they are more fearful of losses and look to invest in safer assets.

In financial jargon, when investors as a whole are willing to take on risk, we call this *low risk aversion,* which means they are in risk-seeking mode. Alternatively, when investors are drawn to more conservative investments and less willing to take on risk, we describe them as *risk-averse.*

Carry trades are the most profitable when investors have *low risk aversion*. This notion makes sense when you consider what a carry trade involves. Remember, a carry trade involves buying a currency that pays a high interest rate while selling a currency that pays a low interest rate. In buying the high interest rate currency, the investor is taking a risk because it is believed that a country needs to offer a higher interest rate to offset the risk of holding the currency. Also, while high interest rates attract investment, they can also hurt growth by raising the cost of borrowing. This creates uncertainty around whether the economy of the country will continue to perform well and be able to pay not just high but even higher interest rates. This risk is something a carry trade investor must be willing to take.

If investors as a whole were not willing to take on this risk, then capital would never move from one country to another, and the carry trade opportunity would not exist. Therefore, in order to return, carry trades require that investors as a group have low risk aversion, or be willing to bear the risk of investing in the higher interest rate currency.

To summarize: Carry trades will be the most profitable when investors are willing to bear the risk of investing in high interest paying currencies.

■ When Will Carry Trades Not Work?

So far, we have shown that a carry trade will work best when investors have low risk aversion. What happens when investors have *high risk aversion*?

Carry trades are the least profitable when investors have *high risk aversion*. When investors have high risk aversion, they are less willing as a group to take chances with their investments. This means they would be less willing to invest in riskier currencies that offer higher interest rates. Instead, when investors have high risk aversion they would actually prefer to put their money in "safe haven" currencies that pay lower interest rates. During this time, they may also opt to close or unwind their carry trades. In doing so, they would be buying the currency with the low interest rate and selling the currency with the high interest rate.

Returning to our earlier example, let's assume the investor suddenly feels uncomfortable holding the foreign currency, the Australian dollar. Now, instead of looking for the higher interest rate, she is more interested in keeping her investment safe. As a result, she swaps her Australian dollars for more familiar Swiss francs.

The net effect of millions of people doing this transaction is that capital flows out of Australia and into Switzerland as investors take their Australian dollars and convert them into Swiss francs. During this period of risk aversion, Switzerland attracts more capital due to the perceived safety of its currency, and the inflow of capital increases the value of the Swiss franc (see Figure 18.3).

When investors have high risk aversion, they prefer to avoid the riskier high interest rate paying currency and instead invest in the safer, lower interest rate paying currency, which is the opposite of a carry trade.

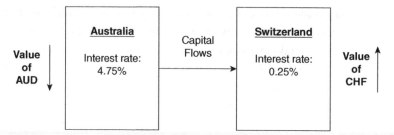

FIGURE 18.3   AUDCHF Carry Trade Example 2

To summarize: Carry trades will be the least profitable in periods of uncertainty when investors are unwilling to bear the risk of investing in high interest paying currencies.

▪ The Importance of Risk Aversion

Carry trades will generally be profitable when investors have low risk aversion, and unprofitable when investors have high risk aversion. So before placing a carry trade it is important to understand the risk environment—whether investors as a whole have high or low risk aversion—and when it *changes*.

Rising risk aversion is generally beneficial for low interest rate paying currencies: Sometimes the mood of investors will change rapidly, and investors' willingness to make risky trades can change dramatically from one moment to the next. Often, these large shifts are caused by significant global events. When periods of risk aversion occur quickly, the result is generally a large capital inflow into low-interest-rate-paying "safe haven" currencies (see Figure 18.2).

For example, in the summer of 1998 the Japanese yen appreciated against the dollar by more than 20% over the span of two months, due to the Russian debt crisis and LTCM hedge fund bailout. Similarly, just after the September 11 terrorist attacks the Swiss franc rose by more than 7% against the dollar over a 10-day period. During the global financial crisis in 2008, we also saw big gains in the yen and the Swiss franc.

These sharp movements in currency values often occur when risk aversion quickly changes from low to high. As a result, when risk aversion shifts, a carry trade can turn from being profitable to unprofitable very quickly.

Risk Aversion and Carry Trade Profitability

As investor risk aversion goes from high to low, carry trades become more profitable as detailed in Figure 18.4.

How do you know if investors as a whole have high or low risk aversion? Unfortunately, it is difficult to measure investor risk aversion with a single number.

Carry Trade Profitability		
(−) ⟶ (+)		
High Risk Aversion	**Risk Neutral**	**Low Risk Aversion**
1. Investors less willing to take risks, remove funds from risky currencies		1. Investors more willing to take greater risks
2. Capital flows out of riskier high-interest currencies and into low interest safe-haven currencies		2. Capital flows away from low-interest currencies and into those that pay higher interest rates
3. Low-interest currencies appreciate as investors get out of risky trades		3. Low-interest currencies tend to remain weak, used in financing risky trades

FIGURE 18.4   Carry Trade Profitability

One way to get a broad idea of risk aversion levels is to look at bond yields. The wider the spread between the yields of bonds from different countries with similar credit ratings, the higher the investor risk aversion. Bond yields are readily available on major financial websites such as Bloomberg.com and Reuters.com. In addition, several large banks have developed their own measures of risk aversion that signal when investors are willing to take risk and when they are not.

Other Things to Bear in Mind When Considering a Carry Trade

While risk aversion is one of the most important things to consider before making a carry trade, it is not the only one. The following are some additional issues to be aware of.

Low Interest Rate Currency Appreciation

By entering into a carry trade, an investor is able to earn a profit from the interest rate difference, or spread, between a high interest rate currency and a low interest rate currency. However, the carry trade can turn unprofitable if for some reason (like the risk aversion examples earlier), the low interest rate currency appreciates by a significant amount.

Aside from rising risk aversion, improving economic conditions within a low interest paying country can also cause its currency to appreciate. An ideal carry trade will involve a low interest currency whose economy is weak and has low expectations for growth. If the economy were to improve, however, the country might then be able to offer investors a higher rate of return through increased interest rates. If this were to occur—again, using the previous example, say that Switzerland increased the interest rates it offered—then investors may take advantage of these higher rates by investing in Swiss francs. As seen in Figure 18.3, an appreciation of the Swiss franc would negatively affect the profitability of the Australian dollar–Swiss franc carry trade. (At the very least, higher interest rates in Switzerland would negatively affect the carry trade's profitability by lowering the interest rate spread.)

This same sequence of events may currently be unfolding for the Japanese yen. Given its zero interest rates, the Japanese yen has for a very long time been an ideal low interest rate currency to use in carry trades (known as *yen carry trades*). This situation however, may be changing. Increased optimism about the Japanese economy has recently led to an increase in the Japanese stock market. Increased investor demand for Japanese stocks and currency has caused the yen to appreciate, and this yen appreciation negatively affects the profitability of carry trades like Australian dollar (high interest rate) versus Japanese yen.

If investors continue to buy the yen, the yen carry trade could start to become unprofitable. This further illustrates the fact that when the low interest rate currency in a carry trade (the currency being sold) appreciates, it negatively affects the profitability of the overall carry trade position.

Trade Balances

A country's trade balance (the difference between imports and exports) can also affect the profitability of a carry trade. We know that when investors have low risk aversion or are risk seeking, capital will flow from the low interest rate paying currency to the high interest rate paying currency (see Figure 18.2) but this does not always happen.

One reason is because countries with large trade surplus can still see their currencies appreciate in low risk environments because running a trade surplus means that the country exports more than it imports. This creates naturally demand for the currency.

The point of this example is to show that even when investors have low risk aversion, large trade imbalances can cause a low interest rate currency to appreciate (as in Figure 18.3). And when the low interest rate currency in a carry trade (the currency being sold) appreciates, it negatively affects the profitability of the carry trade.

Time Horizon

In general, a carry trade is a long-term strategy. Before entering into a carry trade, an investor should be willing to commit to a time-horizon of at least six months. This commitment helps to make sure that the trade will not be affected by the "noise" of shorter-term currency price movements.

To summarize: Carry trade investors should be aware of factors such as currency appreciation, trade balances, and time horizon before placing a trade. Any or all of these factors can cause a seemingly profitable carry trade to become unprofitable.

CHAPTER 19

Fundamental Trading Strategy: Macro Event Driven Trade

Short-term traders are generally focused only on the economic release of the week and how it will impact their day trading activities. This works well for many traders, but it is also important not to lose sight of the big macro events that may be brewing in the economy or the world for that matter. Large-scale macroeconomic events will move markets and will move them in very big ways. Their impact goes beyond a simple one- or two-day price change because depending on their size and scope, these occurrences have the potential to reshape the fundamental perception toward a currency for months or even years at a time. Events such as wars, political uncertainly, natural disasters, and major international meetings or monetary policy changes are so potent due to their irregularity that they can have widespread psychological and physical impacts on the currency market. With these events come both currencies that appreciate vastly and currencies that depreciate just as dramatically. Therefore, keeping on top of global developments, understanding the underlying direction of market sentiment before and after these events occur and anticipating them could be very profitable, or at least can help prevent significant losses.

Know When Big Events Occur: Here Is a List of a Few Important Ones

- Significant G7 finance ministers meetings

- Presidential elections

- Important summits

- Major Central Bank meetings

- Potential changes to currency regimes

- Possible debt defaults by large countries

- Possible wars as a result of rising geopolitical tensions

- Federal Reserve chairman's semiannual testimony on economy

The best way to highlight the significance of these events is look at a few notable macroeconomic examples from the past two decades.

2014 Ukraine–Russia Crisis

The 2014 Ukraine–Russia crisis was one of the biggest geopolitical events of the past decade. The crisis began in 2013 but didn't really hit its peak until March 2014 when Russia signed a bill to absorb Crimea. Leading up to the announcement, the uncertainty put significant pressure on the EURUSD in January 2014 with the currency pair dropping sharply on March 18, 2014, the day that Russia declared that Crimea was now officially apart of their country. This led to a few more weeks of downward pressure for the EURUSD as shown in Figure 19.1 as investors awaited the world's response. Many nations declared their support for Ukraine and war was feared, but eventually Russia was only hit with sanctions, and a few months later, the Ukraine crisis moved to the back burner.

European Sovereign Debt Crisis (2009–2013)

The European Sovereign Debt Crisis started in 2009 and lasted into 2013 with the bulk of the damage being done by February 2012. It was a multiyear debt crisis that was sparked by the inability of many member nations to meet their debt obligations after the global financial crisis. Their banking sectors and economies suffered significant losses, and persistently negative growth prospects made it impossible for countries such as Greece, Ireland, Portugal, and Cyprus to repay or refinance their government debt. Between 2010 and 2012, all of these nations required bailouts or some form of support from the Troika, composed of the ECB, IMF and European Commission. While the problems were concentrated in smaller Eurozone nations, there was fear

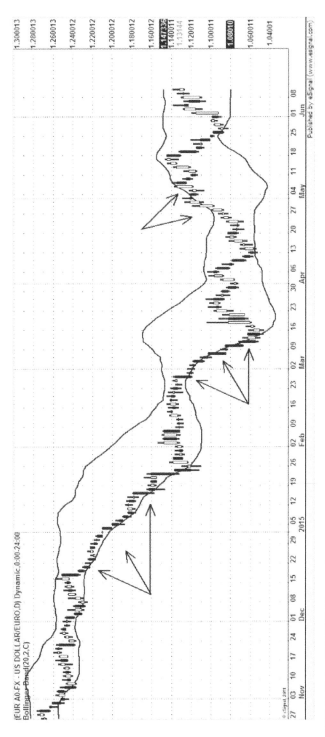

FIGURE 19.1 EURUSD Ukraine Crisis

Source: eSignal

FUNDAMENTAL TRADING STRATEGY: MACRO EVENT DRIVEN TRADE

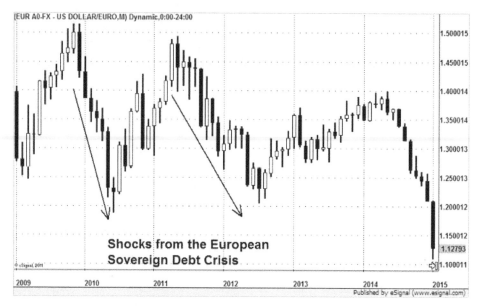

FIGURE 19.2 EURUSD Sovereign Debt Crisis

Source: eSignal

of contagion for the major economies. The country of Spain did not require a bailout but in 2012, a number of banks required additional funding. The crisis posed caused significant volatility for the euro. Figure 19.2 shows two long periods of EURUSD weakness that were caused by bailouts, downgrades, and other negative headlines.

Global Financial Crisis (2007–2009), Subprime

One of the most important macroeconomic events of the twenty-first century was the 2007 to 2009 subprime/global financial crisis. It was triggered by a sharp slide in house prices, default on mortgages, and blowup of subprime mortgage backed securities and collateralized debt obligations. This, in turn, caused massive losses for banks and financial institutions, leading the failure of major firms such as Lehman Brothers, Merrill Lynch, and Bear Stearns. The impact on the financial market and the economy was staggering, with many countries falling into recession. During this period, the stock market lost more than 50% of its value with the S&P 500, falling from a high of 1,565 in October 2007 to a low of 676 in March 2009. As shown in Figure 19.3, USDJPY dropped from a high of 116.47 in October 2007 to a low of 87.13 in January 2009. This was only the beginning of a multiyear decline for the currency pair. EURUSD had a delayed reaction, rallying strongly between October 2007 and April 2008 as money flowed out of the U.S. economy, and then falling sharply between July 2008 and October 2008 as the risk aversion and crisis spread to Europe.

FIGURE 19.3 USDJPY Global Financial Crisis

Source: eSignal

Political Uncertainty: 2004 U.S. Presidential Election

Another example of major events impacting the currency market is the 2004 U.S. presidential elections. In general, political instability causes perceived weakness in currencies. The hotly contested presidential election in November of 2004, combined with the differences in the candidates' stance on the growing budget deficit, resulted in overall dollar bearishness. The sentiment was exacerbated even further, given the lack of international support for the incumbent President (Bush) due to the administration's decision to overthrow Saddam Hussein. As a result, in the three weeks leading up to the election, the euro rose 600 pips against the U.S. dollar. This can be seen in Figure 19.4. With a Bush victory becoming increasingly clear and later confirmed, the dollar sold off against the majors as the market looked ahead to what would probably end up being the maintenance of status quo. On the day following the election, the EURUSD rose another 200 pips and then continued to rise an additional 700 pips before peaking out six weeks later. This entire move took place over the course of two months, which may seem like an eternity for many, but this macroeconomic event really shaped the markets and for those who were following it, big profits could have been made. However, this is important even for short-term traders because given that the market was bearish dollars in general leading up to the U.S. presidential election, a more prudent trade would be to look for opportunities to buy the EURUSD on dips rather than trying sell rallies and look for tops.

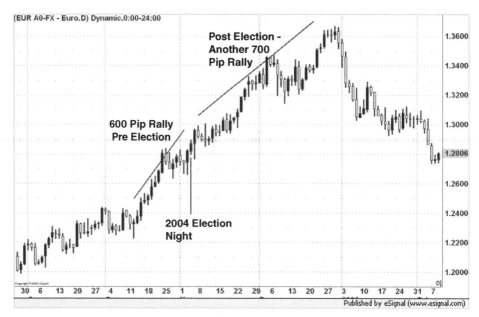

FIGURE 19.4 EURUSD Election Trade

Source: eSignal

G7 Meeting Dubai September 2003

The G7 finance ministers meeting on September 22, 2003, was a very important turning point for the markets. The dollar collapsed significantly following the meeting at which the G7 finance ministers wanted to see "more flexibility in exchange rates." Despite the rather tame nature of these words, the market interpreted this line to be a major shift in policy. The last time changes to this degree had been made was back in 2000. Taking a step back, the countries that constitute the G7 are the United States, United Kingdom, Japan, Canada, Italy, Germany, and France. Collectively, these countries account for two-thirds of the world's total economic output. Not all G7 meetings are important. The only time the market really hones in on the G7 finance ministers meeting is when they expect big changes to be made to the statement. In 2000, the market paid particular attention to the upcoming meeting because there was strong intervention in the EURUSD the day before the meeting. The meeting in September 2003 was also important because the U.S. trade deficit was ballooning and becoming a huge issue. The EURUSD bore the brunt of the dollar depreciation while Japan and China were intervening aggressively in their currencies. As a result, it was widely expected that the G7 finance ministers as a whole would issue a statement that was highly critical of Japan and China's intervention policies. Leading up to the meeting, the U.S. dollar had already begun to sell off as indicated by the chart. At the time of the announcement, the EURUSD shot up 150 pips. Though this initial move was not very substantial, between September 2003 and February

FIGURE 19.5 EURUSD G7 Meeting

Source: eSignal

2004 (which was the next G7 meeting), the dollar fell 8% on a trade-weighted basis, 9% against the British pound, 11% against the euro, 7% against the yen, and 1.5% against the Canadian dollar. To put the percentages into perspective, a move of 11% is equivalent to approximately 1100 pips. Therefore, the longer-term impact is much more significant than the immediate impact as the event itself has the significance to change the overall sentiment in the market. Figure 19.5 is a weekly chart of the EURUSD that illustrates how the currency pair performed following the September 22, 2003 G7 meeting.

U.S. War Against Iraq

Geopolitical risks such as wars can also have a pronounced impact on the currency market. Figure 19.6 shows that between December 2002 and February 2003, the dollar depreciated 9% against the Swiss franc (USDCHF) in the months leading up to war. The dollar sold off because the war itself was incredibly unpopular among the international community. The Swiss franc was one of the primary beneficiaries due to the country's political neutrality and safe-haven status. Between February and March, traders began to believe that the inevitable war would turn into a quick and decisive U.S. victory, so they began to unwind the war trade. This eventually led to a 3% rally in USDCHF as investors exited their short dollar positions.

Each of these events caused large-scale movements in the currency market. Such events are clearly important to follow for all types of traders. Keeping abreast of

FIGURE 19.6   USDCHF Iraq War

Source: eSignal

broad macroeconomic events can help traders make smarter decisions and prevent them from fading large factors that may be brewing in the background. Most of these events are talked about, debated, and anticipated many months in advance by economists, currency analysts, and the international community in general.

CHAPTER 20

Quantitative Easing and Its Impact on Forex

Quantitative easing is such an important topic that it deserves its own chapter. After the global financial crisis many countries fell into recession, and in response central banks around the world lowered interest rates to record lows. When rates could not fall any lower, they had to resort to unprecedented measures, the most powerful of which was quantitative easing (QE). Between 2007 and 2015, the Bank of Japan, Federal Reserve, Bank of England, European Central Bank, and the Swedish National Bank all resorted to QE, and their decision had a significant impact on their currencies on both a short- and long-term basis.

The goal of quantitative easing is to keep yields low and to flood the market with liquidity. To do so, a central bank would create money by buying financial assets such as government bonds from banks using electronic cash. This basically "creates new money." It also keeps yields low because bond prices have an inverse relationship with yields and in giving banks money, the hope is that it will encourage lending and in turn lead to more economic activity. The jury is out on how much QE really helped these economies, but the influence on currencies was undeniable.

U.S. Quantitative Easing

After the financial crisis, the first major central bank to respond with quantitative easing was the U.S. Federal Reserve. In November 2008, the central bank launched a $600 billion bond-buying program. The program was initially effective as the economy improved, prompting the Fed to temporarily halt bond purchases. However, the economy never gained additional momentum and as such, the central bank returned with a second round of QE (dubbed QE2) in November 2010. The size of the program matched the first round. Unfortunately, more bond buys were needed, and QE3 was launched in September 2012. Unlike QE1 and QE2, QE3 was an open-ended program. The central bank announced plans to purchase $40 billion in assets every month, and in December 2012, that amount was increased to $85 billion per month. The program lasted for five years, and purchases were finally halted in October 2014. Figure 20.1 shows how each round of quantitative easing impacted the EURUSD. As you can see, each round triggered a sharp rise in EURUSD and—another way to look at it—weakness in the U.S. dollar. In 2008, the month that QE1 was announced, EURUSD surged 17% from high to low. When QE2 was announced, the EURUSD began a rally that took the pair up more than 20%. QE3 led to a similar uptrend with gains extended when the program was increased.

UK Quantitative Easing

Quantitative easing was launched by the Bank of England in March 2009. At the time, the BoE pledged to spend 75 billion pounds over a three-month period buying UK assets, but the program continued and between March 2009 and January 2010, the central bank had spent 200 billion pounds. In October 2011, growth started to slow more dramatically with the economy facing a double dip recession. In response policymakers voted to increase the QE program by another 75 billion. In February 2012, the central bank added another 50 billion and the same increase was made in July 2012, bringing the total program to 375 billion pounds. Figure 20.2 shows how GBPUSD responded to each round of QE. What is interesting is that the sterling fell sharply in the run up to the March 2009 announcement. It extended lower afterward but rebounded in the months that followed. In 2011, 2012, and 2013, the sterling rallied the month that QE was announced. One important thing to remember is that the Federal Reserve was also buying bonds and expanding its own QE program at the time, so the two offset each other to some degree, limiting the reaction in GBPUSD. More importantly, investors interpreted each round of BoE QE as positive for the currency because they hoped that the central bank's efforts would help to turn around the economy.

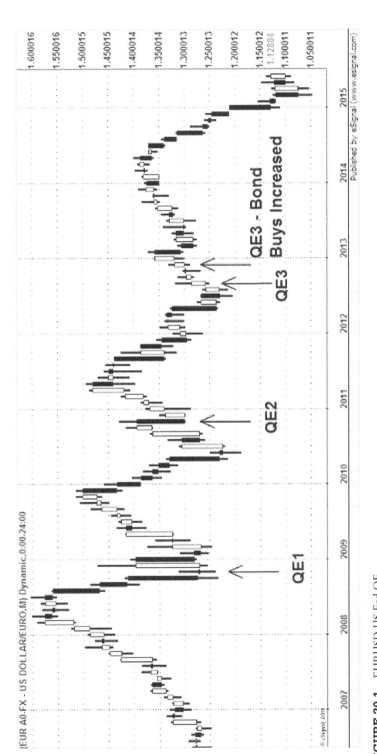

FIGURE 20.1 EURUSD US Fed QE

Source: eSignal

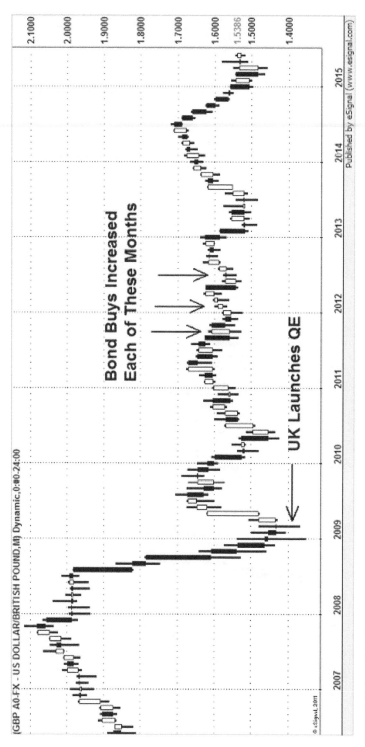

FIGURE 20.2 GBPUSD UK BoE QE

Source: eSignal

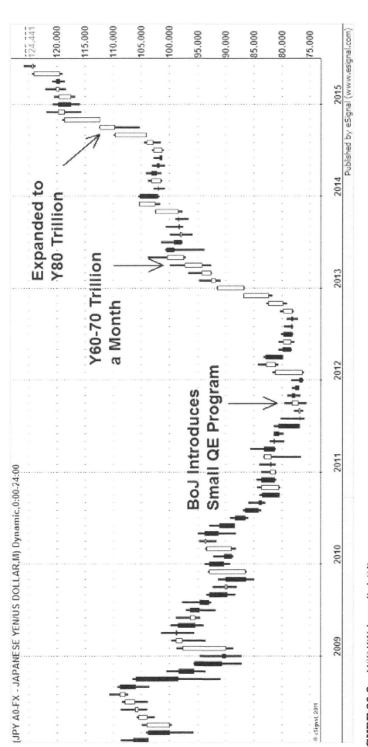

FIGURE 20.3 USDJPY Japan BoJ QE

Source: eSignal

QUANTITATIVE EASING AND ITS IMPACT ON FOREX

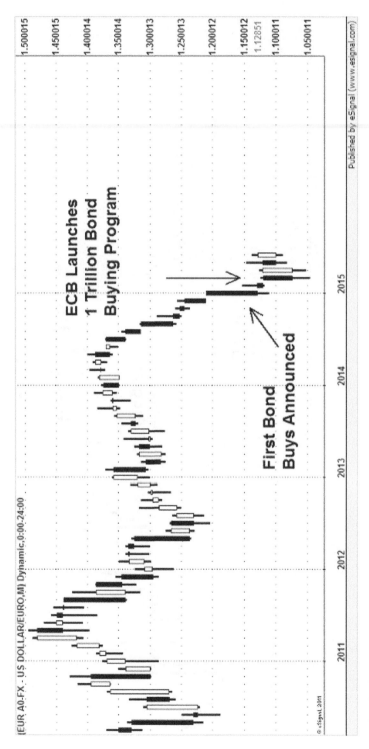

FIGURE 20.4 EURUSD EZ ECB QE

Source: eSignal

Japan Quantitative Easing

The phrase *quantitative easing* was first used by the Bank of Japan in 2001. At the time, they did not believe that the program was effective but after the financial crisis, they said they would examine their asset purchase program. In October 2011 the Bank of Japan increased the program by 5 trillion yen which was a small sum (approximately USD$66 billion) compared to the staggering amounts that other countries were purchasing. Then in April 2013, they announced a bold and aggressive plan to buy 60 trillion to 70 trillion yen a year as part of Prime Minister Abe's economic policies. This program was later expanded to 80 billion yen a year. Unlike other countries where the effectiveness of QE was debated, Japan's bond buying program played a large role in turning around the economy. It also had a significant impact on the currency. In Figure 20.3 we show how the first program yielded a very small response in USDJPY but when the Bank of Japan came out in size, USDJPY reacted quickly and aggressively with a move that extended even further when the program was expanded.

Eurozone Quantitative Easing

The European Central Bank was the last major central bank to roll out quantitative easing. They were reluctant to do so for a very long time because structurally the Eurozone is not set up for quantitative easing. Since there is no *euro-bond,* some critics felt that it was not in line with the central bank's mandate. However faced with sluggish growth, stubbornly low inflation, and an interest rate already at zero, the ECB had very few options. They publicly discussed the option months before the actual decision, giving the market plenty of opportunity to discount the move. In January 2015, the ECB announced that they would spend 60 billion euros per month buying private and public bonds. In March 2015, ECB President Draghi unveiled an aggressive 1 trillion quantitative easing program. As shown in Figure 20.4, both announcements had a significant impact on the currency, but EURUSD stabilized after the second announcement (but only after falling 500 pips) because investors hoped that the aggressive program by the central bank would help turn around the economy.

While no additional quantitative easing programs are expected as of mid-2015, the unwinding of these unprecedented measures in the coming years should have just as much impact on currencies as the initial announcement itself, providing an opportunity for forex traders.

CHAPTER 21

Fundamental Trading Strategy: Commodity Prices as a Leading Indicator

Commodities like gold and oil have an important connection to the FX market. Understanding the nature of these relationship can help traders gauge risk, forecast price changes, and understand exposure. Even if commodities are unfamiliar, they will often move on the same fundamental factors as currencies, particularly when it comes to popular instruments such as gold and oil. As discussed previously, there are four major currencies that are considered *commodity currencies*: the Australian dollar, the Canadian dollar, the New Zealand dollar, and the Swiss franc. However, every one of these currencies is different, as are their correlation with commodities. Take the Canadian dollar, for example; it tends to move in line with oil prices, but the connection is complicated and fickle. There are different reasons for why these currencies mirror commodity prices in their movements; and knowledge of the fundamental drivers behind these movements, their direction, and the strength of their correlation can be an effective way to discover trends in both markets.

Let's start with gold and oil because they have the largest influence on currencies.

Gold

Before looking at the relationship that gold has with commodity currencies, it is important to understand the connection between gold and the U.S. dollar. The United States is the world's second largest producer of gold (behind South Africa), but a rally in gold prices does not always lead to dollar appreciation. Actually, when the dollar falls, gold prices tend to rise, and vice versa. This seemingly illogical occurrence is a byproduct of the perception investor's hold for gold. During periods of geopolitical instability, traders tend to shy away from the dollar and turn to the safety of gold. In fact, many traders coin gold as the *anti-dollar*. Therefore, if the dollar depreciates, gold gets pushed up as wary investors flock from the declining greenback to the steady commodity. AUDUSD mirrors gold movements most closely.

Between June 2010 and June 2015, AUDUSD had a strong 0.83, or 83%, positive correlation with gold as shown in Figure 21.1; so when gold prices rise, the AUDUSD would generally appreciate as well. The relationship comes from the fact that Australia is the world's second largest producer of gold, exporting about $5 billion worth of the precious metal annually. Because of this, the currency pair amplifies the affects of gold prices twofold. If instability is causing an increase in

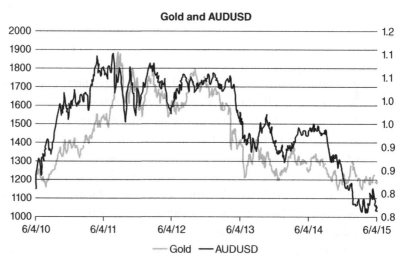

FIGURE 21.1 AUDUSD and Gold

Source: eSignal

prices, this probably signals that the USD has already began to depreciate. The AUDUSD pair will then be pushed down further as importers of gold demand more of Australia's currency to cover higher costs. Surprisingly enough the CADUSD also had a 0.67 correlation with gold during the same period because Canada is the world's fifth largest producer of gold and a risk currency. Thus, rising gold prices could be a precursor to gains in AUD and sometimes even in the CAD.

In the past, there was a strong correlation between the Swiss franc and gold because their reserves were backed by gold; but when the central bank abandoned the gold standard, this relationship broke. Between 2010 and 2015, gold and CHFUSD only had a 0.36, or 36%, positive correlation. Not everyone realizes how much the relationship deteriorated because many still remember the days when both were perceived as safe havens. The Swiss National Bank's 1.20 EURCHF peg also eroded the correlation between gold and the Swissie and it may be some time before this correlation returns.

■ Oil

Oil prices have a huge impact on the global economy, affecting both consumers and producers. The correlation between this commodity and currencies is far more complex and less stable than gold. In fact, of all of the commodity currencies, only one (the CAD) has any meaningful connection with oil prices.

The Canadian dollar is traditionally quoted as USDCAD but to examine the correlation between the Canadian dollar and oil, we find it more valuable to invert the pair and talk about CADUSD. The correlation index between oil and CADUSD is 0.67. The relationship has been stronger in the past but in recent years, the performance of the U.S. economy also played a role in the market's appetite for U.S. dollars. On a day-to-day basis, oil may not have a significant impact on the CAD, but over the medium term, as shown in Figure 21.2, the relationship can be strong, with oil acting as a leading indicator for the Canadian dollar. Canada is the world's fifth largest producer of oil, so the price of oil can have a significant impact on the country's economy.

The price of oil also impacts global inflation. In 2014, oil prices dropped from a high of $107 a barrel to $50 a barrel. This move caused inflation to fall across the globe, prompting easing measures by major central banks and forcing the European Central Bank to introduce quantitative easing in 2015. If oil prices decline in a meaningful way, it generally leads to more expansionary monetary policies, especially if it is driven by weaker growth and not offset by stronger demand. In contrast, rising oil prices can create inflationary pressures, leading to tighter monetary policy conditions. Therefore, the path of oil prices has implications for not only the CAD but all major and minor currencies.

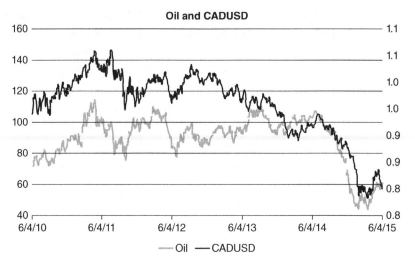

FIGURE 21.2   CADUSD and Oil

Source: eSignal

Iron Ore and Dairy Prices

Iron ore and dairy prices can also influence the price action of commodity currencies. Iron ore is Australia's most important export, which means that a rise in iron ore prices will boost corporate profits and, in turn, the Australian dollar. Meanwhile, a decline in iron ore prices will hurt the currency. Dairy prices can influence the performance of the New Zealand dollar, because milk is the country's number one export.

Trading Opportunity

Now that the relationships have been explained, there are two ways to exploit this knowledge. Taking a look at Figures 21.1 and 21.2, you can see that commodity prices are generally a leading indicator for currency prices. As such, commodity bloc traders should monitor gold and oil prices to help determine where these currencies are headed. The second way to exploit this knowledge is to trade the same view using different products, which helps to diversify risk even when the high correlation. In fact, there is one key advantage of expressing a gold/oil view in currencies over commodities, and that is the opportunity to earn interest on the positions, which is something trading gold or oil futures do not offer.

CHAPTER 22

Fundamental Strategy: Using Bond Spreads as a Leading Indicator for FX

A ny trader can attest that interest rates are an integral part of investment decisions and can drive markets in either direction. FOMC rate decisions are the second most market moving release for currencies, behind nonfarm payrolls. The effects of interest rate changes have not only short-term implications, but also long-term consequences on the currency markets. One central bank's rate decision can affect more than a single pairing in the network of currencies. Yield differentials of fixed-income instruments such as Libor rates and 10-year bond yields can be used as leading indicators for currency movements. In FX trading, an interest rate differential is the difference between the interest rate of a base currency (appearing first in the pair) less the interest rate of the quoted currency (appearing second in the pair). Each day at 5pm EST, the close of the day for currency markets, funds are either paid out or received to adjust for interest rate differences. This is known as *rollover*.

Understanding the correlation between interest rate differentials and currency pairs can be very useful particularly since it is the single most important driver of currency movements. In addition to monetary policy decisions, the future direction of rates along with the expected timing of rate changes is also critical to currency pair movements. The reason why it is important is because the majority of international investors are yield seekers. Large investment banks, hedge funds, and institutional investors have the ability access the global markets and actively shift funds from lower yielding assets to higher yielding assets.

■ Calculating Interest Rate Differentials and Following the Currency Pair Trends

The best way to use interest rate differentials for trading is by keeping track of one-month LIBOR rates and/or 10-year bond yields in Microsoft Excel. These rates are publicly available on websites such as Bloomberg.com. Interest rate differentials are then calculated by subtracting the yield of the second currency in the pair from the yield of the first. It is important to make sure that interest rate differentials are calculated in the order in which they appear for the pair. For instance, the interest rate differentials in GBPUSD should be the 10-year gilt rate minus the U.S. 10-year rate. For euro data, use data from the German 10-year bund. Form a table that looks similar to the one shown in Figure 22.1.

After sufficient data are gathered, you can chart the currency pair values versus yields using a graph with two axes to see if there are any correlations or trends. The date should be used as the x-axis and currency pair price and interest rate differentials as the two y-axes. To fully utilize these data in trading, it is important to monitor the trend of interest rates differentials because they can be used as a guide for the future direction of the currency pair.

Date	EURUSD	German 10Yr Yield	US 10 Year Yield	EZ-US Yield Spread	GBPUSD	UK 10-Yr Yield	UK-US Yield Spread
1-Jan	1.2097	0.541	2.172	−1.631	1.5574	1.756	−0.1986
1-Feb	1.1293	0.302	1.642	−1.34	1.5060	1.33	0.176
1-Mar	1.1195	0.328	1,994	−1993.672	1.5431	1.796	−0.2529
1-Apr	1.0740	0.18	1,924	−1923.82	1.4822	1.576	−0.0938
1-May	1.1212	0.366	2.033	−1.667	1.5344	1.834	−0.2996

FIGURE 22.1 Yield Spread Table

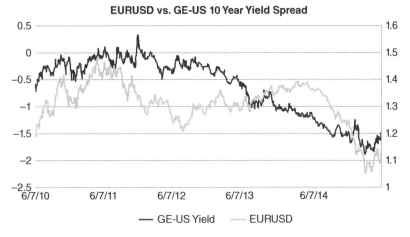

FIGURE 22.2 EURUSD and Bond Spread

To fully appreciate the correlation between interest rates and currencies, let's take a look at a few examples. Figure 22.2 charts the EURUSD against the 10-year German bund and U.S. Treasury yield spread between June 2010 and June 2015. As you can see, there is a very strong correlation between these instruments. However, sometimes the currency pair will have a delayed reaction. For example, the yield spread started to fall in early 2013, and while it led to consolidation in EURUSD, the currency pair did not start to really trend lower until June 2014. Nonetheless, it is clear from the chart that the relationship is strong.

Figure 22.3 shows the relationship between GBPUSD and the 10-year UK Gilt and US Treasury yield spread. In this example, there was no delay in the reaction of GBPUSD to the movement in yields. The yield spread started to fall quickly between June 2014 and June 2015, and it coincided with the decline in GBPUSD.

Figure 22.4 takes a look at a nondollar pair, AUDNZD, and once again, we see a very strong correlation. This chart compares the AUDNZD currency pair with the 10-year Australian and New Zealand yield spread. Sometimes, the interest rate yield will lead the direction of AUDNZD, and other times, AUDNZD will be a leading indicator for the spread.

Interest Rate Differentials: Leading Indicator, Coincident Indicator, or Lagging Indicator?

We know that yield spreads and currencies have a strong correlation, but do currency pair prices predict interest rate movements, or do interest rate movements drive currency pair prices? Leading indicators are economic indicators that predict

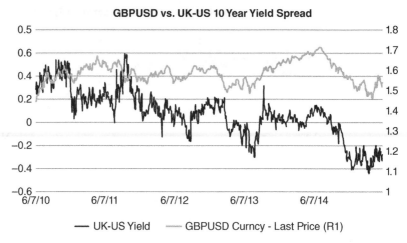

FIGURE 22.3 GBPUSD and Bond Spread

FIGURE 22.4 AUDNZD and Bond Spread

future events; coincident indicators are economic indicators that vary with economic events; lagging indicators are economic indicators that follow an economic event. For instance, if interest rate differentials predict future currency pair prices, interest rate differentials are said to be leading indicators of currency pair prices. Whether interest rate differentials are a leading, coincident, or lagging indicator of currency pair prices depends on how much traders care about future rates versus current rates. Assuming efficient markets, if currency traders only care about current interest rates and not about future rates, one would expect a coincident relationship. If currency traders consider both current and future rates, one would expect interest rate differentials to be a leading indicator of currency prices. The rule of thumb is that when there is a big move in the yield spread, it will coincide with a big move in the currency pair; and if that hasn't happen, then it signals an imminent move in the pair. No correlation is perfect. There will be times when interest rate differentials matter more than others and that tends to be when central banks are at the cusp of or engaging in major monetary policy changes.

CHAPTER 23

Fundamental Trading Strategy: Risk Reversals

Risk reversals are a useful fundamental-based tool to add to your mix of trading indicators. One of the weaknesses of currency trading is the lack of volume data and accurate indicators for gauging sentiment. The only publicly available report on positioning is the *Commitment of Traders Report* published by the Commodity and Futures Commission. Unfortunately, this report is released with a three-day delay. A useful alternative is to use risk reversals—which are provided on a real-time basis on the FXCM News Plugin, under options, or on the Bloomberg/Reuters terminals. As we first introduced in Chapter 7, a risk reversal consists of a pair of options for the same currency (a call and a put). Based on put–call parity, these far out of the money options (25 delta) with the same expiration and strike price should also have the same implied volatility. However, in reality, this is not true. Sentiment is embedded in volatilities, which makes risk reversals a good tool to gauge market sentiment. A number strongly in favor of calls or puts indicates that there is more demand for calls than puts. The opposite is also true; a number strongly in favor of puts over calls indicates that there is a premium built in put options as a result of the higher demand. If risk reversals are near zero, it indicates that there is indecision among bulls and bears and that there is no strong bias in the markets.

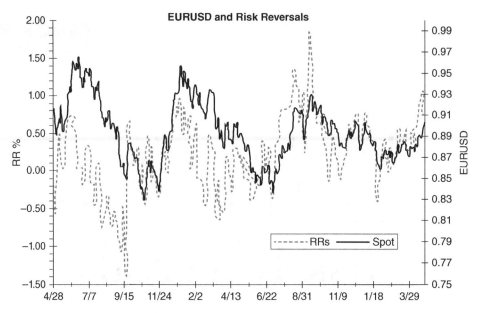

FIGURE 23.1 EURUSD Risk Reversal Chart

What Does a Risk Reversal Table Look Like?

We showed this table before in Chapter 7, but want to present it again to make sure that it is understood well (see Figure 23.1). Each of the abbreviations for the currency options are listed; and as indicated, most risk reversals are near zero, which reflects no major bias for puts or calls. However, for USDJPY, the longer-term risk reversals indicate that the market is strongly favoring yen calls (JC) and dollar puts.

How Can You Use This Information?

For easier graphing and tracking purposes, we use positive and negative integers for calls and put premiums respectively. A positive number indicates that calls are preferred over puts and that the market as a whole anticipates an upward movement in the underlying currency. Likewise, a negative number indicates that puts are preferred over calls and that the market is expecting a down-move in the underlying currency. Used prudently, risk reversals can be a valuable tool in judging market positioning. While the signals generated by a risk reversal system will not be completely accurate, they can help investors judge whether the market is bullish or bearish.

Risk reversals become particularly important when the values are at extreme levels. We identify extreme levels as one standard deviation plus or minus the average risk reversal. When risk reversals are at these levels, they give off contrarian signals, indicating that a currency pair is overbought or oversold based upon sentiment. The indicator is perceived as a contrarian signal because when the entire market is positioned for a rise in a given currency, it makes it harder for the currency to rally and easier for it to fall on negative news or events. As a result, a strongly negative number implies oversold conditions whereas a strongly negative number would imply overbought conditions. Although the buy or sell signals produced by risk reversals are not perfect, they can convey additional information used to make trading decisions.

Examples

Take a look at our first example of the EURUSD (Figure 23.1). Visually, you can see that 25 delta risk reversals have been a leading indicator for EURUSD price action. When risk reversals plunged to –1.39 on September 30, it was a signal that the market had a strong bearish bias. This proved to be a reliable contrarian indicator of what eventually became a 300-pip rebound in the EURUSD over the course of nine days. When prices spiked once again almost immediately to 0.67 in favor of a continuation of the up move, the EURUSD proved bulls wrong by engaging in an even deeper selloff. Although there were many instances of risk reversals signaling contra-trend moves on a smaller scale, the next major spike came a year later. On August 16, risk reversals were at 1.43, which meant that bullish sentiment hit a very high level. This preceded a 260-pip drop in the EURUSD over the course of three weeks. When risk reversals spiked once again a month later to 1.90, we saw another top in the EURUSD, which later became a much deeper descent.

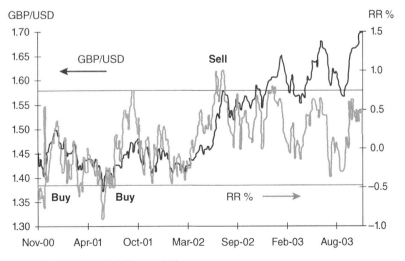

FIGURE 23.2 GBPUSD Risk Reversal Chart

The next example is the GBPUSD. As can be seen in Figure 23.2, risk reversals do a very good job of identifying extreme overbought and oversold conditions. Buy and sell levels are added to the GBPUSD chart for further clarification of how risk reversals can also be used to time market turns. With the lack of price volume data to give us a sense of where the market is positioned, risk reversals can be helpful in gauging general market sentiment.

CHAPTER 24

Fundamental Trading Strategy: Using Option Volatilities to Time Market Movements

U sing option volatilities to time foreign exchange spot movement is a topic that we touched on briefly in Chapter 7. This strategy warrants a more detailed explanation because it has long been a favorite for professional traders and hedge funds. Volatility can be defined as a measure of a currency's expected fluctuation over a given time period based on past price fluctuations. This is typically calculated by taking the historic annual standard deviation of daily price changes. Future prices help to determine implied volatility, which is used to calculate option premiums. Although this sounds fairly complicated, its application is not. Basically, option volatilities measure the rate and magnitude of a currency's price over a given period of time based on historical fluctuations. Therefore, if the average daily trading range of the EURUSD contracted from 100 pips to 60 pips and stayed there for two weeks, in all likelihood, short-term volatility also contracted significantly compared to longer-term volatility during the same time period.

■ How to Use Option Volatilities to Trade Forex

As a guideline, there are two simple rules to follow. The first one is that if short-term option volatilities are significantly lower than long-term volatilities, one should expect a breakout, though the direction of the breakout will not be defined by this rule. Lastly, if short-term option volatilities are significantly higher than long-term volatilities, one should expect a reversion to range trading.

Why Does This Technique Work?

During a period of consolidation, implied option volatilities are either low or on the decline. The inspiration for these rules is that in periods of range trading, there tends to be little movement. We care most about when option volatilities drop sharply, which could be a sign that a profitable break is underway. When short-term volatility is above long-term volatility, it means that near-term price action is more volatile than the long-term average price action. This suggests that the ranges will eventually contract back toward average levels. The trend is most noticeable in empirical data. Below are a few examples of how this rule predicted breakouts that turned into new trends but before analyzing the charts, it is important to note that we use one-month volatilities as our short-term volatilities and three-month volatilities as our long-term volatilities.

In Figure 24.1, the one-month volatility of GBPUSD is generally close to three-month volatilities. However, the first arrow shows an instance where short-term volatility spiked above long-term volatility during a period of GBPUSD weakness. This signaled a correction or relief rally in the currency pair and that was exactly what we saw in September when the GBPUSD bounced more than 200 pips. The second arrow shows an instance where short-term volatility spiked well below long-term volatility and that foreshadowed a major breakdown in the currency pair. In this case, GBPUSD dropped over 600 pips after a period of consolidation.

In Figure 24.2 we have a chart of USDJPY. Like GBPUSD, the one-month and three-month option volatilities move very closely. However in May, one-month volatilities dropped sharply below three-month volatilities and that foreshadowed the first breakout in more than two months.

Who Can Benefit from This Technique?

This strategy is not only useful for breakout traders, but range traders can also utilize this information for their trading. If volatility contracts significantly or becomes very

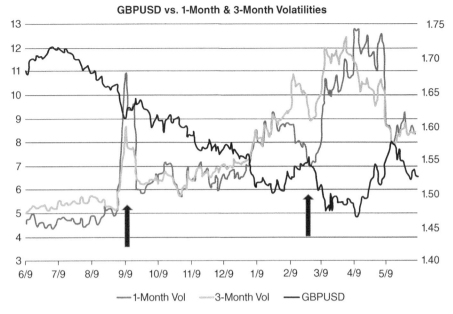

FIGURE 24.1   GBPUSD Volatility Chart

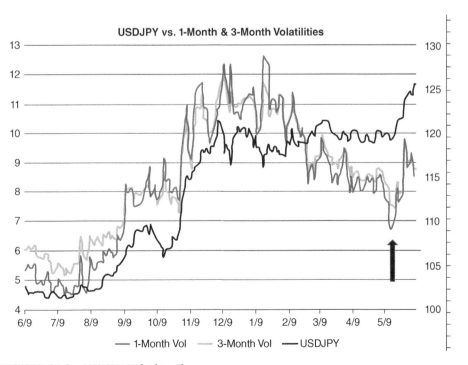

FIGURE 24.2   USDJPY Volatility Chart

low, the likelihood of continued range trading decreases. After eyeing a historical range, traders should look at volatilities to estimate the likelihood that the spot price will remain within this range. Should the trader decide to go long or short this range, he or she should continue to monitor volatility as long as he or she has an open position in the pair to assist them in determining when to close out that position. If short-term volatilities fall well below long-term volatilities, the trader should consider closing their position if the suspected breakout is not in their favor. The potential break is likely to work in the favor of the trader if the current spot is close to the limit and far from the stop. In this hypothetical situation, it may be profitable to move limit prices away from current spot prices to increase profits from the potential break. If the spot price is close to the stop price and far from the limit price, the break is likely to work against the trader, and the trader should close his or her position immediately.

Breakout traders can monitor volatilities to verify a breakout. If traders suspect a breakout, he or she can verify this breakout though implied volatilities. Should implied volatility be constant or rising, there is a higher probability that the currency will continue to trade in range than if volatility is low or falling. In other words, breakout traders should look for short-term volatilities to be significantly lower than long-term volatilities before making a breakout trade.

Aside from being a key component for pricing, option volatilities can also be a useful tool for forecasting market activities. Option volatilities measure the rate and magnitude of the changes in a currency's prices. Implied option volatilities, on the other hand, measure the expected fluctuation of a currency's price over a given period of time based on historical fluctuations.

◼ Tracking Volatilities on Your Own

Volatility tracking typically involves taking the historic annual standard deviation of daily price changes. Generally speaking, we use three-month volatilities for long-term volatilities numbers and one-month volatilities for the short term. Volatilities can be found on Bloomberg or Reuters.

The next step is to start compiling a list of data with the date, currency pair price, implied one-month volatility, and implied three-month volatility for the various currency pairs in Excel. It might also be beneficial to find the difference between the one-month and three-month volatilities to look for large differentials or to calculate one-month volatility as a percentage of three-month volatility.

Once a sufficient amount of data is compiled, one can graph the data as a visual aid. The graph should use two y-axes, with spot prices on one and short- and long-term volatilities on the other. If desired, the differences in short- and long-term volatilities can be graphed as well in a separate, single y-axis graph.

CHAPTER 25

Fundamental Trading Strategy: Intervention

Intervention by central banks is one of the most important short- and long-term fundamentally driven market movers for the currency market. For short-term traders, intervention can lead to sharp intraday movements on the scale of 150–250 pips in a matter of minutes. For longer-term traders, intervention can signal a significant change in trend because it suggests that the central bank is shifting or solidifying its stance and sending a message to the market that they are backing certain directional move in their currency. There are basically two types of intervention: sterilized and unsterilized. Sterilized intervention requires offsetting intervention with the buying or selling of government bonds while unsterilized intervention involves no changes to the monetary base to offset intervention. Many argue that unsterilized intervention has a more lasting effect on the currency than sterilized intervention.

Taking a look at some of the following case studies, it is apparent that interventions in general are important to watch and can have large impacts on a currency pair's price action. Although the actual timing of an intervention tends to be a surprise, quite often the market will begin talking about the need for intervention days or weeks before the actual intervention occurs. The direction of an intervention is almost always known in advance because the central bank will typically come across the newswires complaining about too much strength or weakness in their currency.

These warnings give traders a window of opportunity to participate in what could be significant profit potentials or to stay out of the markets. The only thing to watch out for, which you will see in our case study is that the sharp intervention based rallies or selloffs can quickly be reversed as speculators come into the market to "fade the central bank." Whether or not the market fades, the central bank depends on the frequency of central bank intervention, the success rate, the magnitude of the intervention, the timing of the intervention, and whether fundamentals support intervention. Intervention is much more prevalent in emerging market currencies than in the G7 currencies because these countries need to prevent their local currencies from appreciating too significantly such that it would hinder economic recovery and reduce the competitiveness of the country's exports. Nonetheless, G7 interventions will happen and its rarity is exactly what makes them significant.

■ Japan

In the past two decades, the central bank most willing to engage intervention is the Bank of Japan. As an export dependent country, a strong yen poses a major risk to the export sector. While the Bank of Japan conducts the intervention, the decision is made by the Ministry of Finance. The most recent case of intervention by the Japanese government was in 2011. The BoJ largely stayed out of the market between 2012 and 2015 because Abenomics helped to drive a recovery in the economy. On October 31, 2011, USDJPY hit a record low, which means that the Japanese yen hit a record high. Frustrated with the currency's strength after the 2011 earthquake and tsunami, the Japanese government came into the forex market aggressively to sell the yen and buy the dollar. On that day, their intervention efforts drove USDJPY from a low of 75.575 to a high of 79.50, almost 400 pips. As shown in Figure 25.1, 90% of this move happened in the first 35 minutes.

FIGURE 25.1 USDJPY Chart

The Bank of Japan also bought USDJPY in August 2011, but one of their biggest intervention programs was in March 2011, when central banks around the world joined the BoJ to sell the yen as a sign of solidarity after an earthquake and tsunami drove the currency to a record high. On that day, intervention only drove USDJPY from 79.18 to 82, but a few weeks later it hit a high of 85.50, as shown in Figure 25.2.

The Bank of Japan also intervened in September 2015 and as shown in Figure 25.3, a daily chart, USDJPY jumped nearly 300 pips that day. Typically, USDJPY will move 75 to 150 pips on an average day, so a 300-pip move that happens in minutes is significant. In all but one of these four cases, the intervention move was reversed almost immediately. The only reason why USDJPY extended its rally in March 2011 was because the intervention was coordinated with other central banks, making it more powerful.

While the Japanese government has been quieter in recent years, they were very active in the early twenty-first century. The frequency and strength of BoJ intervention during this period created an *invisible floor* under USDJPY. Although there has been no more mention of this floor in recent years, the BoJ/MoF instilled enough fear that intervention is always a worry. This fear is well justified because in the event of BoJ intervention, the average 100-pip daily range can easily triple.

Japanese intervention can be traded one of two ways—ride the move on the day of intervention or fade it in the days that follow. The key is not to be greedy, because the Japanese government can always step in again. Committing to take a solid 100-pip profit (of a 150–200 pip move) or using a very short-term intraday trailing stop of 15–20 pips, for example, can be helpful.

Switzerland

The Swiss National Bank's 1.20 EURCHF floor is another form of intervention. Faced with a high level of uncertainty in the financial markets, an overvalued currency, and deflation risks in 2011, the SNB introduced a minimum exchange rate of CHF 1.20 per euro. At the time, they pledged to sell francs in an unlimited quantity to maintain the peg. The goal was to stabilize the Swiss economy by capping the gain in the franc. As shown in Figure 25.4, the peg was very effective in keeping EURCHF above 1.20 between late 2012 and 2014. However, in January 2015, the prospect of quantitative easing from the European Central Bank pushed the SNB to abandon their peg, and their surprise announcement caused a 30% one-day decline in EURCHF. Many foreign exchange brokers were unprepared for the move and experienced massive losses as a result.

Other central banks have also intervened in their currency in the past decade including the Reserve Bank of New Zealand. Unfortunately, for the RBNZ, most of their efforts failed with the currency rising after each round of intervention. For

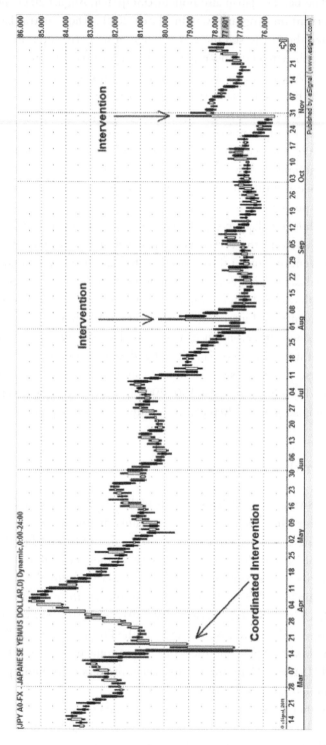

FIGURE 25.2 USDJPY Chart BoJ Intervention

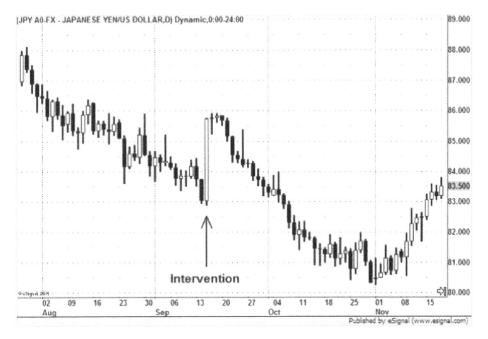

FIGURE 25.3   USDJPY Chart BoJ Intervention

FIGURE 25.4   EURCHF 1.20 Peg

forex traders, this creates an opportunity in that it provides the case for buying the currency after intervention.

Eurozone

The European Central Bank on the other hand is fairly quiet. They have only intervened a few times before, the most recent of which was in 2000. The ECB came into the market to buy euros when the single currency dropped from 90 cents to 84 cents. In January 1999, when the euro was first launched it was valued at 1.17 against the U.S. dollar. Due to the sharp slide, the European Central Bank (ECB) convinced the United States, Japan, the United Kingdom, and Canada to join them in coordinated intervention to prop up the euro for the first time ever. The Eurozone felt concerned that the market was lacking confidence in their new currency but also feared that the slide in their currency was increasing the cost of the region's oil imports. With energy prices hitting 10-year highs at the time, Europe's heavy dependence on oil imports necessitated a stronger currency. The U.S. agreed to intervention because buying euros and selling dollars would help to boost the value of European imports and aid in the funding of an already growing U.S. trade deficit. Tokyo joined in the intervention because they were becoming concerned that the weaker euro was posing a threat to their own exports. Although the ECB did not release details on the magnitude of their intervention, the Federal Reserve reported having purchased 1.5 billion euros against the dollar on behalf of the ECB. Even though the actual intervention itself caught the market by surprise, the ECB gave good warning to the market with numerous bouts of verbal support from ECB and EU officials. For trading purposes, this would have given traders an opportunity to buy euros in anticipation of intervention or to avoid shorting the EURUSD.

Figure 25.5 shows the price action of the EURUSD on the day of intervention. Unfortunately, there is no minute data available dating back to September 2000, but from the daily chart, we can see that on the day that the ECB intervened in the euro (September 22, 2000), with the help of its trade partners, the EURUSD had a high-low range of over 400 pips.

Even though intervention does not happen often, it is a very important fundamental trading strategy because each time it occurs, price movements are substantial.

For traders, intervention has three major implications for trading:

1. *Bet on intervention*: Heed the warnings from central bank officials and use it as a signal for possible intervention—the invisible floor created by the Japanese government gave USDJPY bulls plenty of opportunity to pick short-term bottoms.

2. *Avoid betting against intervention*: Betting against intervention can be dangerous because one bout of intervention by a central bank could easily trigger a

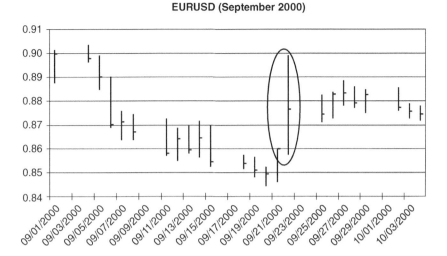

FIGURE 25.5 EURUSD Intervention

sharp 100–150 plus pip move in the currency pair, taking out stop orders and exacerbating the move.

3. *Use stops when intervention is a risk*: With the 24-hour nature of the market, intervention can occur at any time of the day. Although stops should *always* be entered into the trading platform immediately after the entry order is triggered, having stops in place are even more important when intervention is a major risk.

CHAPTER 26

Currency Profiles and Outlook

In order to understand how to trade currencies effectively, it is important to have a firm grasp of the general economic characteristics of the most commonly traded currencies. This includes understanding which economic reports and factors have the most significant impact on a currency's movements. For example, some currencies are extremely sensitive to commodity price movements and others are not. Learning the characteristics or personalities of each currency will help traders understand what factors influence the exchange rate on a short- and long-term basis. We will look at the eight most actively traded currencies—the U.S. dollar, euro, British pound, Swiss franc, Japanese yen, and Australian, New Zealand, and Canadian dollars. Of course, the most important currency of them all is the U.S. dollar.

Currency Profile: U.S. Dollar (USD)

Broad Economic Overview

The United States is the world's leading economic power, with gross domestic product valued at over US$17 trillion as of 2014. This is the highest in the world, and based on the purchasing power parity model, it is four times the size of Japan's output, five times the size of Germany's, and seven times the size of the United Kingdom's. The United States is primarily a service-oriented country, with nearly

80% of its GDP coming from real estate, transportation, finance, health care, and business services. Yet, the sheer size of the U.S. manufacturing sector still makes the U.S. dollar particularly sensitive to developments in the manufacturing sector. With the United States having the largest and most liquid equity and fixed income markets in the world, foreign investors have consistently increased their purchases of U.S. assets. According to the IMF, foreign direct investments into the U.S. are equal to approximately 40% of total global net inflows for the United States. On a net basis, the United States absorbs 71% of total foreign savings. This means that if foreign investors are not satisfied with their returns in the U.S. asset markets and they decide to repatriate their funds, this would have a significant effect on U.S. asset values and the U.S. dollar. More specifically, if foreign investors sell their U.S. dollar denominated assets holdings in search of higher yielding assets elsewhere, this would typically result in a decline in the value of the U.S. asset, as well as the U.S. dollar.

The import and export volume of the United States also exceeds that of any other country. This is due to the country's sheer size, as true import and export volume represent a mere 12% of GDP. Despite this large activity, on a netted basis, the United States is running a very large current account deficit of over $113 billion as of Q4 2014. This is a major problem that the U.S. economy has been struggling with for decades, as the large current account deficit makes the U.S. dollar highly sensitive to changes in capital flows. In fact, in order to prevent a decline in the U.S. dollar as a result of trade, the United States needs to attract a significant amount of capital inflows per day. Thankfully, the U.S. bond market is the largest in the world, and Treasuries remain an attractive investment due to the lack of suitable alternatives.

Most major economies also count the United States as its largest trading partner, with U.S. trade representing 20% of total world trade. These rankings are very important because changes in the value of the dollar and its volatility will impact the U.S. trading activities with these respective countries. More specifically, a weaker dollar will encourage more U.S. exports, whereas a stronger dollar could curb foreign demand for American goods. However, since the United States is not a trade-dependent economy, the strength of a dollar is less troublesome. Here's a breakdown of the most important trading partners for the United States, in order of importance:

Leading Export Markets
1. Canada
2. Mexico
3. China
4. European Union
5. Japan

Leading Import Sources

1. China
2. Canada
3. Mexico
4. European Union
5. Japan

Source: US Trade.gov 2014

Monetary and Fiscal Policy Makers—The Federal Reserve

The Federal Reserve Board (Fed) is the monetary policy authority of the United States. The Fed is responsible for setting and implementing monetary policy. The board consists of a 12-member Federal Open Market Committee (FOMC). The voting members of the FOMC are the seven governors of the Federal Reserve Board, plus five presidents of the 12 district reserve banks. The FOMC holds eight meetings per year, which are widely watched for interest rate announcements or changes in growth expectations. After four of those meetings, the head of the Central Bank holds a press conference, and typically that is when major monetary policy changes are made.

The Fed has a high degree of independence to set monetary authority. They are less subject to political influences, as most members are accorded long terms that allow them to remain in office through periods of alternate party dominance in both the presidency and Congress.

The Federal Reserve issues a biannual *Monetary Policy Report* in February and July followed by the Humphrey–Hawkins testimony where the Federal Reserve chairman responds to questions from both the Congress and the Banking Committees in regards to this report. This report is important to watch, as it contains the FOMC forecasts for GDP growth, inflation, and unemployment.

The Fed, unlike most other central banks, has a mandate or "long-run objectives" of "price stability and sustainable economic growth." In order to adhere to these goals, the Fed has to use monetary policy to limit inflation and unemployment and achieve balanced growth. The most popular tools that the Fed uses to control monetary policy include the following.

Open Market Operations

Open market operations involve Fed purchases of government securities, including Treasury bills, notes and bonds. This is one of the most popular methods for the Fed to signal and implement policy changes. Generally speaking, increases in Fed purchases of government securities decreases interest rates, while selling of government securities by the Fed boosts interest rates.

The Fed Funds target rate is the key policy target of the Federal Reserve. It is the interest rate for borrowing that the Fed offers to its member banks. The Fed tends to increase this rate to curb inflation or decrease this rate to promote growth and consumption. Changes to this rate are closely watched by the market and tend to imply major changes in policy and will typically have large ramifications for global fixed income and equity markets. The market also pays particular attention to the statement released by the Federal Reserve as it can offer guidance for future monetary policy actions.

Fiscal policy is in the hands of the U.S. Treasury. Fiscal policy decisions include determining the appropriate level of taxes and government spending. In fact, although the markets pay more attention to the Federal Reserve, the U.S. Treasury is the actual government body that determines dollar policy. That is, if they feel that the USD rate on the foreign exchange market is under- or overvalued, the U.S. Treasury is the government body that gives the NY Federal Reserve Board the authority and instructions to intervene in the foreign exchange market by physically selling or buying USD. Therefore, the Treasury's view on dollar policy and changes to that view can be important to the currency market.

Over the past few decades, the Treasury and Fed officials have maintained a "strong dollar" bias. While a weak dollar helps to promote growth for political reasons, the government is unlikely to change their stance in support of a weak dollar policy.

Important Characteristics of the U.S. Dollar

■ *Over 80% of all currency deals involve the dollar.* The most liquid currencies in the foreign exchange market are the EURUSD, USDJPY, GBPUSD, and USDCHF. These currencies represent the most commonly traded currencies in the world, and it is no coincidence that all of these currency pairs involve the U.S. dollar. In fact, 80% of all currency deals, which include currency conversion, hedging, and trade settlement, involve the U.S. dollar. This explains why U.S. data, the U.S. dollar, and U.S. fundamentals are so important to foreign exchange traders.

■ *Prior to the introduction of the euro and the growing utilization of the Chinese renminbi, the U.S. dollar was considered one the world's premier "safe-haven" reserve currencies.* The U.S. dollar has long been one of the world's premier "safe-haven" currencies, with 76% of global currency reserves held in dollars. To this day, the dollar is still the preferred currency of choice, but in recent years its safe haven, reserve currency status has been challenged by the euro and Chinese renminbi. We are still a very long way from the dollar being usurped by either currency, but in the past decade, many central banks have slowly diversified their reserves by reducing their dollar holdings and increasing their euro and renminbi holdings. This trend will only accelerate in the years to come, but until European and Chinese bond markets are large and developed enough to handle the reserve diversification flows, the dollar and U.S. Treasuries will still be the investment of choice for reserve managers.

■ *The U.S. dollar moves in the opposite direction of gold prices.* One of the unique characteristics of the U.S. dollar is that there is a strong inverse relationship between the price of gold and the value of the U.S. dollar as shown in Figure 26.1. These two instruments are near-perfect mirror images of each other, which means that when the value of the dollar declines, the price of gold rises; and when the dollar appreciates, the price of gold falls. There is, of course, a good reason—gold is priced in U.S. dollars. The correlation is not perfect—in times of geopolitical uncertainty, investors generally prefer hard versus fiat currencies or gold versus the dollar.

■ *Many emerging market countries "peg" their local currencies to the dollar.* Pegging a currency to the dollar refers to the idea that a government agrees to maintain their currency at a specific rate or range to the U.S. dollar. As the value of the dollar changes, this requires the central bank to buy or sell their local currency and the U.S. dollar to maintain the peg. For example, let's imagine that Country A pledges to maintain a fixed currency peg of 7.5 versus the U.S. dollar. If the dollar weakens, causing downward pressure on the exchange rate, the central bank would have to buy U.S. dollars and sell their local currency to maintain the peg. After buying dollars, they would typically invest those funds into U.S. Treasuries.

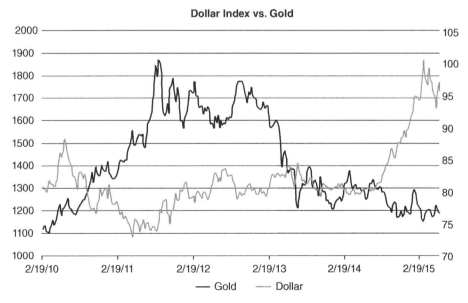

FIGURE 26.1 Dollar Index vs. Gold

This process is exactly how China and other Asian economies became large holders of US Treasuries. Through the years, many countries have switched from a fixed to floating rate peg and in some cases a peg that references a basket of currencies, but in each case, the dollar is still the leading component. However, the movement from fixed U.S. dollar pegs to a basket reduces the amount of dollars that a country like China needs to buy, and as their currency regime and others in the region are loosened further, the impact on the dollar will grow.

- *Interest rate differentials between U.S. Treasuries and foreign bonds strongly followed.* The interest rate differentials between U.S. Treasuries and foreign bonds are a very important relationship that professional FX traders need to follow. It can be a strong indicator of potential currency movements because the U.S. market is one of the largest markets in the world, and investors are very sensitive to the yields that the offered by U.S. assets. Large investors are constantly looking for assets with the highest yields. As yields in the U.S. decrease or if yields abroad increase, this would induce investors to sell their U.S. assets and purchase foreign assets. Selling U.S. fixed income or equity assets would influence the currency market because that would require selling U.S. dollars and buying the foreign currency. If U.S. yields rise or foreign yields decrease, investors in general would be more inclined to purchase U.S. assets, therefore boosting the value of the dollar (USD).

- *Keep an eye on the dollar index.* Market participants closely follow the U.S. dollar index as a gauge of overall dollar strength or weakness. The USD index is a futures contract traded on the Intercontinental Exchange (ICE) that is calculated using the trade-weighted geometric average of six currencies. It is important to follow this index because when market participants are reporting general dollar weakness or a decline in the trade-weighted dollar, they are typically referring to this index. Unfortunately, the weighting does not accurately reflect U.S. trade activity. Nonetheless, the DXY is closely followed and actively traded. Also, even though the dollar may have moved significantly against a single currency, it may have not moved as significantly on a trade-weighted basis. This is important because some central bankers may choose to focus on the trade-weighted index instead of the individual currency pair's performance against the dollar.

- *The dollar is impacted by equities and Treasuries.* In earlier chapters, we have established that there is a strong correlation between a country's equity and fixed-income markets and its currency: If the equity market is rising, generally speaking, foreign investment dollars should be coming in to seize the opportunity. If equity markets are falling, domestic investors will be selling their shares of local companies and looking for opportunities abroad. With fixed-income markets, economies boasting the most valuable fixed income opportunities with the highest yields will be capable of attracting more foreign investment. Daily fluctuations and developments in any of these markets reflect movement of foreign portfolio investments, which would require foreign exchange transactions. Cross border merger and acquisition activities can also influence the price action of currencies. Large M&A deals, particularly those that involve a significant cash portion, will have a notable impact on the currency markets. The reason is that the acquirer will need to buy or sell dollars to fund their cross-border acquisition.

Important Economic Indicators for the United States

Economic data is always important, but U.S. data tends to have the greatest impact on currencies because more than 80% of currency transactions involve the U.S. dollar. Here are some of the most important and market moving pieces of U.S. data:

Employment: Nonfarm Payrolls

The employment report is the most important and widely watched indicator on the economic calendar. Its importance is mostly due to political influences rather than pure economic reasons, as the Fed is under strict pressure to keep unemployment under control. As a result, interest rate policy is directly influenced by employment conditions. The monthly jobs report consists of data compiled from two different surveys: the establishment survey and the household survey. The establishment survey provides data on nonfarm payroll employment, average hourly workweek, and the aggregate hours index. The household survey provides information on the labor force, household employment, and the unemployment rate. When this report is released on the first Friday of every month, forex traders will immediately hone in on the nonfarm payrolls number, the unemployment rate, and average hourly earnings. However, any revisions or seasonal adjustments can also impact the dollar's reaction to the overall report.

Consumer Price Index

The Consumer Price Index is a key gauge of inflation. The index measures the prices on a fixed basket of consumer goods. Economists tend to focus more on the CPI-U or the core inflation rate, which excludes the volatile food and energy components. The indicator is widely watched by the FX markets as it drives a lot of activity because job growth and inflation is the key to monetary policy.

Retail Sales

The key to growth is consumer spending and for this reason, the retail sales report is also extremely market moving. The Retail Sales Index measures the total goods sold by a sampling of retail stores over the course of a month. This index is used as a gauge of consumer consumption and consumer confidence. The most important number to watch is retail sales less autos, as auto sales can vary month-to-month. While retail sales can be quite volatile due to seasonality, it is one of the most important indicators on the health of the economy along with a key input for GDP.

Nonmanufacturing and Manufacturing ISM

The monthly nonmanufacturing and manufacturing reports released by the Institute for Supply Management is also important because it generally provides the most current information on activity in the economy. ISM releases a monthly composite index based on surveys of 300 purchasing managers nationwide representing 20 different industries. An index value above 50 reflects expansion, while values below 50 are indicative of contraction. The ISM nonmanufacturing index is particularly important because the United States is a services economy, and typically this report is released ahead of nonfarm payrolls; and the employment subcomponent can provide early clues on the health of the labor market.

Consumer Confidence

The Consumer Confidence Survey measures how individuals feel about the economy. There are two popular reports—one released by the Conference Board and one by the University of Michigan. In the Conference Board survey, questionnaires are sent out to a nationwide representative sample of 5,000 households, of which approximately 3,500 respond. Households are asked five questions:

1. A rating of business conditions in the household's area
2. A rating of business conditions in six months
3. Job availability in the area
4. Job availability in six months
5. Family income in six months

Responses are seasonally adjusted and an index is constructed for each response, and then a composite index is fashioned based on the aggregate responses. The University of Michigan Survey, on the other hand, only polls 500 people, but since it is released before the Conference Board's report, it can have a larger impact on currencies. Rising consumer confidence is viewed as a precursor to stronger consumer spending and growth.

Producer Price Index

The Producer Price Index (PPI) is a family of indexes that measures average changes in selling prices received by domestic producers for their output. PPI tracks changes in prices for nearly every goods producing industry in the domestic economy, including agriculture, electricity and natural gas, forestry, fisheries, manufacturing, and mining. Foreign exchange markets tend to focus on seasonally adjusted finished goods PPI and how the index has reacted on a monthly, quarterly, and annualized basis.

Gross Domestic Product

Gross domestic product, or GDP, is a measure of the total production and consumption of goods and services. In the United States, the Bureau of Economic

Analysis (BEA) constructs two complementary measures of GDP, one based on income and one based on expenditures. The advance release of GDP, which occurs the month after each quarter ends, contains some BEA estimates for data not yet released, inventories and trade balance, and is the most important release. Other releases of GDP, which are the revisions, are typically not very significant unless a major change is made.

International Trade

The balance of trade represents the difference between exports and imports of foreign trade in goods and services. Merchandise data are provided for U.S. total foreign trade with all countries and details for trade with specific countries and regions of the world, as well as for individual commodities. Traders tend to focus on seasonally adjusted trade numbers over a three-month period as single month trade periods are regarded as volatile and less reliable.

Employment Cost Index (ECI)

The employment cost index data is based on a survey of employer payrolls in the third month of the quarter for the pay period ending on the twelfth day of the month. This survey is a probability sample of approximately 3,600 private industry employers and 700 state and local governments, public schools, and public hospitals. The big advantage of ECI is that it includes nonwage costs, which adds as much as 30% to total labor costs. Reaction to the ECI, however, is often muted as it is generally very stable. It should be noted however that it is one of the Federal Reserve's favorite indicators.

Industrial Production

The Index of Industrial Production is a set of indexes that measures the monthly physical output of U.S. factories, mines, and utilities. The index is broken down by industry type and market type. Foreign exchange markets focus mostly on the seasonally adjusted monthly change in aggregate figure. Increases in the index are typically dollar positive.

Treasury International Capital Flow Data (TIC Data)

The Treasury International Capital flow data measures the amount of capital flow into the United States on a monthly basis. This economic release has become increasingly important over the past few years since the funding of the U.S. deficit is becoming more of an issue. Aside from the headline number itself, the market also pays close attention to the official flows, which represents the demand for U.S. government debt by foreign central banks.

CHAPTER 27

Currency Profile: Euro (EUR)

▊ Broad Economic Overview

The European Union (EU) was developed as an institutional framework for the construction of a united Europe. As of May 2015, the EU consists of 28 member countries with 19 of these nations sharing the euro as a common currency. The Eurozone consists of Austria, Belgium, Cyprus, Estonia, Finland, France, Germany, Greece, Ireland, Italy, Latvia, Lithuania, Luxembourg, Malta, the Netherlands, Portugal, Slovakia, Slovenia, and Spain. With the exception of Denmark and the United Kingdom, other EU states are obliged to join the monetary union when they meet the criteria to do so. Aside from a common currency, these countries also share a single monetary policy dictated by the European Central Bank (ECB). These common currency countries constitute the European Monetary Union (EMU).

The EMU is the world's second largest economic power, with gross domestic product valued at approximately US$18 trillion in 2014. With a highly developed fixed income, equity, and futures market, the EMU is the second most attractive investment market for domestic and international investors. In its early days, the EMU found difficulty attracting foreign direct investment or large capital flows because, historically, the U.S. markets are larger with more consistent returns. As a result, the U.S. absorbs 71% of total foreign savings. However, with the euro becoming an established currency and the European Monetary Union incorporating more members, the euro's importance as a reserve currency is rising and translating into greater capital flows. The only problem is that European bond markets are fragmented, and there are not enough quality assets for central banks to invest in. Unless there are euro bonds, foreign central banks could be slow to diversify their reserve holdings. Nonetheless, they will do so gradually, providing ongoing support for the euro.

Trade is extremely important to Eurozone nations and most countries conduct the majority of their trade with other states in the region. This is important because one of the most valuable aspects of the euro is its facilitation of trade activity through the elimination of exchange rate risk. Large Eurozone nations such as Germany, France, Italy, and Spain also conduct significant trade activity with countries like the United States and China. This makes the value of the euro particularly important to economic activity. A country like the United States is less sensitive to exchange rate fluctuations because most of its demand is internal, but Europe is extremely sensitive to its exchange rate because many Eurozone nations rely on external demand. The size and scope of the EMU's trade with the rest of the world provides it with significant power in the international trade arena. International clout is also one of the primary goals in the formation of the European Union, because it allows individual nations to negotiate as a group on an equal playing field with the United States and China, their two largest trading partners. The breakdowns of the most important trading partners for the European Union are the following:

Leading Export Markets

1. United States
2. China
3. Switzerland
4. Russia
5. Turkey

Leading Import Sources

1. China
2. Russia
3. United States
4. Norway
5. Switzerland

While trade is extremely important, the service sector has the largest share of total output followed by manufacturing. In fact, a large number of the companies whose primary purpose is to produce finished products still concentrate their EU activity on innovation, research, design, and marketing, while outsourcing most of their manufacturing activities to Asia.

The EU's growing role in international trade has major implications for the role of the euro as a reserve currency. As more countries conduct trade with the Eurozone, they will be motivated to accumulate more euros to reduce exchange risk and transaction costs. Traditionally, most international trade transactions involve the British pound, the Japanese yen, and/or the U.S. dollar. Before the establishment of the euro, it was unreasonable to hold large amounts of every individual EU national currency. As a result, currency reserves tended toward the dollar. At the end of the 1990s, approximately 65% of all world reserves were held in U.S. dollars, but after the introduction of the euro, foreign reserve assets slowly shifted towards the euro. This trend will only continue as the world becomes more globalized.

Monetary and Fiscal Policy Makers—The European Central Bank

The European Central Bank (ECB) is the governing body responsible for determining the monetary policy of the countries participating in the EMU. The Executive Board of the EMU consists of the president of the ECB, the vice president of the ECB, and four other members. These individuals, along with the governors of the national central banks, comprise the Governing Council. The ECB is set up such that the Executive Board implements the policies dictated by the Governing Council. New monetary policies decisions are typically made by majority vote, with the president having the casting vote in the event of a tie in their monthly meeting. After each meeting the Central Bank president holds a press conference to answer questions. This is also used as an opportunity to clarify their monetary policy stance.

The EMU's primary objective is to maintain price stability and promote growth. Monetary and fiscal policy changes are made to ensure that this objective is met. With the formation of the EMU, the Maastricht Treaty was developed by the Union to apply a number of criteria for each member country. These criteria were developed by the Union to help them achieve their objective. Deviations from these criteria by any one country will result in heavy fines. Listed below are the EMU criteria. It is apparent based on these criteria that the ECB has a strict mandate focused on inflation and deficit. Generally, the ECB strives to maintain annual growth in HCPI (Harmonized Consumer Price Index) below 2% and M3 (Money Supply) annual growth around 4.5%.

The EMU Criteria

In the 1992 Treaty on European Union (the Maastricht Treaty) the following preconditions were created for any EU member state looking to join the economic and monetary union (EMU).

- A rate of inflation no more than 1.5% above the average of the three best performing member states, taking the average of the 12-month year-on-year rate preceding the assessment date.

- Long-term interest rates not exceeding the average rates of these low-inflation states by more than 2% for the preceding 12 months.

- Exchange rates which fluctuate within the normal margins of the exchange-rate mechanism (ERM) for at least two years.

- A general government debt/GDP ratio of not more than 60%, although a higher ratio may be permissible if it is "sufficiently diminishing."

- A general government deficit not exceeding 3% of GDP, although a small and temporary excess can be permitted.

If a country meets the convergence criteria and joins the EMU, their monetary policy will be determined by the European Central Bank (ECB). The ECB and the ESCB (European System of Central Banks) are independent institutions from both national governments and other EU institutions, granting them complete control over monetary policy. This operational independence is accorded to them as per Article 108 of the Maastricht Treaty, which states that any member of the decision-making bodies cannot seek or take instructions from any Community Institutions, any government of a member state, or any other body. In other words, no one country can pressure the ECB into making a monetary policy change that is in only their best interest. The primary tools the ECB uses to control monetary policy is the following.

Open Market Operations

The ECB has four main categories of open market operations to steer interest rates, manage liquidity, and signal monetary policy stance. This includes:

- *Main refinancing operations.* These are regular liquidity-providing reverse transactions conducted weekly with a maturity of two weeks, which provide the bulk of refinancing to the financial sector.

- *Longer-term refinancing operations.* These are liquidity-providing reverse transactions with a monthly frequency and a maturity of three months, which provide counterparties with additional longer-term refinancing.

- *Fine-tuning operations.* These are executed on an ad-hoc basis, with the aim of both managing the liquidity situation in the market and steering interest rates, in particular in order to smooth the effects on interest rates caused by unexpected liquidity fluctuations.

- *Structural operations.* These involve the issuance of debt certificates, reverse transactions, and outright transactions. These operations will be executed whenever the ECB wishes to adjust the structural position of the Eurosystem vis-à-vis the financial sector (on a regular or nonregular basis).

ECB Minimum Bid Rate (Repo Rate)

The ECB minimum bid rate is the key policy target for the ECB and the level of borrowing that the ECB offers to the central banks of its member states. This is also the rate that is subject to change at the monthly ECB meetings. Since inflation is a major concern for European policy makers, they are generally more inclined to keep interest rates at lofty levels to prevent inflation. Changes in the ECB's minimum bid rate can have large ramifications for the EUR.

The ECB does not have an exchange rate target, but will factor in exchange rates in their policy deliberations because they can affect price stability. A high exchange rate lowers inflationary pressures while a low exchange rate promotes it. The ECB is not prohibited from intervening in the foreign exchange markets if they believe that inflation is a concern. As a result, comments by members of the Governing Council are closely watched by forex traders and can have a significant impact on the euro.

In addition to their monthly meetings, the Central Bank will also publish a monthly bulletin and release staff forecasts and minutes from past meetings. The president of the Central Bank holds a press conference after the policy meeting and that, along with each of these event risks, can cause volatility in the currency.

Now let's take a look at some of the important characteristics of the euro:

■ *EURUSD cross is the most liquid and actively traded currency.* The euro was introduced as an electronic currency in January 1999. At the time, the euro replaced all pre-EMU currencies, except for Greece's currency, which was converted to the euro in January 2001. As a result, the EURUSD cross is now the most liquid currency in the world and its movements are used as the primary gauge of the health of both the European and U.S. economies. Figure 27.1 highlights the 10 year performance of EUR-USD. The euro is most frequently known as the "anti-dollar" since dollar or U.S. fundamentals generally have a greater impact on the movement of the currency.

  EURJPY and EURCHF are also very liquid currencies that can be used as a gauge of the health of the Japanese and Swiss economies. Many new traders will start with the EURUSD because of its orderly movements, tight spread, and liquidity.

■ *Euro: A currency without a country.* One of the greatest problems of the euro is that it is currency without a country. Instead, it bears the economic, political, and social risks of 19 different nations. This is its greatest strength and its greatest weakness. In the past decade, we have seen how the debt crisis in smaller Eurozone nations have affected the currency as a whole. It undermines confidence and has, on many occasions, put the entire monetary union at risk.

■ *Spread between 10-year U.S. Treasuries and 10-year Bunds can indicate euro sentiment.* Ten-year government bonds can serve as an important indicator of where the euro

CURRENCY PROFILE: EURO (EUR)

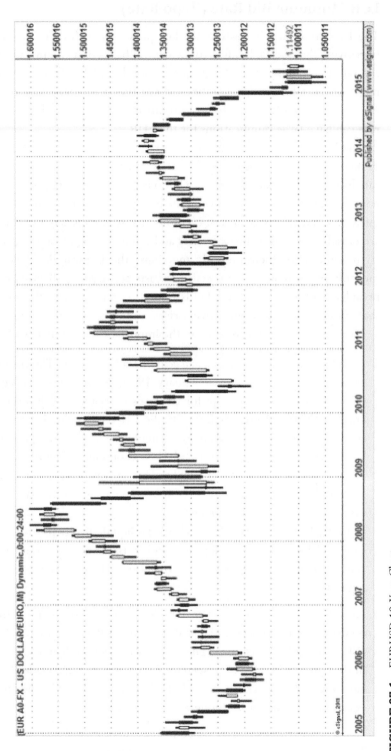

FIGURE 27.1 EURUSD 10-Year Chart

Source: eSignal

is headed, especially against the U.S. dollar. The differential between the 10-year U.S. government bond and the 10-year German Bund rates can provide a good indication for EURUSD's movement. If Bund rates are higher than U.S. Treasury rates and the differential increases, or the spread widens, this is generally positive for the EURUSD. Alternatively, a decrease in the differential or a tightening of the interest rates is generally bearish for EURUSD. As there is no Euro bond, the 10-year German Bund yield is typically used as the benchmark bond for the Eurozone because Germany is the largest country in the monetary union.

■ *Predictions for euro area money flows.* Another useful rate to follow is the three-month interest rate, also known as the euro interbank offer rate or the Euribor rate. This is the rate offered from one large bank to another on interbank term deposits. Traders tend to compare the Euribor futures rate with the Eurodollar futures rate. Eurodollars are deposits denominated in U.S. dollars at banks and other financial institutions outside the United States. Because investors like high-yielding assets, European fixed-income assets become more attractive as the spread between Euribor futures and Eurodollar futures widens in favor of Euribors. As the spread narrows, European assets become less attractive, whereby implying a potential decrease in money flows into the Euro.

Mergers and acquisition activity can also affect how the EURUSD moves. In recent years we have seen increased M&A activity between EU and U.S. multinationals. Large deals, especially with a large cash component, can lead to a sudden burst in the EURUSD, but the reaction is generally short-lived.

■ Important Indicators for the Euro

When it comes to Eurozone economic reports, the only ones that affect the euro are German or Eurozone data. The largest countries in the Eurozone in order of GDP contribution are Germany, France, Italy, and Spain. While French and Italian data are important, they rarely move the currency. So what forex traders should focus on are the broader regional reports and German data. Central bank rate decisions are the most important, but here are some additional economic reports that can have meaningful impact on the currency.

PMIs

Every month, Markit Economics releases the PMI indices for the Manufacturing and Service sectors. For the Eurozone, they provide this data for the four largest economies and a composite index for the region. These numbers are extremely market moving because they provide the most up-to-date information on how each of the economies are performing in the current month and not how the economies performed the previous month like many other reports. However, since the reports are for the current period, they are usually subject to revisions so the euro will move on the preliminary and secondary reports. A reading above 50 represents expansion, and a reading below 50 represents contraction. For the Eurozone, the manufacturing PMI index is the most important along with the composite index, which aggregates how the manufacturing and service sector are performing. Since the German data are released shortly before the Eurozone report, they can have a greater impact on the currency.

IFO Survey

Germany is by far the largest economy in Europe and is responsible for approximately 20% of total GDP. Any insight into German business conditions is seen as an insight into Europe as a whole. The IFO is a monthly survey conducted by the IFO institute. They survey over 7,000 German businesses, asking for their assessment of the German business climate and their short-term plans. The initial publication of the results consists of the business climate headline figure and its two equally weighted subindices: current business conditions and business expectations. The typical range is from 80 to 120, with a higher number indicating greater business confidence. The report is most valuable, however, when measured against previous data.

Inflation Indicators—HICP

Since the ECB has an inflation mandate, the EU Harmonized Index of Consumer Prices (HICP) published by Eurostat is very important. This harmonized index is designed for international comparison as required by EU law. The index is compiled with information on prices retrieved by each national statistical agency. Individual countries are required to provide Eurostat with the 100 indices used to compute the HICP. The national HICPs are totaled by Eurostat as a weighted average of these subindices, and the weights used are country-specific. The HICP is released at the end of the month following the reference period, which is about 10 days after the publications of the national CPIs from Spain and France, the final EMU-5 countries to release their CPIs. Even if part of the information is already known when the HICP is released, it is an important release because it serves as the reference inflation index for the ECB who aims to keep Eurozone consumer price inflation between 0% and 2%.

German Industrial Production

Industrial production data are seasonally adjusted (SA) and include a breakdown into four major subcategories: mining, manufacturing, energy, and construction. The manufacturing aggregate comprises four main product groups: basic and producer goods, capital goods, consumer durables, and consumer nondurables. The market tends to pay attention to the annual rate of change and the seasonally adjusted month-on-month figure. Germany's figure is most important since it is the largest country in the Eurozone; however, the market can also react to the French industrial production report. The initial industrial production release is based on a narrower data sample and hence subject to revision when the full sample has become available. The ministry occasionally provides insight on the expected direction of the revision in the initial data release.

German Unemployment

Labor market numbers are important for every country and in the case of the Eurozone, German unemployment is the most important. Released by the Labor Office, the data contain information on the number of unemployed, as well as the changes on the previous month, on both seasonally (SA) and nonseasonally (NSA) adjusted terms. The NSA unemployment rate is provided, along with data on vacancies, short-shift working arrangements, and the number of employees (temporarily suspended in 1999). Within an hour after the FLO release, the Bundesbank releases the SA unemployment rate. The day ahead of the release, there is often a leak of the official data from a trade-union source. The leak is usually of the NSA level of unemployment in millions. When a precise figure is reported on Reuters, as given by "sources" for the NSA level of unemployment, the leak usually reflects the official figures. Rumors often circulate up to one week before the official release, and they are notoriously imprecise. Regardless, a drop in unemployment along with an improvement in the jobless rate is positive for the currency, whereas a rise in jobless claims or increase in the unemployment rate is negative for the currency.

Preliminary GDP

Preliminary GDP is issued when Eurostat has collected data from a sufficient number of countries to produce an estimate. This usually includes France, Germany, and the Netherlands. However, Italy is not included in the preliminary release and is only added in the final number. The yearly aggregates for EU-15 and EMU-11 are a simple sum of national GDP. For the quarterly accounts, the aggregation is more complex since some countries (Greece, Ireland, and Luxembourg) do not yet produce quarterly national accounts data. Moreover, Portugal produces only partial quarterly accounts with a significant lag. Thus, both the EU-15 and EMU-11 quarterly paths are the result of estimates from quarterly data based on a group of countries accounting for more than 95% of total EU GDP (see the Foreword for a detailed description of the weights of each country in the EU).

M3

M3 is a broad measure of money supply, which includes everything from notes and coins to bank deposits. The ECB closely monitors M3 as they view it as a key measure of inflation. At its session in December 1998, the governing council of the ECB set its first reference value for M3 growth at 4.5%. This value supports inflation below 2%, trend growth of 2% to 2.5%, and a long-term decline in the velocity of money by 0.5% to 1%. The growth rate is monitored on a three-month moving average basis in order to prevent monthly volatility to distort the information given by the aggregate. The ECB's approach to monetary targeting leaves considerable room for maneuver and interpretation. Because the ECB does not impose bands on M3 growth, as the Bundesbank used to do, there will be no automatic action when M3 growth diverges from the reference value. Moreover, although the ECB considers M3 to be the key indicator, it will also take into account the changes in other monetary aggregates.

Individual Country Budget Deficits

The Stability and Growth Pact states that budget deficits for every country in the monetary union must be kept below 3% of GDP. Failure to meet these targets will be punished. However through the years many Eurozone nations have had deficits in excess of 3% and penalties have not been enforced.

CHAPTER 28

Currency Profile: British Pound (GBP)

■ Broad Economic Overview

The United Kingdom is the world's fifth largest economy with GDP valued at approximately US$3 trillion in 2014 according to the IMF. With one of the most dynamic central banks in the world, the UK economy benefited from many years of strong growth, low unemployment, expanding output, and resilient consumption. The strength of consumer consumption has been largely due to the strong housing market. The United Kingdom is a service-oriented economy, with manufacturing representing an increasingly smaller portion of GDP, now equivalent to only one-fifth of national output. Their capital market system is one of the most developed in the world, with finance and banking being the strongest contributors to GDP. Although the majority of the UK's GDP is from services, it is also one of the largest producers and exporters of natural gas in the European Union. The energy production industry accounts for 10% of GDP, which is one of the highest shares of any industrialized nation. This is particularly important, as increases in energy prices (such as oil) will significantly benefit the large number of UK oil exporters. (The United Kingdom became a net oil importer for a brief period due to disruptions in the North Sea in 2003, but it has already resumed its status as a net oil exporter.)

Overall, the United Kingdom is a net importer of goods with a consistent trade deficit. Its largest trading partner is the EU, with trade between the two constituencies accounting for over 50% of all of the country's import and export activities. The United States, on an individual basis, still remains the United

Kingdom's largest trading partner. The breakdowns of the most important trading partners for the United Kingdom are the following:

Leading Export Markets
1. United States
2. Germany
3. Switzerland
4. Netherlands
5. France

Leading Import Sources
1. Germany
2. Netherlands
3. China
4. United States
5. France

Since the launch of the euro in 1999, the single currency's troubles have become increasingly apparent, and this has made the UK's decision to maintain its own currency and monetary authority increasingly intelligent. Yet the possibility of euro adoption will remain a question in the minds of pound traders for many years to come, although in 2015 into 2016, the more relevant question is whether the United Kingdom will remain in the EMU. A decision on euro entry has significant ramifications for the UK economy—the most important of which is that UK interest rates would have to be adjusted to reflect the equivalent interest rate of the Eurozone. One of the primary arguments against adopting the euro is that the UK government has sound macroeconomic policies that have worked very well for the country for decades. Its successful monetary and fiscal policies have led it to outperform most major economies during economic downturns, including the European Union.

The UK Treasury has previously specified five economic tests that must be met prior to euro entry, which are the following:

UK's Five Economic Tests for Euro
1. Is there sustainable convergence in business cycles and economic structures between the United Kingdom and other EMU members, so that the UK citizens could live comfortably with euro interest rates on a permanent basis?
2. Is there enough flexibility to cope with economic change?
3. Would joining the EMU create an environment that would encourage firms to invest in the United Kingdom?
4. Would joining the EMU have a positive impact on the competitiveness of the UK's financial services industry?
5. Would joining the EMU be good for promoting stability and growth in employment?

The United Kingdom is a very political country where government officials are highly concerned with voter approval. If voters do not support euro entry, the likelihood of EMU entry would decline. The following are some of the arguments for and against adopting the euro:

Arguments in Favor of Adopting the Euro

- There would be reduced exchange rate uncertainty for UK businesses and lower exchange rate transaction costs or risks.

- The prospect of sustained low inflation under the governance of the European Central Bank should reduce long-term interest rates and stimulate sustained economic growth.

- Single currency promotes price transparency.

- The integration of national financial markets of the EU will lead to higher efficiency in the allocation of capital in Europe.

- The euro is the second most important reserve currency after the USD.

- With the United Kingdom joining the euro, the political clout of the EMU would increase dramatically.

Arguments against Adopting the Euro

- Currency unions have collapsed in the past.

- Economic or political instabilities of one country would impact the Euro, which would have exchange rate ramifications for otherwise healthy countries.

- Strict EMU criteria outlined by the Stability and Growth Pact.

- Entry would mean a permanent transfer of domestic monetary authority to the European Central Bank.

- Joining a currency union with no monetary flexibility would require the United Kingdom to have more flexibility in the labor and housing markets.

- There are fears about which countries might dominate the ECB.

- Adjusting to new currency will require large transaction costs.

◼ Monetary and Fiscal Policy Makers— Bank of England

For the United Kingdom, the Bank of England (BoE) controls monetary policy, and the Monetary Policy Committee (MPC) is a nine-member committee responsible for setting interest rate policy in the United Kingdom. It consists of a governor, two deputy governors, two executive directors of the central bank, and four outside experts. The committee was granted operational independence in 1997, which means they won't be influenced by the governing party. Despite this independence, monetary policies have centered on achieving an inflation target dictated by the Chancellor of the Treasury. Currently, this target is RPIX (Retail Price Index) inflation of 2.5%. The central bank has the power to change interest rates to levels that will allow them to meet this target. The MPC holds monthly meetings, which are closely followed for announcements on changes in monetary policy, including changes in the interest rate (bank repo rate). When no changes are made, no details are provided. In this case, the rate decision is generally a nonevent for the currency, with traders shifting their focus to the minutes released two weeks later.

The MPC publishes statements after every meeting, along with a quarterly *Inflation Report* that details the MPC's two-year forecast for growth and inflation along with justification for policy movements. In addition, another publication, the *Quarterly Bulletin,* provides information on past monetary policy movements and analysis of the international economic environment and its impacts on the UK economy. All of these reports can provide guidance of future policy changes. The main policy tools used by the MPC and BoE are the following.

Bank Repo Rate

This is the key rate used in monetary policy to meet the Treasury's inflation target. This rate is set for the Bank's own operations in the market, such as its short-term lending activities. Changes to this rate affect the rates set by the commercial banks for their savers and borrowers. In turn, this rate will affect spending and output in the economy, and eventually costs and prices. An increase in this rate would imply an attempt to curb inflation and slow growth, while a decrease in this rate would be aimed at stimulating growth and expansion.

Open Market Operations

The goal of open market operations is to implement changes in the bank repo rate, while assuring adequate liquidity in the market and continued stability in the banking system. This is reflective of the three main objectives of the BoE: maintaining the integrity and value of the currency, maintaining the stability of the financial system, and seeking to ensure the effectiveness of the United Kingdom's financial services. To ensure liquidity, the Bank conducts daily open market operations to buy or sell short-term government fixed-income instruments. If this is not sufficient to meet liquidity needs, the Bank would also conduct additional overnight operations.

Important Characteristics of the British Pound

- *GBPUSD is very liquid.* The GBPUSD is one of the most liquid currencies in the world, with 6% of all currency trading involving the British pound as either the base or counter currency. It is also one of the three most liquid currencies alongside EURUSD and USDJPY. One of the reasons for the currency's liquidity is the country's highly developed capital markets. Many foreign investors seeking opportunities other than the United States have sent their funds to the United Kingdom for investment. In order to create these transactions, foreigners will need to sell their local currency and buy British pounds.

■ *GBP has three names.* The UK's currency has three names: the British pound, sterling, and cable. All of these are used interchangeably.

■ *GBP is laden with speculators.* At the time of publication, the British pound has one of the highest interest rates among the developed nations. Although Australia and New Zealand have higher interest rates, their financial markets are not as developed as that of the United Kingdom. As a result, many investors who already have positions or are interested in initiating new carry trades positions frequently use the GBP as the lending currency and will go long the pound against currencies such as the U.S. dollar, Japanese yen, and Swiss franc. A carry trade involves buying or lending a currency with a higher interest and selling or borrowing a currency with a lower interest rate. In recent years, carry trades have increased in popularity, which helped spur demand for the British pound. However, should the interest rate yield differential between the pound and other currencies narrow, an exodus of carry traders will increase volatility in the British pound.

■ *Interest rate differentials between Gilts and foreign bonds are closely followed.* Interest rate differentials between UK Gilts—U.S. Treasuries and UK Gilts and German Bunds are widely watched by FX market participants. Gilts versus Treasuries can be a barometer of GBPUSD flows, while Gilts versus Bunds can be used as a barometer for EURGBP flows. More specifically, these interest rate differentials indicate how much premium yield UK fixed-income assets are offering over U.S. and European (German Bunds are usually used as a barometer for European yield) fixed-income assets, or vice versa. This differential provides traders with indications of potential capital flow or currency movements, as global investors are always shifting their capital in search of the assets with the highest yields. The United Kingdom can provide these yields with the safety of having the same credit stability as the United States.

■ *Euro sterling futures can give indications for interest rate movements.* Since the UK interest rate or bank repo rate is the primary tool used in monetary policy, it is important to keep abreast of potential changes to the interest rate. Comments from government officials is one way to gauge biases for potential rate changes, but the Bank of England is one of the only central banks that requires members of the Monetary Policy Committee to publish their specific voting records. This personal accountability indicates that comments by individual committee members represent their own opinions and not that of the BoE. Therefore, it is necessary to look for other indication of potential BoE rate movements. Three-month euro sterling futures reflect market expectations on euro sterling

FIGURE 28.1 GBPUSD 10-Year Chart

Source: eSignal

interest rates three months into the future. These contracts are also useful in predicting UK interest rate changes, which will ultimately affect the fluctuations of the GBPUSD. Figure 28.1 illustrates 10 year performance of GBP-USD.

- *Comments on euro by UK politicians will impact the euro.* Any speeches, remarks (especially from the Prime Minister or Treasury Chancellor), or polls in regards to the euro will impact currency trade. Indication of adoption of the euro tends to put downward pressure on GBP, while further opposition to euro entry will typically boost the GBP. Reason being that in order for the GBP to come in line with the euro, interest rates would have to decline and monetary policy would have to be subjected to a foreign entity. A decrease in the interest rate would induce carry trade investors to close their positions or sell pounds. The GBPUSD would also decline because of the uncertainties involved with Euro adoption. The UK economy is performing very well under the direction of its current monetary authority. The EMU is currently encountering many difficulties with member countries breaching EMU criteria. With one monetary authority dictating 19 countries (plus UK would be 20), the EMU has yet to prove that they have developed a monetary policy suitable for all member states.

- *GBP has positive correlation with energy prices.* The UK houses some of the largest energy companies in the world, including British Petroleum. Energy production represents 10% of GDP. As a result, the British pound tends to have a positive correlation with energy prices. Specifically, since many members of the EU import oil from the United Kingdom, as oil prices increase, they will, in turn, have to buy more pounds to fund their energy purchases. In addition, rises in the price of oil will also benefit the earnings of the nations' energy exporters.

- *GBP crosses*. Although the GBP/USD is a more liquid currency than EURGBP, EURGBP is typically the leading gauge for GBP strength. The GBPUSD currency pair tends to be more sensitive to U.S. developments, while EURGBP is a more pure fundamental pound trade since Europe is Britain's primary trade and investment partner. However, both currencies are naturally interdependent, which means movements in the EURGBP can affect movements in the GBPUSD. The reverse is also true—that is, movements in GBPUSD will also affect trading in EURGBP. Therefore, it is important for pound traders to be consciously aware of the trading behavior of both currency pairs. The EURGBP rate should be exactly equal to the EURUSD divided by the GBPUSD rate. Small differences in these rates are often exploited by market participants and quickly eliminated.

Important Economic Indicators for the United Kingdom

All of the following indicators are important for the United Kingdom. However, since the United Kingdom is primarily a service-oriented economy, it is particularly important to pay attention to service sector data.

PMIs

Every month, Markit Economics releases the PMI indices for the manufacturing, service, and construction sectors. These numbers are extremely market moving because they provide the most up-to-date information on how each of the economies is performing in the current month and not how the economies performed the previous month, like many other reports. However since the reports are for the current period, they are usually subject to revisions, so the euro will move on the preliminary and secondary reports. A reading above 50 represents expansion, and a reading below 50 represents contraction. For the United Kingdom, the PMI services index is the most important, along with the composite index, which aggregates how the manufacturing and service sector are performing.

Employment Situation

The employment report is a monthly survey of the labor market conducted by the Office of National Statistics. The objectives of the survey are to divide the working-age population into three separate classifications (employed, unemployed, and not in the labor force), and to provide descriptive and explanatory data on each of these categories. Data from the survey provide market participants with information on major labor market trends such as shifts in employment across industrial sectors, hours worked, labor force participation, and unemployment rates. The timeliness of the survey makes it a closely watched statistic by the currency market as it is a good barometer of the strength of the UK economy and an important input into monetary policy.

Retail Sales

The key to growth is consumer spending, and for this reason, the retail sales report is also extremely market moving. The Retail Sales Index measures the total goods sold by a sampling of retail stores over the course of a month. This index is used as a gauge of consumer consumption and consumer confidence. While retail sales can be quite volatile due to seasonality, it is one of the most important indicators on the health of the economy, along with a key input for GDP.

Consumer or Retail Price Index

CPI or RPI is a measure of the change in prices of a basket of consumer goods. The markets however focus on the underlying RPI or RPI-X, which excludes mortgage interest payments. The RPI-X is closely watched as the treasury sets inflation targets for the BoE, currently defined as 2.5% annual growth in RPI-X.

GDP

GDP is a quarterly report conducted by the Bureau of Statistics. GDP is a measure of the total production and consumption of goods and services in the UK. GDP is measured by adding expenditures by households, businesses, government, and net foreign purchases. The GDP price deflator is used to convert output measured at current prices into constant-dollar GDP. The data are used to gauge where in the business cycle the United Kingdom finds itself. Fast growth often is perceived as inflationary, while low (or negative) growth indicates a recessionary or weak growth.

Industrial Production

The industrial production (IP) index measures the change in output in the United Kingdom of manufacturing; mining and quarrying; and electricity, gas, and water supply. Output refers to the physical quantity of items produced, unlike sales value, which combines quantity and price. The index covers the production of goods and power for domestic sales in the United Kingdom and for export. Because IP is responsible for close to a quarter of gross domestic product, IP is widely watched as it can provide good insight into the current state of the economy.

UK Housing Starts

Housing starts measures the number of residential building construction projects that have begun during any particular month. This is important for the United Kingdom as the housing market is the primary industry that sustains the economy.

CHAPTER 29

Currency Profile: Swiss Franc (CHF)

■ Broad Economic Overview

Switzerland is the twentieth largest economy in the world, with a GDP valued at over US$685 billion as of 2014. Although the economy is relatively small, it is one of the wealthiest in the world on a GDP per capita basis. The country is prosperous and technologically advanced with economic and political stability that rivals many larger economies. The country's prosperity stems primarily from technological expertise in manufacturing, tourism, and banking. More specifically, Switzerland is known for their chemicals and pharmaceuticals industries, machinery, precision instruments, watches, and a financial system historically known for protecting the confidentiality of its investors. This coupled with the country's lengthy history of political neutrality earned Switzerland the Swiss franc safe haven status and as a direct result of that, it is the one world's most popular destinations for offshore capital. Even when the central bank introduced a temporary 1.20 EURCHF peg and lowered interest rates to negative levels, Switzerland still managed to attract safe haven flows.

It is estimated that Switzerland holds over US$2 trillion in offshore assets as of 2014 and attracts over 35% of the world's private wealth management business. A large and highly advanced banking and insurance industry has developed to support this demand, and the sector employs over 50% of the population and comprises over 70% of total GDP. Since Switzerland's financial industry thrives on its safe haven status and renowned confidentiality, capital flows tend to drive the economy during times of global risk aversion, while trade flows drive the economy in a risk-seeking environment. Trade flows are extremely important, with nearly two thirds of all trade conducted with Europe. With this in mind, Switzerland's most important trading partners are the following:

Leading Export Markets

1. Germany
2. India
3. United States
4. Hong Kong
5. France

Leading Import Sources

1. Germany
2. Italy
3. United States
4. France
5. China

Traditionally, Switzerland has a strong trade and current account surplus that lends support to the currency. Most of the surplus can be attributed to the large amount of foreign direct investment into the country, in seek of safety of capital, despite the low to negative yields offered by Switzerland.

◼ Monetary and Fiscal Policy Makers— Swiss National Bank

Monetary policy in Switzerland is determined by the Swiss National Bank (SNB). They are a completely independent authority with a three-person committee responsible for determining monetary policy. This committee consists of a chairman, a vice chairman, and one other (member) who constitute the Governing Board of the SNB. Due to the small size of the committee, all decisions are based on a consensus vote. The Board reviews monetary policy at least once a quarter, but decisions on monetary policy can be made and announced at any point in time. Unlike most other central banks, the SNB does not set one official interest rate target, but instead sets a target range for their three-month Swiss Libor rate.

Central Bank's Goals

In December of 1999, the SNB shifted from focusing on monetary targets (M3) to an inflation target of less than 2% inflation per year. This measure is taken based on the national consumer price index. Monetary targets still remain important indicators and are closely watched by the central bank, because they provide information on the long-term inflation. This new inflation focus also increases the central bank's transparency. In their mandate, they have clearly stated, "Should inflation exceed 2% in the medium term, the National Bank will tend to tighten its monetary stance." If there is danger of deflation, the National Bank would loosen monetary policy. The SNB also closely monitors exchange rates, as excessive strength in the Swiss franc can cause inflationary conditions. This is especially true in environments of global risk aversion, as capital flows into Switzerland increases significantly during those times. As a result, the SNB typically favors a weak franc, and is not hesitant to use intervention as liquidity tool. SNB officials intervene in the franc using a variety of methods including verbal remarks on liquidity, money supply, and the currency.

Their Tools

The most commonly used tools by the SNB to implement monetary policy include the following.

Target Interest Rate Range

Traditionally, the SNB implements monetary policy by setting a target range for their three-month interest rate known as the Swiss Franc Libor rate. According to the SNB, "The Libor is a reference interest rate in the interbank market for unsecured loans." It is a trimmed mean of the rates charged by 12 leading banks and is published daily by the British Bankers' Association. The National Bank publishes its target range regularly. As a rule, this range extends over 1 percentage point, and the SNB generally aims to keep the Libor in the middle of the range. The SNB undertakes quarterly economic and monetary assessments at which it reviews its monetary policy. If circumstances so require, it will also adjust the Libor target range in between these quarterly assessments. It sets out the reasons for its decisions in press releases.

Open Market Operations

Repo transactions are the SNB's major monetary policy instrument. A repo transaction involves a cash taker (borrower) selling securities to a cash provider (lender), while agreeing to repurchase the securities of the same type and quantity at a later date. This structure is similar to a secured loan, whereby the cash taker must pay the cash provider interest. These repo transactions tend to have very short maturities ranging from one day to a few weeks. The SNB uses these repo transactions to manipulate undesirable moves in the three-month Libor rate. To prevent increases in the three-month Libor rate above the SNB's target, the bank would supply the commercial banks with additional liquidity through repo transactions at lower repo rates, and in essence create additional liquidity. Conversely, the SNB can reduce liquidity or induce increases in the three-month Libor rate by increasing repo rates.

In addition to the quarterly monetary policy decision, the SNB publishes a *Quarterly Bulletin* with a detailed assessment of the current state of the economy and a review of monetary policy. A *Monthly Bulletin* is also published containing a short review of economic developments. These reports are important to watch, as they may contain information on changes in the SNB's assessment of economy and guidance on monetary policy.

1.20 EUR/CHF Peg Implementation and Abandonment

Few would have expected that one of the seminal developments in the forex market was the Swiss National Bank's decision to implement and later abandon its 1.20 EURCHF peg. This decision transformed the foreign exchange industry, bankrupted many brokers, and led to tighter regulations across the globe. Faced with a high level of uncertainty in the financial markets, an overvalued currency and deflation risks in 2011, the SNB introduced a minimum exchange rate of CHF 1.20 per euro. At the time, it pledged to sell francs in an unlimited quantity to maintain the peg. The goal was to stabilize the Swiss economy by capping the gain in the franc. However, in January 2015, the prospect of quantitative easing from the European Central Bank pushed the SNB to abandon the peg. It also accumulated significant foreign exchange reserves that irritated critics, but more importantly, the franc became less overvalued through the years, giving the SNB fewer reasons to maintain the peg. SNB's decision was a complete surprise, and caused a 30% drop in EURCHF in a single day. Many foreign exchange brokers were unprepared for the move and experienced massive losses as a result.

◼ Important Characteristics of the Swiss Franc

- *Safe haven status.* This is perhaps the most unique characteristic of the Swiss franc. Switzerland's safe haven status is continually stressed because this and the secrecy of the banking system are the key advantages of Switzerland. The Swiss franc moves primarily on external events rather than domestic economic conditions. That is, as mentioned earlier, due to its political neutrality, the franc is considered the world's premier safe haven currency. Therefore, in times of global instability and/or uncertainty, investors tend to be more concerned with capital retention than appreciation. At such times, funds will flow into Switzerland, which would cause the Swiss franc to appreciate regardless of whether growth conditions are favorable.

- *Swiss franc is closely correlated with gold.* Switzerland is the world's third largest official holder of gold. In the past, a Swiss constitutional mandate required the currency to be backed 40% with gold reserves. The mandate is now removed but the positive correlation between the Swiss franc and gold remains because the relationship has been engrained into the minds of forex traders; therefore, both gold and the Swiss franc are perceived as safe haven instruments. Before the SNB abandoned the EURCHF 1.20, Swiss franc had an 80% positive correlation with gold. These days, the correlation is still there but in a smaller magnitude. Generally speaking, if the price of gold appreciates, the Swiss franc has a high likelihood of rising in value. In addition, since gold is also viewed as the ultimate safe haven form of money, both gold and the Swiss franc benefit during periods of global economic and geopolitical uncertainty.

- *Carry trades effects.* With one of the lowest interest rates in the industrialized world, over the past few years, the Swiss franc has become one of the most popular funding currencies for carry trades. As mentioned in this book, the popularity of carry trades has increased significantly over the past two decades, as investors are actively seeking high yield. A carry trade involves buying or lending a currency with a high interest rate and selling or borrowing a currency with a low interest rate. With CHF having one of the lowest interest rates of all industrialized countries, it is one of the primary currencies sold or borrowed in carry trades. This results in the need to sell CHF against a higher yielding currency. Carry trades are typically done in cross-currencies such as GBPCHF or AUDCHF, but these trades can impact both EURCHF and USDCHF. The unwinding of carry trades involves the need for investors to buy back the Swiss franc.

- *Interest rate differentials between euro Swiss futures and foreign interest rate futures are closely followed.* One of the favorite indicators of professional Swiss franc traders is the interest rate differential between three-month euro Swiss futures and eurodollar futures. These differentials can provide guidance on potential money flows as they indicate how much premium yield U.S. fixed-income assets are offering over Swiss fixed-income assets, or vice versa. This differential provides traders with indications of potential currency movements, as investors are always looking for assets with the highest yields. This is particularly important to carry traders who enter and exit their positions based on the positive interest rate differentials between global fixed-income assets.

- *Potential changes in banking regulations.* Over the past few years members of the European Union have been exerting significant pressure on Switzerland to relax the confidentiality of their banking system and to increase transparency of their customers' accounts. The European Union is pressing this issue because of its active measures to persecute EU tax evaders. This should be a concern for many years to come. However, this is a difficult decision for Switzerland to make because the confidentiality of their customers' accounts represents the core strength of their banking system. The EU has threatened to impose severe sanctions on Switzerland if they do not comply with their proposed measures. Both countries are currently working to negotiate an equitable resolution. Any news or talk of changing banking regulations will impact both Switzerland's economy and the Swiss franc.

- *Mergers and acquisition activity.* Switzerland's primary industry is banking and finance. In this industry, merger and acquisition activities (M&A) are very common, especially as consolidation continues in the overall industry. As a result, these M&A activities can have significant impact on the Swiss franc. If foreign firms purchase Swiss banks or insurance companies, they will need to buy Swiss francs and in turn, sell their local currency. If Swiss banks purchase foreign firms, they would need to sell Swiss francs and buy the foreign currency. Either way, it is important for Swiss franc traders to frequently watch for notices on M&A activity involving Swiss firms.

- *Trading behavior, cross currency characteristics.* The EURCHF is the most commonly traded currency for traders who want to participate in CHF movements. USDCHF is less frequently traded because of its greater illiquidity and volatility. However, day traders may tend to favor USDCHF over EURCHF because of its volatile movements. In actuality, the USDCHF is a synthetic currency derived from EURUSD and EURCHF because more transactions are done between the euro and Swiss franc. Market makers or professional traders tend to use those pairs as leading indicators for trading USDCHF or to price the current USDCHF level when the currency pair is illiquid. Theoretically, the USDCHF rate should be exactly equal to the EURCHF rate divided by EURUSD. Only during times of unusual circumstances, such as the Iraq War, September 11, or the EURCHF peg, will USDCHF develop a market of its own. Any small differences in these rates are quickly exploited by market participants. Figure 29.1 highlights the 10 year performance of EUR-CHF.

■ Important Economic Indicators for Switzerland

Economic data from Switzerland tends to have limited impact on the currency, but these are the most important pieces of Swiss data.

KoF Leading Indicators

The KoF leading indicators report is released by the Swiss Institute for Business Cycle Research. This index is generally used to gauge the future health of the Swiss economy. It contains six components: (1) change in manufacturers' orders; (2) the expected purchase plans of manufacturers over the next three months; (3) the judgment of stocks in wholesale business; (4) consumer perception of their financial conditions; (5) backlog in the construction sector; and (6) orders backlog for manufacturers.

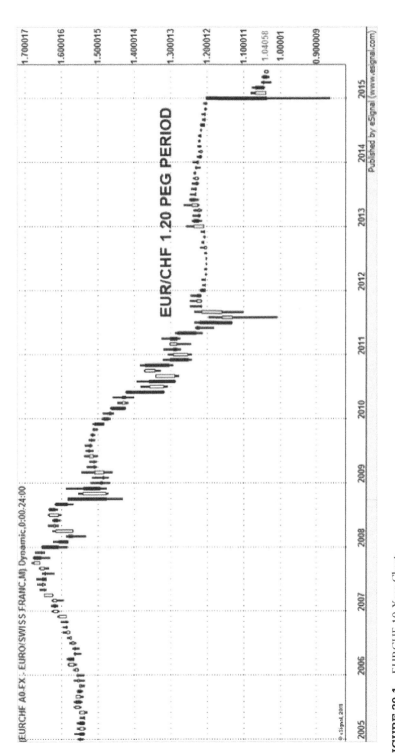

FIGURE 29.1 EURCHF 10-Year Chart

Source: eSignal

CURRENCY PROFILE: SWISS FRANC (CHF)

Consumer Price Index

The Consumer Price Index is calculated monthly, on the basis of retail prices paid in Switzerland. In accordance with prevalent international practice, the commodities covered are distinguished according to the consumption concept, which includes in the calculation of the CPI of those goods and services that are part of the private consumption aggregate according to the National Accounts. The basket of goods does not include *transfer expenditure* such as direct taxation, social insurance contributions, and health insurance premiums. The index is a key measure of inflation.

Gross Domestic Product

GDP is a measure of the total production and consumption of goods and services in the Switzerland. GDP is measured by adding expenditures by households, businesses, government, and net foreign purchases. The GDP price deflator is used to convert output measured at current prices into constant-dollar GDP. The data are used to gauge where in the business cycle Switzerland finds itself. Fast growth often is perceived as inflationary, while low (or negative) growth indicates a recessionary or weak growth period.

Balance of Payments

Balance of payments is the collective term for the accounts of Swiss transactions with the rest of the world. The current account is the balance of trade plus services portion. BoP is an important indicator for Swiss traders, as Switzerland has always kept a strong current account balance. Any changes to the current account, positive or negative, could see substantial flows.

Production Index (Industrial Production)

The production index is a quarterly measure of the change in the volume of industrial production (or physical output by producers).

Retail Sales

Switzerland's retail sales report is released on a monthly basis 40 days after the reference month. The report is an important indicator of consumer spending habits and is not seasonally adjusted.

CHAPTER 30

Currency Profile: Japanese Yen (JPY)

Economic Overview

Japan is the third largest economy in the world with GDP valued at over US$4.6 trillion in 2014 (behind the United States and China). If we count the European Union as a whole, it would be considered the fourth largest economy. Japan is one of the world's largest exporters and is responsible for over US$690 billion in exports per year. Manufacturing and exports of products such as electronics and cars are the signature drivers of the economy, accounting for nearly 17% of GDP. As a result, Japanese growth is extremely sensitive to the value of the currency. For many years, Japan has maintained a trade surplus, but the earthquake followed by tsunami in 2011 turned the country into a net oil importer and created a long period of trade imbalances, where oil imports exceeded exports in value. This began to change in early 2015, when a weakening yen and falling oil prices helped to turn around trade activity, returning Japan to a surplus nation. Having a trade surplus means that there will be inherent demand for the Japanese yen even when interest rates are low and there are structural deficiencies. Japan's most important trade partners are the United States and China:

Leading Export Markets

1. China
2. United States
3. South Korea
4. Taiwan
5. Hong Kong

Leading Import Sources:

1. China
2. United States
3. South Korea
4. Australia
5. Saudi Arabia

■ Abenomics

In the 1980s, Japan's capital market was one of the most attractive markets for international investors seeking investment opportunities in Asia. Japan had the most developed capital markets in the region, and its banking system was considered to be the one of the strongest in the world. At the time, the country was experiencing above-trend economic growth and near zero inflation. This resulted in rapid growth expectations, boosted asset prices, and rapid credit expansion, leading to the development of an asset bubble. Between 1990 and 1997, the asset bubble collapsed, inducing a US$10 trillion decline in asset prices, with the fall in real estate values accounting for nearly 65% of the total decline, nearly two years of national output. This fall in asset prices sparked the banking crisis in Japan. It began in the early 1990s and developed into a full-blown systemic crisis in 1997 following the failure of a number of high-profile financial institutions. Many of these banks and financial institutions extended loans to builders and real estate developers at the height of the asset bubble in the 1980s, with land as collateral. A number of these developers defaulted after the asset bubble collapse, leaving the country's banks saddled with bad debt and collateral worth sometimes 60% to 80% less than when the loans were taken out. Due to the large size of these banking institutions and their role in corporate funding, the crisis had profound effects on Japan and the global economy. Enormous bad debts, falling stock prices, and a collapsing real estate sector crippled Japan's economy for more than two decades.

It was not until the rollout of Abenomics that the economy began to turn around. When Shinzo Abe became prime minister for the second time in 2012, he rolled out a three-pronged plan to stimulate growth and pull the economy out of stagnation through monetary policy, fiscal policy, and economic growth strategies. This was known as *Abenomics*. In the first few weeks of the program, Abe announced a massive stimulus package that involved significant government spending and a strong dose of quantitative easing. The effects were almost immediate, with the Japanese yen falling significantly across the board. Not soon after, the unemployment rate started to fall and growth slowly returned.

Monetary and Fiscal Policy Makers

Monetary policy in Japan is determined by the Bank of Japan (BoJ). In 1998, the Japanese government passed laws giving the BoJ operational independence from the Ministry of Finance (MoF) and complete control over monetary policy. However, despite the government's attempts to decentralize decision making, the MoF still remains in charge of foreign exchange policy. The BoJ is responsible for executing all official Japanese foreign exchange transactions at the direction of the MoF. The Bank of Japan's Policy Board consists of the BoJ governor, two deputy governors, and six other members. Monetary policy meetings are held twice a month, with briefings and press releases provided immediately. The BoJ also publishes a *Monthly Report* issued by the Policy Board, and a *Monthly Economic Report*. These reports are important to watch for changes in BoJ sentiment and signals of new monetary or fiscal policy measures, as the government is constantly trying to develop fresh initiatives to stimulate growth.

The MoF and the BoJ are very important institutions, and they both can influence currency movements. Since the MoF is the director of foreign exchange interventions, it is important to watch and keep abreast of the comments made from MoF officials. Being an export driven economy, the government tends to favor a weaker currency. So if the Japanese yen appreciates significantly or too rapidly against the dollar, members of the BoJ and MoF will become increasingly vocal about their concerns or disapproval in regards to its current level or recent movements. These comments can affect how the yen moves, but if government officials flood the market with comments and there is no follow-up action, the market would start to become immune to these concerns. However, the MoF and BoJ have a lengthy history of interventions in the currency markets to manipulate the value of the yen value in Japan's best interests, so their comments cannot be completely ignored.

The most popular tool that the BoJ uses to control monetary policy is open market operations.

Open Market Operations

These activities are focused on controlling the uncollateralized overnight call rate. The Bank of Japan has maintained a zero interest rate policy (ZIRP) for some time now, which means that the Bank of Japan cannot lower this rate further to stimulate growth, consumption, or liquidity. Therefore, in order to maintain zero interest rates, the BoJ has to manipulate liquidity through open market operations, targeting zero interest on the overnight call rate. It manipulates liquidity by the outright buying or selling of bills, repos, or Japanese government bonds. A repo transaction involves a cash taker (borrower) selling securities to a cash provider (lender), while agreeing to repurchase the securities of the same type and quantity at a later date. This structure is similar to a secured loan, whereby the cash taker must pay the cash provider interest. These repo transactions tend to have very short maturities, ranging from one day to a few weeks.

Important Characteristics of the JPY

- *Proxy for Asian strength / weakness.* Japan tends to be seen as a proxy for broad Asian strength because the country has the largest GDP in Asia outside of China. With the most developed capital markets, Japan was once the primary destination for all investors who wanted access into the region. Japan also conducts a significant amount of trade with its Asian partners. As a result, economic problems or political instability in Japan tend to spill over into the other Asian countries. However, this spillover is not one-sided. Economic or political problems in other Asian economies, particularly China, can also have dramatic impacts on the Japanese economy and in turn movements in the Japanese yen. For example, North Korean political instability poses a great risk to Japan and the Japanese yen due to the country's geographic proximity.

- *Bank of Japan intervention practices.* The BoJ and MoF are active participants in the foreign exchange markets. That is, they have a lengthy history of entering the FX markets if they are dissatisfied with the value of the Japanese yen. While they have not intervened since 2011, they won't be reluctant to do so if the currency strengthens significantly. As Japan is a very political economy, with close ties between government officials and principals of large private institutions, the MoF can have a very narrow segment in mind when it decides to intervene in the currency. Since the BoJ is such an active participant, it is very in tune with the market movements and its participants. Periodically, the BoJ receives information on large hedge fund positions from banks and likes to intervene when speculators are on the other side of the market, allowing them to get the most "bang for the bucks." The MoF and BoJ always considers three main factors before intervention:

  1. *Amount of appreciation / depreciation in JPY*—Intervention has historically occurred when the yen moves by 7 or more yen in less than 6 weeks. Using the USDJPY as a barometer, 7 yen would be equivalent to 700 pips, which would represent a move from 120.00 to 127.00.
  2. *Current USDJPY rate*—Historically, only 11% of all BoJ interventions that were conducted to counter a strong JPY occurred above the 115 level.
  3. *Speculative positions*—In order to maximize the impact of intervention, the BoJ and MoF prefer to intervene when market participants hold massive positions in the opposing direction because the flow of stops will exacerbate

the reversal in the currency pair. The CFTC provides a weekly report on existing speculative positions that can be found at www.cftc.gov.

- *JPY movements are sensitive to time.* The Japanese yen can be particularly active towards the end of Japan's fiscal year (March 31), as exporters repatriate their dollar denominated assets to window dress their balance sheets. This is particularly important for Japanese banks because they need to rebuild their balance sheets to meet FSA guidelines that require the banks to mark to market their security holdings. In anticipation of the need for repatriation-related purchases, Japanese yen speculators frequently bid the yen higher in attempt to take advantage of this increased inflow. As a result, following fiscal year end, the Japanese yen tends to have a bias toward depreciation as speculators close their positions.

  Aside from the fiscal year end, time is also a factor on a day-to-day basis. Unlike traders in London or New York who typically have lunch at their trading desk, Japanese traders tend to take hour-long lunches, leaving only a junior trader in the office. On occasion, this can translate into additional volatility in the yen during this period as the market becomes illiquid. In addition to this period, the JPY tends to move fairly orderly during Japanese and London hours, unless there are official comments or major surprises in economic data. During U.S. hours, however, the JPY tends to have higher volatility, as U.S. traders are actively engaging in dollar and yen positions.

- *Stocks and bonds have a positive correlation with USDJPY.* The Nikkei has a positive correlation with USDJPY, which means that when the currency pair appreciating, equities are generally on the rise as well. For Japan, the currency typically leads equities because a weak yen is positive for the economy, but there can be times when equities lead currencies. The spread between U.S. 10-year Treasury and JGB yields is also very important for the currency. Typically, when the yield spread is on the rise, we see USDJPY move higher, and when the yield spread declines, it creates pressure on USDJPY. Figure 30.1 highlights the 10 year performance of USDJPY.

- *Carry trade effects.* The popularity of carry trades has increased in recent years, as investors are actively seeking high-yielding assets. With the Japanese yen having the lowest interest rate of all industrialized countries, it is the primary currency sold or borrowed in carry trades. The most popular carry trade currencies included GBPJPY, AUDJPY, NZDJPY, and even USDJPY. Carry traders would go short the Japanese yen against the higher yielding currencies. Unwinding of carry trades as result of spread narrowing is typically beneficial for the Japanese yen, as the reversal process involves purchasing the yen and buying back other currencies. Since there is so much demand to sell the yen for carry, in periods of risk aversion, these trades can be unwound quickly creating a significant rally in the currency.

■ Important Economic Indicators for Japan

Since Japan is a manufacturing-oriented economy, manufacturing data tend to have the most significant impact on the yen. However, on a monthly basis, unless there is a big surprise, Japanese data do not typically move the currency. The most influential event risk is always the monetary policy announcement and trade balance. Aside from that, these are the numbers to watch.

Tankan Survey

If there is one piece of Japanese data to follow, it should be the quarterly Tankan Report. The Tankan is an economic survey of Japanese enterprises published four times a year. The survey includes more than 9,000 enterprises, which are divided into four major groups: large, small, and medium-sized companies, as well as principal enterprises. The survey provides us with an overall impression of the business climate in Japan and is widely watched and anticipated by foreign exchange market participants.

Balance of Payments

The monthly balance of payments report provides investors with insight into Japan's international economic transactions that include goods, services, investment income, and capital flows. The current account side of BoJ can be used a good gauge of international trade. Figures are released on a monthly and semiannual basis.

Employment

Employment figures are reported on a monthly basis by the Management and Coordination Agency of Japan. The employment release measures the number of jobs and unemployment rate for the country as a whole. The data are obtained through a statistical survey of the current labor force. This release is a closely watched economic indicator because of its timeliness and its importance as a leading indicator of economic activity.

Industrial Production

The industrial production (IP) index measures trends in the output of Japanese manufacturing, mining, and utilities companies. *Output* refers to the total quantity of items produced. The index covers the production of goods for domestic sales in Japan and for export. It excludes production in the agriculture, construction, transportation, communication, trade, finance, and service industries; government output; and imports. The IP index is then developed by weighting each component according to its relative importance during this base period. Investors feel IP and

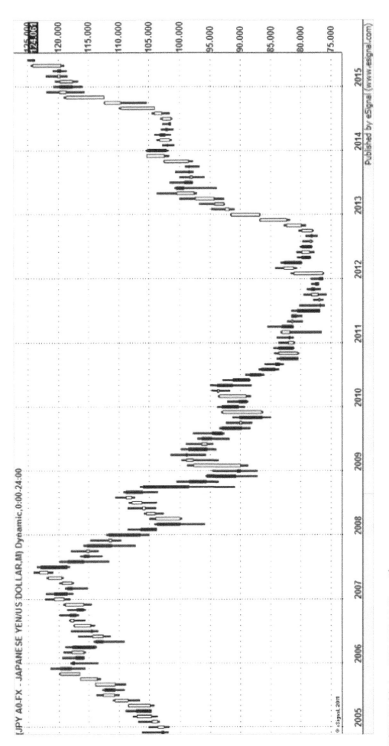

FIGURE 30.1 USDJPY 10-Year Chart

Source: eSignal

inventory accumulation have strong correlations with total output and can provide valuable insight into the current state of the economy.

GDP

Gross domestic product (GDP) is a broad measure of the total production and consumption of goods and services measured over quarterly and yearly periods in Japan. GDP is measured by adding total expenditures by households, businesses, government, and net foreign purchases. The GDP price deflator is used to convert output measured at current prices into constant-dollar GDP. Preliminary reports are the most significant for FX market participants.

CHAPTER 31

Currency Profile: Australian Dollar (AUD)

Broad Economic Overview

Australia is the twelfth largest country in the world, with a gross domestic product of approximately US$1.5 trillion. In Asia, it ranks as the third largest economy in the region. On a relative basis, the economy is very small, only one-tenth that of the United States and less than one-fifth the size of China. However on a per capita basis, Australia ranks right up there with many industrialized Western European countries. Australia has a service-oriented economy with close to 70% of GDP coming from industries such as finance, property, and business services. However, the country has a trade deficit, with manufacturing dominating the country's exporting activities. Rural and mineral exports account for over 60% of all manufacturing exports and 12% of GDP. The economy is therefore highly sensitive to changes in commodity prices. As a country heavily dependent on exports, the pace of growth of Australia's largest trade partners is extremely important because downturns or rapid growth abroad can impact import and export demand. Here's a breakdown of Australia's most important trading partners:

Largest Export Markets
1. China
2. Japan

3. South Korea
4. United States
5. New Zealand

Largest Import Sources

1. China
2. United States
3. Japan
4. Singapore
5. Germany

As you can see, Australia's number one trading partner is China. In fact, Chinese demand represents a third of the country's trade activity. In terms of products, the Chinese are major importers of Australian iron ore, coal, natural gas, and gold. Asia Pac is extremely important to Australia, as more than 70% of its exports are destined for countries within the region. This makes Australia's economy highly sensitive to the performance of countries in the Asian Pacific region. Hiccups in China's economy can have a significant impact on Australia, not only in terms of exporting activities but also on housing market activity. At the same time, growth in China is positive for Australia's economy. During the global financial crisis, exports to China helped shelter Australia from a major downturn. The relationship between China and Australia is known as Sino-Australian relations. China has recently taken steps to produce its own resources, and if this trend continues, it could dramatically change the landscape of Australia's economy.

■ Monetary and Fiscal Policy

The Reserve Bank of Australia (RBA) is the central bank of Australia. The monetary policy committee within the central bank consists of the governor (chairman), the deputy governor (vice chairman), secretary to the treasurer, and six independent members appointed by the government. Changes to monetary policy are made on consensus within the committee.

Central Bank's Goals

The RBA's charter states that the mandate of the Reserve Bank Board is to focus monetary and banking policy on ensuring:

1. The stability of the currency of Australia;
2. The maintenance of full employment in Australia; and
3. The economic prosperity and welfare of the people of Australia

In order to achieve these objectives, the government has set an informal consumer price inflation target of 2% to 3% per year. The RBA believes that the key to long-term sustainable growth in the economy is to control inflation, which would preserve the value of money. In addition, an inflation target provides a discipline for monetary policy making and guidelines for private-sector inflation expectations. This also increases the transparency of the banks' activities. Should inflation or inflation expectations exceed the 2% to 3% target, traders should know that it would raise red flags at the RBA and prompt the central bank to favor a tighter monetary policy or, in the other words, further rate hikes.

Monetary policy decisions involve setting the interest rate on overnight loans in the money market. Other interest rates in the economy are influenced by this interest rate to varying degrees, so that the behavior of borrowers and lenders in the financial markets is affected by monetary policy (though not only by monetary policy). Through these channels, monetary policy affects the economy in pursuit of the goals just outlined.

Cash Rate

The cash rate is the RBA's target rate for open market operations and is the rate charged on overnight loans between financial intermediaries. This means the cash rate should have a close relationship with the prevailing money market interest rates. Changes in monetary policy directly affect the interest rate structure of the financial system. They also affect sentiment in a currency. Figure 31.1 graphs the AUDUSD

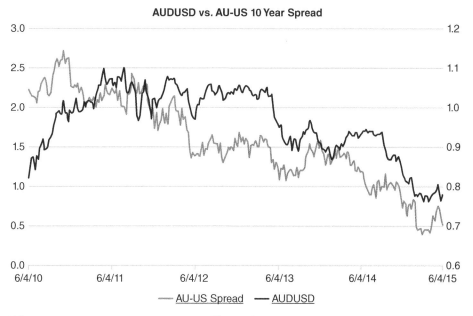

FIGURE 31.1 AUDUSD vs. 10-Year Yield Spread

against the interest rate differential between Australia and the United States between 2010 and 2015. There is clearly a positive correlation between the 10-year yield spread and the currency. Between June 2014 and June 2015, for example, the yield spread dropped from 1.5% to 0.5%, and this coincided with a drop in the AUDUSD from 95 to 76 cents.

Maintaining the Cash Rate: Open Market Operations

The focus of daily open market operations is to keep the cash rate close to the target, by managing money market liquidity provided to commercial banks. If the Reserve Bank wishes to decrease the cash rate, it would increase supply of short-dated repurchase agreements at a lower interest rate than the prevailing cash rate, which would in essence decrease the cash rate. If the Reserve Bank wishes to increase the cash rate, it would decrease supply of short-dated repurchase agreements, which would increase the cash rate. A repurchase agreement involves a cash taker (commercial bank) selling securities to a cash provider (RBA), while agreeing to repurchase the securities of the same type and quantity at a later date. This structure is similar to a secured loan, whereby the cash taker must pay the cash provider interest. These repo transactions tend to have very short maturities, ranging from one day to a few weeks.

Australia has had a floating exchange rate since 1983, and the Reserve Bank of Australia may undertake foreign exchange market operations when the market threatens to become excessively volatile or when the exchange rate is clearly inconsistent with underlying economic fundamentals. The RBA monitors a trade-weighted index (TWI), as well as the cross-rate with the U.S. dollar. Intervention operations are invariably aimed at stabilizing market conditions rather than meeting exchange rate targets.

Monetary Policy Meetings

The RBA meets every month (except for January), on the first Tuesday of each month, to discuss potential changes in monetary policy. Following each meeting, the RBA issues a press release outlining justifications for its monetary policy changes. If it leaves rates unchanged, no statement is published. The RBA also publishes a monthly *Reserve Bank Bulletin*. The May and November issues of the *Reserve Bank Bulletin* include the semiannual statement on the Conduct of Monetary Policy. The February, May, August, and November issues contain a Quarterly Report on the Economy and Financial Markets. It is important to read these bulletins for signals on potential monetary policy changes.

Important Characteristics of the Australian Dollar

■ *Commodity linked currency*. Historically, the Australian dollar has had a very strongly correlation (approximately 80%) with commodity prices and, more specifically, gold and iron ore prices. The correlation stems from the fact that Australia is the world's second largest gold producer and the world's largest producer of iron ore. Therefore, the price of iron ore and gold is extremely important to Australia's economy. However, unless there is a sharp movement in gold or iron ore prices, it generally takes time for the AUDUSD to adjust to changes in the price of commodities. Generally speaking, if commodity prices are strong, inflationary fears start to appear, and the RBA would be inclined to raise rates to curb inflation. However, this is a sensitive topic, as gold prices tend to increase in times of global economic or political uncertainty. If the RBA increases rates during those conditions, it leaves Australia more vulnerable to spillover effects.

■ *Carry trade effects*. Australia has one of highest interest rates among the developed countries. With a fairly liquid currency, the Australian dollar is one of the most popular currencies to use for carry trades. A carry trade involves buying or lending a currency with a high interest rate and selling or borrowing a currency with a low interest rate. The popularity of the carry trade has contributed to the 57% rise of the Australian dollar against the U.S. dollar between 2001 and 2005. While the carry trade suffered greatly in 2008, it came back strongly between 2009 and 2011. During this time, many foreign investors were looking for high yield when equity investments offered minimal returns. However, carry trades only last as long as the actual yield advantage remains. If global central banks increase their interest rates and the positive interest rate differential between Australia and other countries narrow, the AUDUSD could suffer from an exodus of carry traders.

■ *Drought effects*. Since the majority of Australia's exports are commodities, the country's GDP is highly sensitive to severe weather conditions that may damage the country's farming activities. For example, 2002 was a particularly difficult year for Australia, because the country was experiencing a severe drought. The drought took an extreme toll on Australia's farming activities, with dry conditions hampering the economy throughout the twenty-first century. This is important because agriculture accounts for 3% of the country's GDP. The RBA estimates that the "decline in farm production could directly reduce GDP growth by around 1 percentage point." Aside from exporting activities, a drought also has indirect effects on other aspects of Australia's economy. Industries that supply and service agriculture, such as the wholesale and transport sectors, as well as retail operations in rural farming areas, may also be negatively affected by a drought. However, it is also important to note that the Australian economy has a history of recovering strongly after a drought. The 1982–1983 drought first subtracted then subsequently added around 1% to 1 1/2% to GDP growth. The 1991–1995 drought reduced GDP by around 1/2 to 3/4 percentage points in 1991–1992 and 1994–1995, but the recovery boosted GDP by 3/4 percentage points.

■ *Interest rate differentials.* Interest rate differentials between the cash rates of Australia and the short-term interest rate yields of other industrialized countries should also be closely watched by Australian dollar traders. These differentials can be good indicators of potential money flows as they indicate how much premium yield Australian dollar short-term fixed-income assets are offering over foreign short-term fixed-income assets, or vice versa. This differential provides traders with indications of potential currency movements, as investors are always looking for assets with the highest yields. This is particularly important to carry traders who enter and exit their positions based on the positive interest rate differentials between global fixed-income assets.

■ Important Economic Indicators for Australia

GDP

GDP is a measure of the total production and consumption of goods and services in Australia. GDP is measured by adding expenditures by households, businesses, government, and net foreign purchases. The GDP price deflator is used to convert output measured at current prices into constant-dollar GDP. The data are used to gauge where in the business cycle Australia finds itself. Fast growth often is perceived as inflationary, while low (or negative) growth generally coincides with a weak growth period.

CPI

The Consumer Price Index (CPI) measures quarterly changes in the price of a basket of goods and services, which account for a high proportion of expenditure by the CPI population group (i.e., metropolitan households). This basket covers a wide range of goods and services, including food, housing, education, transportation, and health. This is an important indicator to watch, as it is a key input for monetary policy decisions.

Balance of Goods and Services

This number is a monthly measure of Australia's international trade in goods and services on a balance of payments basis. General merchandise imports and exports

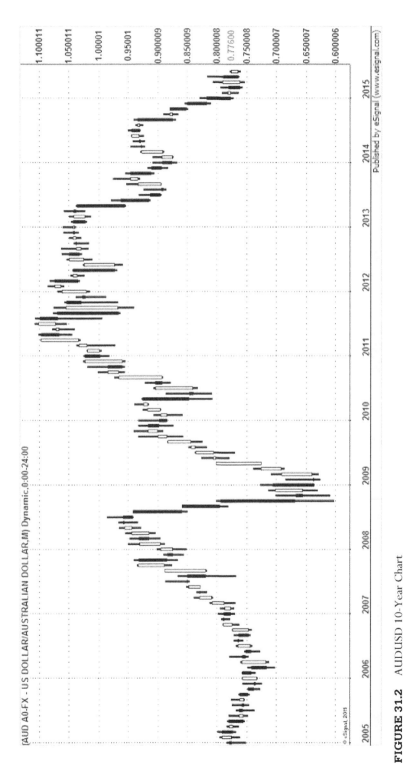

[AUD A0-FX - US DOLLAR/AUSTRALIAN DOLLAR,M) Dynamic,0:00-24:00

© eSignal 2011

Published by eSignal (www.esignal.com)

FIGURE 31.2 AUDUSD 10-Year Chart

Source: eSignal

are derived mainly from international trade statistics, which are based on Australian Customs Service records. The current account is the balance of trade plus services.

Private Consumption

This is a national accounts measure that reflects current expenditure by households and producers of private nonprofit services to households. It includes purchases of durable as well as nondurable goods. However, it excludes expenditure by persons on the purchase of dwellings and expenditure of a capital nature by unincorporated enterprises. This number is important to watch, as private consumption or consumer consumption is the foundation for resilience in the Australian economy.

Producer Price Index

The Producer Price Index (PPI) is a family of indexes that measures average changes in selling prices received by domestic producers for their output. The PPI tracks changes in prices for nearly every goods-producing industry in the domestic economy, including agriculture, electricity and natural gas, forestry, fisheries, manufacturing, and mining. Foreign exchange markets tend to focus on seasonally adjusted finished goods PPI and how the index has reacted on an m/m, q/q, h/h and y/y basis. Australia's PPI data are released on a quarterly basis.

Figure 31.2 illustrates the 10 year performance of AUDUSD.

CHAPTER 32

Currency Profile: New Zealand Dollar (NZD)

■ Broad Economic Overview

New Zealand is a very small economy with GDP valued at approximately US$183 billion in 2013. In fact, there are less people living in New Zealand than in New York City. It was once one of the most regulated countries within the OECD (Organization for Economic Co-operation and Development), but over the past two decades the country has been moving toward a more open, modern, and stable economy. With the passing of the Fiscal Responsibility Act of 1994, the country is shifting from an agricultural farming community to one that seeks to become a leading knowledge-based economy with high skills, high employment, and high value-added production. This act sets legal standards that hold the government formally responsible to the public for its fiscal performance. It also sets the framework for the country's macroeconomic policies. The following are the five principles outlined under the Fiscal Responsibility Act:

1. Debt must be reduced to "prudent" levels; by achieving surpluses on the operating budget every year until such a level is reached.
2. Debt must be reduced to "prudent" levels; and the government must ensure that expenditure is lower than revenue.

3. Sufficient levels of Crown net worth must be achieved and maintained to guard against adverse future events.
4. Reasonable taxation policies must be followed.
5. Fiscal risks facing the government must be prudently managed.

New Zealand also has highly developed manufacturing and services sectors, with the agricultural industry driving the bulk of the country's exports. The economy is strongly trade-oriented, with exports of goods and services representing approximately one third of GDP. Due to the small size of the economy and its significant trade activities, New Zealand is highly sensitive to global performance, especially of its key Asian trading partners, Australia, China, United States, and Japan. Together, Australia, China, and Japan represent 42% of New Zealand's trading activity. It is also extremely sensitive to exchange rate fluctuations, particularly against the Australian dollar. The following lists are a breakdown of the New Zealand's most important trading partners:

Leading Export Markets
1. Australia
2. China
3. European Union
4. United States
5. Japan

Leading Import Sources
1. European Union
2. China
3. Australia
4. United States
5. Japan

◼ Monetary and Fiscal Policy Makers— Reserve Bank of New Zealand

Monetary policy in New Zealand is determined by the Reserve Bank (RBNZ). The Monetary Policy Committee is an internal committee of bank executives who review monetary policy on a weekly basis. Meetings to decide on changes to monetary policy occur eight times a year, or approximately every six weeks. Unlike most other central banks, the decision for rate changes rests ultimately on the bank's governor. The current policy target agreements set by the minister and the governor focus on maintaining policy stability and avoiding unnecessary instability in output, interest rates, and the exchange rate. Price stability refers to maintaining the annual

CPI inflation at 1.5%. If the RBNZ does not meet this target, the government has the ability to dismiss the governor of the RBNZ. This is rarely done, but this serves as a strong incentive for the RBNZ to meets its inflation target. The most common tools used by the RBNZ to implement monetary policy changes are the following.

Official Cash Rate (OCR)

The Official Cash Rate is the rate set by the RBNZ to implement monetary policy. The Bank lends overnight cash at 25 basis points above the OCR rate and receives deposits or pays interest at 25 basis points below this rate. By controlling the cost of liquidity for commercial banks, the RBNZ can influence the interest rates offered to individuals and corporations. This effectively creates a 50 basis point corridor that bounds the interbank overnight rate. The idea is then that banks offering funds above the upper bound will attract few takers, because funds can be borrowed for a lower cost from the RBNZ. Also, banks offering rates below the lower bound will also attract few takers, because they are offering lower yields than the RBNZ. The official cash rate is reviewed and manipulated with the goal of maintaining economic stability.

Objectives for Fiscal Policy

Open market operations on the other hand are used to meet the cash target. The cash target is the targeted amount of reserves held by registered banks. The RBNZ prepares forecasts of daily fluctuations on the cash target and will then use these forecasts to determine the amount of funds to inject or withdraw in order to meet the cash target. The following government objectives provide a guideline for fiscal and monetary policy measures:

- *Expenses*: Expenses will average around 35% of GDP over the horizon used to calculate contributions toward future New Zealand Superannuation (NZS) costs. During the buildup of assets to meet future NZS costs, expenses plus contributions will be around 35% of GDP. In the longer term, expenses less withdrawals to meet NZS costs will be around 35% of GDP.

- *Revenue*: Raise sufficient revenue to meet the operating balance objective. A robust, broad-based tax system that raises revenue in a fair and efficient way.

- *Operating balance*: Operating surplus on average over the economic cycle sufficient to meet the requirements for contributions toward future NZS costs and ensure consistency with the debt objective.

- *Debt*: Gross debt below 30% of GDP on average over the economic cycle. Net debt, which excludes the assets to meet future NZS costs, below 20% of GDP on average over the economic cycle.

- *Net worth*: Increase net worth consistent with the operating balance objective. This will be achieved through a buildup of assets to meet future NZS costs.

Source: New Zealand Treasury

Important Characteristics of the New Zealand Dollar

Strong Correlation with AUD—Competition with Australia

Australia is New Zealand's largest trading partner. This coupled with their geographic proximity and New Zealand's high dependence on trade, creates strong ties between the economies of the two countries. When the Australian economy is healthy and Australian corporations increase their importing activities, New Zealand will be one of the first to benefit. When it is weak, New Zealand suffers but in recent years its sensitivity has diminished because of the country's growing trade with China and other nations. Nonetheless, 22% of trade is still conducted with Australia, and this explains why there is a positive correlation between the two currencies. Figure 32.1 shows how closely AUDUSD and NZDUSD have moved between 2005 and 2015.

Commodity-Linked Currency

New Zealand is an export driven economy with commodities representing over 40% of the country's exports, and as a result the New Zealand dollar has a strong correlation with commodity prices, particularly dairy. Fonterra is one of the world's

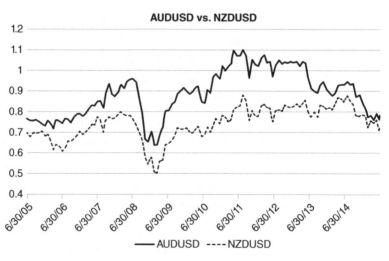

FIGURE 32.1   AUDUSD versus NZDUSD

leading dairy producer and also largest company in New Zealand. Twice a month the Global Dairy Trade will conduct an auction and if prices rise, it will be positive for the New Zealand dollar. If prices fall, it will be negative for the currency because it can mean reduced payout and profit for dairy producers. The correlation between Australian and New Zealand dollars also contributes to the NZD's status as a "commodity linked" currency. Therefore, the New Zealand dollar's correlation with commodity prices is not only limited to its own trade activities. Therefore, as commodity prices increase, the Australian economy benefits, translating into increased activity in all aspects of the country's operations, including trade with New Zealand.

Carry Trades

Of the industrialized countries, New Zealand tends to maintain the highest interest rate as it needs to offer investors a higher yield to compensate for the risk of investing in a small economy. This yield advantage along with its secure credit rating has made the New Zealand dollar one of the most popular currencies to purchase for carry trades. A carry trade involves buying or lending a currency with a high interest rate and selling or borrowing a currency with a low interest rate. The popularity of the carry trade has contributed to the rise of the New Zealand dollar in an environment where many global investors are looking for opportunities to earn high yield. However, this also makes the New Zealand dollar particularly sensitive to changes in interest rates. That is, when the United States begins increasing their interest rates, while New Zealand stays on hold or reduces their interest rates, the carry advantage of the New Zealand dollar would narrow. In such situations, the New Zealand dollar could come under pressure as speculators reverse their carry trade positions.

Interest Rate Differentials

Interest rate differentials between the cash rates of New Zealand and the short term interest rate yields of other industrialized countries are closely watched by professional NZD traders. These differentials can be good indicators of potential money flows as they indicate how much premium yield NZD short-term fixed-income assets are offering over foreign short-term fixed income assets, or vice versa. This differential provides traders with indications of potential currency movements, as investors are always looking for assets with the highest yields. This is particularly important to carry traders who enter and exit their positions based on the positive interest rate differentials between global fixed-income assets.

Population Migration

As mentioned earlier, New Zealand has a very small population, less than half of New York City. Therefore, changes in migration can have significant effects on the economy. Between 2013 and 2014, the population of New Zealand increased by 78,800 people, which was the largest net migration in at least 90 years. Between 2011 and 2012, for example, the population only grew by 26,400 people. Although these absolute numbers appear small, it is fairly significant for New Zealand because of the size of the population. In fact, this strong population migration into New Zealand has contributed significantly to the performance of the economy, because as the population increases, the demand for household goods increases, leading to an increase in overall consumer consumption.

Drought Effects

Since the bulk of New Zealand's exports are commodities, the country's GDP is highly sensitive to severe weather conditions that may damage the country's farming activities. In 2013, droughts cost the country over $1.3 billion. In addition, droughts are also very frequent in Australia, New Zealand's largest trading partner, and when they occur it can have a negative impact on the New Zealand economy.

■ Important Economic Indicators for New Zealand

New Zealand does not release economic indicators often; however, when they do, the following items are the most important:

Gross Domestic Product

GDP is a quarterly measure of the total production and consumption of goods and services in New Zealand. GDP is measured by adding expenditures by households, businesses, government, and net foreign purchases. The GDP price deflator is used to convert output measured at current prices into constant-dollar GDP. This data are used to gauge where in the business cycle New Zealand finds itself. Fast growth often is perceived inflationary, while low (or negative) growth indicates a recessionary or weak growth period.

Consumer Price Index

The Consumer Price Index (CPI) measures quarterly changes in the price of a "basket" of goods and services that account for a high proportion of expenditure by the CPI population group (i.e., metropolitan households). This basket covers a wide range of goods and services, including food, housing, education, transportation, and health. This is an important indicator to watch, as monetary policy changes are highly influenced by this index as it is a measure of inflation.

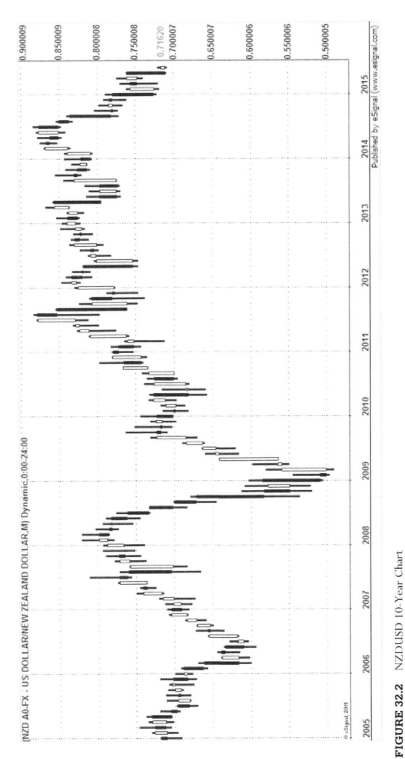

FIGURE 32.2 NZDUSD 10-Year Chart

Source: eSignal

Balance of Goods and Services

New Zealand's Balance of Payments statements are records of the value of New Zealand's transactions in goods, services, income, and transfers with the rest of the world, and the changes in New Zealand's financial claims on (assets), and liabilities to, the rest of the world. New Zealand's International Investment Position statement shows, at a particular point in time, the stock of a country's international financial assets and international financial liabilities.

Retail Sales Ex Inflation

Credit card spending numbers are released for New Zealand on a monthly basis but the retail sales data is quarterly on an ex inflation basis. This measure tracks the resale of new and used goods to the public for personal or household consumption. It is also an important input into GDP.

Producer Price Index

The Producer Price Index (PPI) is a family of indexes that measures average changes in selling prices received by domestic producers for their output. The PPI tracks changes in prices for nearly every goods producing industry in the domestic economy, including agriculture, electricity and natural gas, forestry, fisheries, manufacturing, and mining. Foreign exchange markets tend to focus on seasonally adjusted finished goods PPI and how the index has reacted on a m/m, q/q, h/h, and y/y basis. New Zealand's PPI data is released on a quarterly basis.

Figure 32.2 illustrates the 10-year performance of NZDUSD.

CHAPTER 33

Currency Profile: Canadian Dollar (CAD)

Broad Economic Performance

Canada is the world's eleventh largest country with GDP valued at US$1.8 trillion as of 2014. As a resource-based economy, the country's early economic development hinged on the development, exploitation, and exports of natural resources. It is now the world's fifth largest producer of oil and gold. However, in actuality, nearly two-thirds of the country's GDP comes from the service sector, which also employs three out of four Canadians. The strength in the service sector is partly attributed to the trend by businesses to subcontract a large portion of their services. This may include a manufacturing company subcontracting delivery services to a transportation company. Despite this, manufacturing and resources are still very important for the Canadian economy, as it represents over 25% of the country's exports and is a primary source of income for a number of provinces.

The Canadian economy started to advance with the depreciation of its currency against the U.S. dollar and the Free Trade Agreement that came into effect in January 1989. This agreement eliminated almost all trade tariffs between the United States and Canada. As a result, Canada now exports over 85% of its goods to the United States. Further negotiations to incorporate Mexico created the North American Free Trade Agreement (NAFTA), which took effect on January 1994. This more advanced treaty eliminated most tariffs on trading between all three countries. Canada's close trade relationship with the United States makes it particularly sensitive to the health of the U.S. economy. If the U.S. economy sputters, demand for Canadian exports would suffer. The same is true for the opposite scenario; if U.S. economic growth is robust, Canadian exports will benefit. In the past decade, trade with China has also increased significantly, rising in the ranks from the fifth to the second most important trade partner for Canada. The following is a breakdown of Canada's key export and import markets:

Leading Export Markets

1. United States
2. China
3. United Kingdom
4. Japan
5. Mexico

Leading Import Sources

1. United States
2. China
3. Japan
4. Mexico
5. United Kingdom

■ Monetary and Fiscal Policy

The Governing Council of the Bank of Canada is the board that is responsible for setting Canadian monetary policy. This council consists of seven members: the governor and six deputy governors. The Bank of Canada meets approximately eight times per year to discuss changes in monetary policy. They also release a monthly monetary policy update every quarter, but the rate decision itself is the big market mover for the currency.

Central Bank Goals

The Bank of Canada's primary focus is on maintaining the "integrity and value of the currency," and this involves ensuring price stability. Price stability is maintained by adhering to an inflation target currently set by the Department of Finance at 1% to 3%. The Bank believes that high inflation can damage the functioning of the economy. In their opinion, low inflation on the other hand equates to price stability, which can help to foster sustainable long-term economic growth. The BoC controls inflation through short-term interest rates. If inflation is above the target, the Bank will apply tighter monetary conditions. If it is below the target, the Bank will loosen monetary policy. Overall, the central bank has done a pretty good job of keeping the inflation target within the band since 1998.

The Bank measures monetary conditions using its Monetary Conditions Index, which is a weighted sum of changes in the 90-day commercial paper rate and G-10 trade-weighted exchange rates. The weight of the interest rate versus the exchange rate is 3 to 1, which is the affect of a change in interest rates on the exchange rate based on historical studies. This means that a 1% increase in short-term interest rates is the same as a 3% appreciation of the trade-weighted exchange rate. To change monetary policy, the BoC manipulates the Bank Rate, which can in turn affect the exchange rate. If the currency appreciates to undesirable levels, the BoC can decrease interest rates to offset the rise. If it depreciates, the BoC can raise rates. However, interest rate changes are not used for the purposes of manipulating the exchange rate. Instead, they are used to control inflation but an excessively strong currency and lower inflationary pressures can accelerate the changes. The following are the most commonly used tools by the BoC to implement monetary policy.

Bank Rate

The Bank Rate is the main rate used to control inflation. This is the rate of interest that the Bank of Canada charges to commercial banks. Changes to this rate will affect other interest rates, including mortgage rates and prime rates charged by commercial banks. Therefore, changes to this rate will filter into the overall economy.

Open Market Operations

The Large Value Transfer System (LVTS) is the framework for the Bank of Canada's implementation of monetary policy. It is through this framework that Canada's commercial banks borrow and lend overnight money to each other in order to fund their daily transactions. The LVTS is an electronic platform through which these financial institutions conduct large transactions. The interest rate charged on these overnight loans is called the overnight rate or bank rate. The BoC can manipulate the overnight rate by offering to lend at rates lower or higher than the current market rate if the overnight lending rate is trading above or below the target banks.

On a regular basis, the bank releases a number of publications that are important to follow. This includes a biannual *Monetary Policy Report* that contains an assessment of the current economic environment and implications for inflation and a quarterly *Bank of Canada Review* that includes economic commentary, featured articles, speeches by members of the Governing Council, and important announcements.

Important Characteristics of the Canadian Dollar

■ *Commodity linked currency*. As the world's fifth largest producer of oil and gold, Canada's economy is highly dependent on commodities. This creates a strong positive correlation between the Canadian dollar and oil prices. Generally speaking, when oil prices rise, it benefits domestic producers and increases their income from exports. However at the same time, strong commodity prices can hurt growth abroad; so while rising oil prices are initially positive for Canada, the negative impact on global growth could lead to a decline in demand over the medium term. On the flip side, falling oil prices are negative for the Canadian dollar; but if prices remain low and global growth benefits, it can eventually neutralize the negative impact.

- *Strong correlation with the United States.* Since the 1980s, Canada has been running merchandise trade surpluses with the United States and now approximately 77% of Canadian exports are bound for the Untied States. This heavy reliance on U.S., demand makes Canada extremely sensitive to changes in the U.S. economy. As the U.S. economy accelerates, trade increases with Canadian companies, lifting overall economic activity. However, as the U.S. economy slows, the Canadian economy will be hurt significantly as U.S. companies reduce their importing activities.

- *Mergers and acquisitions.* Due to the proximity of the United States and Canada, cross-border mergers and acquisitions are very common, as companies worldwide strive for globalization. These mergers and acquisitions lead to money flowing between the two countries, which ultimately impacts the currencies. In 2001, the significant U.S. acquisition of Canadian energy companies infused US$25 billion into Canada. This led to a strong rally in USDCAD, as the U.S. companies needed to sell USD and buy CAD to pay for their acquisitions. Any similar type of M&A flow in the future will also have a significant but short-term impact on the Canadian dollar.

- *Interest rate differentials.* Interest rate differentials between the cash rates of Canada and the short-term interest rate yields of other industrialized countries are closely watched by professional Canadian dollar traders. These differentials can be good indicators of potential money flows as they indicate how much premium yield Canadian short-term fixed-income assets are offering over foreign short-term fixed-income assets, and vice versa. This differential provides traders with indications of potential currency movements, as investors are always looking for assets with the highest yields. This is particularly important to carry traders who enter and exit their positions based on the positive interest rate differentials between global fixed-income assets.

- *Carry trades.* A carry trade involves buying or lending a currency with a high interest rate and selling or borrowing a currency with a low interest rate. When Canada has a higher interest rate than the United States, the short USDCAD carry trade becomes more attractive; but if the United States embarks on a tightening campaign or Canada lowers rates, the positive interest rate differential between the Canadian dollar and other currencies would narrow. In such situations, the Canadian dollar could come under pressure if the speculators begin to exit out of their carry trades.

■ Important Economic Indicators for Canada

Canadian economic reports can have a significant impact on the currency. Here are a handful of the most important releases.

Canadian Employment

Every month, Canada releases its labor market report and this report provides more details than that of the United States. Job growth is expressed as net job growth and then split into full- and part-time hirers. Generally speaking, the market prefers that the bulk of job growth is full time, because it represents real long-term employment and not short-term hires that can be laid off at any time. The unemployment rate is also released, and the number of unemployed persons is expressed as a percentage of the labor force.

Consumer Price Index (CPI)

The monthly consumer price report measures the average rate of increase in prices. When economists speak of inflation as an economic problem, they generally mean a persistent increase in the general price level over a period of time, resulting in a decline in a currency's purchasing power. Inflation is often measured as a percentage increase in the Consumer Price Index (CPI). Canada's inflation policy, as set out by the federal government and the Bank of Canada, aims to keep inflation within a target range of 1% to 3%. If the rate of inflation is 10% a year, $100 worth of purchases last year will, on average, cost $110 this year. At the same inflation rate, those purchases will cost $121 next year, and so on.

Gross Domestic Product (GDP)

The gross domestic product measures the total value of all goods and services produced within Canada during a given year. It is a measure of the income generated by production within Canada. GDP is also referred to as economic output. To avoid counting the same output more than once, GDP includes only final goods and services—not those that are used to make another product. For example, GDP would not include the wheat used to make bread, but would include the bread itself.

Trade Balance

The balance of trade is a statement of a country's trade in goods (merchandise) and services. It covers trade in products such as manufactured goods, raw materials, and agricultural goods, as well as travel and transportation. The balance of trade is the difference between the value of the goods and services that a country exports and the value of the goods and services that it imports. If a country's exports exceed its imports, it has a trade surplus and the trade balance is said to be positive. If imports

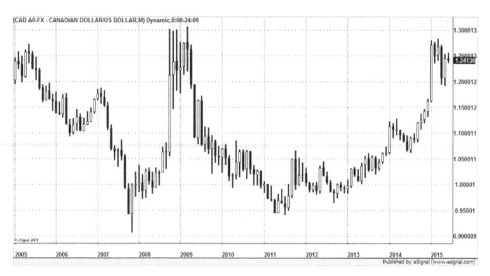

FIGURE 33.1 USDCAD 10-Year Chart
Source: eSignal

exceed exports, the country has a trade deficit, and its trade balance is said to be negative.

Retail Sales

Retail sales is a monthly national accounts measure that calculates current expenditure by households and producers of private nonprofit services to households. It includes purchases of durable as well as nondurable goods. However, it excludes expenditure by persons on the purchase of dwellings and expenditure of a capital nature by unincorporated enterprises. Stronger consumer spending is positive for Canada's economy and, in turn, the Canadian dollar, whereas weaker consumer spending is negative for Canada's economy and currency.

Producer Price Index

The Producer Price Index (PPI) is a family of indexes that measures average changes in selling prices received by domestic producers for their output. The PPI tracks changes in prices for nearly every goods producing industry in the domestic economy, including agriculture, electricity and natural gas, forestry, fisheries, manufacturing, and mining. Foreign exchange markets tend to focus on seasonally adjusted finished goods PPI and how the index has reacted on a monthly, quarterly, and annual basis.

Figure 33.1 illustrates the 10-year performance of USDCAD

INDEX

Note: Page references followed by ''f'' indicate an illustrated figure.

Printed and bound by CPI Group (UK) Ltd, Croydon, CR0 4YY

16/04/2025

14658467-0001